1/05 6r 3/01

☑ P9-BHY-554

The Comparative Imagination

The Comparative Imagination

On the History of Racism, Nationalism, and Social Movements

George M. Fredrickson

UNIVERSITY OF CALIFORNIA PRESS
Berkeley · Los Angeles · London

Permission to reprint several chapters is gratefully acknowledged as follows:

(1) Reprinted from *The Past Before Us: Contemporary Historical Writing in the United States,* edited for the American Historical Association by Michael Kammen. Copyright © 1980 by Cornell University. Used by permission of the publisher, Cornell University Press.

(2) Reprinted with permission from *The New York Review of Books.* Copyright © 1991, 1982 Nyrev, Inc.

(3) Fredrickson, George, M. "From Exceptionalism to Variability: Recent Developments in Cross-National Comparative History," *Journal of American History,* 82(2) (Sept. 1995), pp. 587–604.

(4) *Reviews in American History,* 1994, pp. 379–386. © Johns Hopkins University Press.

(7) Gispen, Kees, ed. *What Made the South Different?,* 1990, pp. 129–147. Reprinted with permission of the University Press of Mississippi.

(10) "Non-violent Resistance to White Supremacy; A Comparison of the American Civil Rights Movement and the South African Defiance Campaigns of 1950." Ward, Brian and Badger, Tony, eds. *The Making of Martin Luther King and the Civil Rights Movement.* Houndmill, England: Macmillan Press (1996). U.S. permission rights by New York University Press.

University of California Press
Berkeley and Los Angeles, California

University of California Press, Ltd.
London, England

Library of Congress Cataloging-in-Publication Data

Fredrickson, George M., 1934–
   The comparative imagination : on the history of
racism, nationalism, and social movements / George
M. Fredrickson.
      p.   cm.
   Includes bibliographical references and index.
   ISBN 0-520-20996-6 (alk. paper)
      1. Racism—United States—History. 2. Racism—
South Africa—History. 3. United States—Race re-
lations. 4. South Africa—Race relations. 5. Black
nationalism—United States—History. 6. Black na-
tionalism—South Africa—History. 7. Afro-
Americans—Civil rights—History. 8. Blacks—Civil
rights—South Africa—History.
I. Title.
E185.61.F838   1997
305.8′00973—dc21   97-18528
                                                CIP

Printed in the United States of America

9 8 7 6 5 4 3 2 1

For Jasper and Zoë

Contents

PART THREE. TWENTIETH-CENTURY
FREEDOM STRUGGLES

Introduction

This collection brings together eleven essays written over the past fifteen years or so that either reflect on the current practice of comparative history or represent my own efforts to do this kind of work.
The latter essays emerged from a topical interest in racism and antiracism that antedates my explicitly comparative scholarship. Most
concern black-white relations in the United States and South Africa;
but one, published here for the first time as chapter 6, deals with
mid-nineteenth-century ideas about race and empire in Alexis de
Tocqueville's writings on American democracy and the French colonization of Algeria. Earlier versions of the piece, called "Understanding
Racism" (chapter 5), which attempted to define and historicize racism
in a general way, appeared in places where few readers are likely to
have seen them; this essay has been substantially expanded and refor-
mulated.[1]

The other essays either were published before 1997 or were originally prepared for symposia or edited books of essays and may appear in slightly different form in the resulting volumes. Except in the
case of "From Black Power to Black Consciousness" (chapter 11),
which has been condensed from a longer piece, these essays have not
been significantly revised. Either they are recent enough to reflect my
current thinking, or, as in the case of the survey of comparative historiography from 1980 (chapter 1), an essay is juxtaposed with a
later essay of similar scope (chapter 3) to show how my assessment

of the field has evolved in light of subsequent scholarship, including my own.

Introducing this volume prompts some autobiographical reflections. Comparative historians are still rare enough to evoke curiosity about how they came to embrace that role. When I am asked, as I often am, how I first got interested in comparative history, I am never able to provide a very good answer because I cannot remember a time when I did not take a comparative approach to almost everything I was thinking seriously about. I instinctively assimilate new experience by first asking what familiar thing it resembles and then how it differs. Everyone does this to some extent, but in my case the urge to compare things may be especially intense and possibly a bit obsessive. Perhaps my comparative bent stems ultimately from the fact that my family made several major moves when I was child, and I was always contrasting where I was with where I had previously been.

As an undergraduate majoring in History and Literature at Harvard, I concentrated on what amounted to American studies, partly because at that time I did not have enough French to pursue my original plan to study the United States, England, and France since 1800. (I had the misfortune to attend a public high school that offered neither French nor German.) When I came to write a senior honors thesis, I chose a topic with a comparative dimension—an investigation of Norwegian-American writing that compelled me to assess the Old World background as well as the New World experiences of an articulate group of first- and second-generation immigrants. A chapter on the ethnic dimension of Thorstein Veblen's thought was later published in *The American Quarterly*.[2]

At this point I was uncertain whether to pursue historical or literary studies in graduate school. A Fulbright to Norway that was supposed to involve a further study of immigration history actually became an excursion into comparative literature. The fruit of this year was a published article on Ibsen's *Hedda Gabler* that compared the ideas at work in the play with Nietzsche's "neopagan" ethics. I also attempted a comparative study of Ibsen and Melville based on their shared experience when, as children, both writers suffered a loss of status and security when their fathers went bankrupt. My enterprise also failed, but its insolvency taught me the valuable lesson that comparison must be based on substantive rather than incidental or superficial similarities.[3]

Although it is clear to me now that my interest in literature was historical rather than aesthetic, I seriously considered doing graduate work in comparative literature. But I was again foiled by language requirements. Although I now had some French and Norwegian, the latter was not in demand, and I therefore lacked the second "major" European language and the Greek or Latin that was then also required. I decided eventually on the American Civilization program at Harvard because it allowed me to defer the choice between literary and historical studies and also seemed to have a comparative aspect in that secondary fields were required in the history or literature of two other societies. It soon became apparent, however, that this requirement was pro forma and not meant as an invitation to sustained comparative work. I therefore became a thoroughgoing Americanist and put my cross-national interests on the back burner: my dissertation was on that seemingly most American of subjects—the Civil War.[4]

My one significant foray into comparative history as a graduate student occurred when I took Louis Hartz's seminar on comparative political thought. In it Hartz expounded at length the ideas that would inform his *Founding of New Societies*. It was my first exposure to a frame of reference that would include both South Africa and the United States. My seminar paper, however, compared the Utopian socialism of Edward Bellamy and William Morris on the very Hartzian basis that the lack of a tradition of communalism handed down from the Middle Ages made American radical thought more individualistic than the English equivalent. There may have been some validity to the argument, but I am glad that I did not attempt to publish this first attempt at comparative history. I had made the mistake of taking Hartz's concept of American exceptionalism as an established truth to be applied and exemplified rather than as a debatable hypothesis to be tested.[5]

When I left graduate school, I had seemingly found a professional identity as an intellectual historian of nineteenth-century America with a special interest in the issues raised by the North–South conflict and the Civil War. My second book concentrated on the great unresolved issue arising from the war—the place of emancipated blacks in the American republic. What turned out to be a lifelong commitment to the study of race and racism was driven by the strong emotions aroused in me by the civil rights struggle of the 1960s and its disappointing aftermath. White supremacy struck me then—and still strikes me today—as America's most persistent problem and its greatest shame, the most glaring and lamentable contradiction of what were supposed to be its fundamental values. I resolved to probe the intellectual and ideological foundations of what Gunnar Myrdal called "the American dilemma."

This field of study also invited comparison with slavery and race relations in other societies.

The Black Image in the White Mind, published in 1971, was not
comparative in any sustained way. But a reading of sociologist Pierre
van den Berghe's incisive cross-cultural study *Race and Racism* provided
me with the concept of "*Herrenvolk* democracy," an illuminating and
provocative key to the question of how white Americans, particularly
defenders of slavery and segregation, had managed to resolve in their
own minds the conflict between the egalitarian values of the Declaration
of Independence and the practice of racial domination. I was struck by
the fact that van den Berghe had found a similar pattern in South Africa,
and at some point the thought occurred to me that a full historical comparison of the development of white supremacist attitudes, ideologies,
and policies in the two countries might prove valuable.[6]

The decision to devote nearly a decade to this project came only after
I had been persuaded to give a paper comparing white supremacy in the
United States and South Africa at a session on comparative race relations at the 1972 convention of the American Historical Association.
As I plunged into South African historiography, I became fascinated
with the extent to which the two national experiences were similar in
some respects and different in others. I soon realized that a conference
paper would barely scratch the surface of the subject and that I would
have to undertake research in South Africa to do it justice. After two
years of exploring South African history in the incomparable
Herskovitz collection at the Northwestern University Library, I went to
South Africa for five months in 1975. I had temporarily narrowed the
subject to race relations in the U.S. South (hereafter referred to as "the
South") and the Cape Colony of South Africa before 1910, and I therefore spent most of that time doing research in the libraries and archives
of Cape Town. The parallels between the growth of white supremacy
in the South and the Cape of Good Hope in the seventeenth, eighteenth,
and nineteenth centuries were quite strong, and the comparisons could
be controlled and precise. As a general rule, comparison works best
when the two cases being considered show a demonstrably high degree
of similarity.

The first chapter of *White Supremacy,* which deals with the expansion of white settlement in the South and the Cape Colony before 1840,
would have fit well into the study as I conceived it in 1975 (as would
the subsequent two chapters on slavery and race mixture). Since chapter 1 deals with the relations of European settlers to indigenous peoples,

its American component addresses the experience of Native Americans rather than that of African Americans. I compared the process leading to the forced removal of the "civilized tribes" from the southern states in the 1830s with the events that led up to the Great Trek in South Africa during the same decade. Although I did not pursue the history of Native American–white relations in the remainder of the book, this research and writing aroused my interest in the comparative study of frontiers, which I addressed briefly in the 1980 survey of comparative history. It also formed the subject of a review essay on recent work on American and South African frontiers, published in 1982, which appears as chapter 2 of this collection. Not a great deal has been done on this subject since, except for James Gump's illuminating comparison of the context and consequences of frontier wars in the 1870s—the conflict between the Sioux and the United States Army on the Great Plains and the clash of the Zulu and British regulars in eastern South Africa.[7]

As the work on *White Supremacy* progressed, however, I concluded that a broader geographical and chronological canvas, one that necessarily involved some sharp contrasts, would more effectively illuminate the historical roots of contemporary U.S. and South African situations than would a more narrow focus on the South and the Cape before 1910. As a result, the last half of the book covers the United States and South Africa as a whole and extends the chronology to the present. The massacre of African teenagers at Soweto in 1976 and the murder of Steve Biko in 1978 horrified much of the world and contributed to my decision to deal more directly with the roots of the current crisis than the more limited comparison would have allowed. I wanted a chance to address more fully the origins and evolution of apartheid and to examine how it compared or contrasted with "the strange career of Jim Crow" in the United States. Although I found that the differences almost overwhelmed the commonalities, I felt that such a study in contrast was a way of countering illusions about the possibility that apartheid might be reformed out of existence, as Jim Crow had been.

In studying a subject like white supremacy it is difficult to avoid thinking about contemporary implications; thus it was a desire to be relevant and topical that, more than anything else, caused the book to overflow the dikes that I had originally constructed to keep it under control. The first three chapters, which were based in part on my intensive research in Cape Town and my prior work on racism in the United States before 1914, were written with more authority and a deeper knowledge of the sources than the last three. The book as a whole may have been less solid and definitive than the more focused study that I had originally projected, but it was clearly more provocative and of greater general interest.

I do not regret this decision to address contemporary concerns at the expense of some historical precision and authoritativeness. The search for a "usable past" and a willingness to generalize about it in ways that subsequent research may call into question does not have to be an invitation to distortion and propaganda, provided that one is asking open-ended questions of the historical record rather than seeking evidence to support a preconceived political position and ignoring whatever contradicts it. The questions are ours and are properly influenced by what we consider important to know right now, even when the answers must be tentative or provisional. The most valuable findings are the ones that convey a realistic sense of possibilities and not false assurances that may bolster our morale while they feed our illusions. No essay in this volume demonstrates more fully my desire for a usable past than "Understanding Racism," although contemporary concerns are evident in most of the pieces—especially in my overview of American and South African freedom struggles (chapter 8) and the review essay on some black American and South African leaders of the 1960s (chapter 9).

When I started working on *White Supremacy* in the early 1970s, I had few models to follow, having given little thought to what comparative history was and how it should be done. As part of a generation of historians who disdained theory and simply went about their business of examining the sources and drawing conclusions from them, I went to work without worrying much about theory and method. But I did have to know what I was writing about, and I turned to the sociological literature on race and racism in search of definitions and concepts.

It was not until I had finished a first draft and began to think about an introduction that I gave serious thought to comparative methodology. What I had been doing felt right to me, but I realized that others would want to know about my procedures and assumptions. If I could not justify what I was doing, I would have to go back and rethink the whole enterprise. One conclusion that I drew was that my methodology differed significantly from that of the comparative historical studies then being produced by sociologists and political scientists. I did not begin with a well-defined model or hypothesis with a fixed number of variables. Rather I put my study in an interpretive context that historians and others had established to expose and explain the differing patterns of race relations in the United States and Latin America. But this was merely a point of departure. I also found new themes dictated by the American and South African materials and sought variations on them. Social theory came into the picture mainly as a heuristic device whenever it seemed applicable. I described and attempted to justify this "historicist" approach to comparative studies both in the introduction to *White Supremacy* and in my 1980 survey of work in comparative history written for a volume summing up the recent endeavors of American historians. The latter essay is reprinted as chapter 1 of this book.

In that essay I was trying to say that comparative history can be done in a manner quite compatible with normal or traditional historical method. It can make use of narrative as well as analysis and manifest a concern for the particular as well as (if not more than) a search for general truths about human experience.

In explaining my own practice in 1980 and 1981, I may have offered too restrictive a view of comparative history. At a 1985 conference at Northwestern University I gave a paper—parts of which were eventually incorporated into the 1995 historiographic essay that became chapter 3 of this book—that distinguished between comparative history in the grand manner and other historical writing employing a comparative method. In this essay I defined the former as book-length studies of developments over time in two or more societies in which each case is treated with a similar degree of depth and specificity. Although systematic comparisons within a single nation have been made between regions, communities, and even the biographies of major historical actors or thinkers, I chose not to consider these because, as the published essay makes clear, I was really interested in "cross-national comparative history." From my perspective, historical comparison is not merely a method or procedure but also an antidote to the parochialism that may accompany a fixation on the history of one nation. For me, comparative analysis is a means of viewing history from a cosmopolitan or international perspective, which in turn makes the experience of individual nations more meaningful.

In-depth bilateral comparison is not, however, the only way to accomplish this objective. Increasingly historians have been utilizing what I would call "comparative perspective" as a tool of analysis. This approach employs general knowledge of an external example or examples of a phenomenon to determine what is characteristic or distinctive about the manifestation of that phenomenon within a single society.

This body of work is extremely valuable and undoubtedly represents the type of comparison that is most compatible with the expectation that academic historians will specialize in the past of one country. As I pointed out in the 1980 essay, such career patterns present a major obstacle to the type of cross-national comparative history that seeks to provide new insights into the history of two or more nations. This is still generally the case, although—as I show in the 1995 historiographic survey (chapter 3) and the review essay of two of the most important comparative works of the past few years (chapter 4)—the number and quality of systematic cross-national histories are on the rise.[8]

I was of course an Americanist before I was a comparativist and for most professional purposes am still one. Not only do I involve the United States in whatever comparison I am attempting, but so do most of the works that I discuss in the "historiographic explorations" in part one of this book. The essays in part two, especially chapters 5 and 7, explicitly privilege the American experience over those with which it is being compared and are closer in method and spirit to "comparative perspective" than to "cross-national comparative history." "Understanding Racism" and "Black-White Relations since Emancipation" use the experience of Brazil and South Africa mainly to illuminate the American pattern rather than for their own sake, although they try to establish some general principles that would apply to all three cases and perhaps to others as well. Part three reverts to detailed bilateral comparison between the United States and South Africa in which neither case is privileged.

In the 1985 paper I also distinguished between "historicist" and "structuralist" approaches to comparative history. The former, which is closer to the normal disciplinary practice of historians, stresses differences, peculiarities, and multiple, continuous causation (i.e., that which is not easily reducible to a fixed set of variables.) It tends to focus more on culture and ideology than on institutions or structures. The aim of this approach is the better understanding of particular societies rather than the establishment or testing of universally, or at least broadly, applicable social scientific theories. The second approach tends to be more congenial to historical sociologists and political scientists. It identifies a limited number of structural or institutional variables operating in a small number of historical situations and uses comparison to isolate the ones that account for similarities and differences.[9]

In the 1985 paper I stressed the gulf between the two methods and presented myself, for the most part, as a spokesman for the historicist approach. But a decade later when I revised and updated it for publication as "From Exceptionalism to Variability," the essay included here, I determined on the basis of new comparative work, including my own, that there is a middle ground, a type of comparative history that combines elements of cultural contrast and structural analysis. I concluded therefore that the historical social scientists and the historians had a lot to learn from each other and that the work of both could and should involve the interaction between the peculiarities of culture and ideology on the one hand and recurrent and generalizable structural factors on the other.

The research and writing for *Black Liberation,* my second extended treatment of the United States and South Africa, made it clear that a natural and persuasive way to do comparative history was to establish a common international context and keep it in mind throughout the study. Awareness of the larger international struggle against imperialism and racism in the twentieth century permitted me to treat black resistance to white supremacy in the United States and South Africa as case studies of a more general phenomenon. The essays in part three of this collection, especially chapters 8, 10, and 11, exemplify this contextualist approach. Beyond the insights into the development of each of the societies being examined, comparative work contributes to a general understanding of the dynamics of world history.[10]

Although *White Supremacy* located American and South African developments within the larger context of the expansion of Europe, it moved quickly to American and South African peculiarities. In a piece published in my 1988 collection of essays on slavery and race, I attempted to contextualize these developments more fully by relating them to the larger history of Western colonialism and racism. In two of the essays in this book, "Understanding Racism" and "Race and Empire in Liberal Thought: The Legacy of Tocqueville," I attempt to use cross-national comparisons (my own or Tocqueville's) to exemplify some general tendencies of recent world history. I now feel much more strongly than I did that comparative history, besides showing the special features of particular national experiences, can contribute much to a broad understanding of the forces that have shaped the modern world as a whole—although the last section of the racism essay betrays again my special concern as an American to provide useful insights into our particular version of racial injustice.[11]

Students and others frequently ask my advice about the practice of comparative history. I have learned a few things from my twenty-five years as a comparative historian that might be of practical help to students or established historians who are considering doing work of this type (and at the same time perhaps make it easier for serious readers to appreciate and evaluate comparative histories). First of all, it is probably advisable to master one nation's history before undertaking extensive cross-national comparisons. Unless a graduate student has prior training in a second case, say an M.A. in a national history other than the chosen area of specialization for the Ph.D., it would be prudent to choose a dissertation topic that involves at most "historical perspective" rather than full-blown bilateral comparison. But excellent comparative dissertations in the fullest sense have been written by those who have made the extra effort to complete what amounts to a double major. It can be done, but its difficulties should not be underestimated.

Besides learning a second history, would-be comparativists originally trained as conventional historians need to become interdisciplinary. They should immerse themselves in the literature on their thematic interest (race relations in my case) produced by sociologists, political scientists, anthropologists, and even those in the new and controversial field of cultural studies. One does not have to become a theorist to use theory productively as a way of developing hypotheses or provisional generalizations.

One should also be willing to learn the languages essential to in-depth historical research. For *White Supremacy,* I taught myself a reading knowledge of Dutch and Afrikaans. For *Black Liberation,* however, I did not find it essential to learn any of the African languages, because English was the lingua franca of black protest in South Africa in the twentieth century. Some sociologists and political scientists have written comparative histories involving countries whose languages they do not read, but the depth of cultural penetration that sophisticated historical work normally requires obliges the comparative historian to read the languages of scholarship and public discourse employed in both cases.

I have been preoccupied with two-sided comparisons because historians can do them with the best effect. Another piece of advice, therefore, is to avoid spreading oneself too thin by trying to deal extensively and in detail with more than two cases. I once attempted a three-way comparison of emancipation in the U.S. South, the Cape Colony of South Africa, and Jamaica in an essay that appeared in an earlier collection, and chapters 5 and 7 of this volume triangulate the histories of race relations in the United States, South Africa, and Brazil. But I would not pretend that my knowledge of Brazilian or Caribbean history would suffice for more than a very general and schematic comparison, suitable for an essay but not for a book-length study. If the aim is to have one's work respected and found useful by scholars in all the fields that one treats comparatively, it is generally advisable to stick to two cases. A third might be possible, but to do it with the same depth as the other two would be a formidable task, and organizing the finished study would be difficult. There are good reasons, I think, that those who profess history as a discipline have rarely attempted to treat three or more cases in a detailed and sustained way.[12]

The need for such depth might lead some readers to conclude that comparative history is so difficult and time-consuming that no sane person would attempt it. I do not wish to underestimate the effort required, but it is nevertheless possible to exaggerate it. Although it is essential to master the relevant historiography on one's topic, a good comparative history need not involve extensive research in archival or primary sources on each case. If the topic is broad, and the secondary literature voluminous and of high quality, there is no reason not to rely heavily upon it. *White Supremacy* made substantial use of secondary sources (at some points, especially in the last half of the book, they were virtually the only sources used to support an argument). My previous knowledge of primary materials on the United States and what I could learn from published memoirs, travel accounts, and official records or reports reflecting the evolving racial attitudes and policies in South Africa added a great deal to my critical synthesis of the two historiographies, especially in the first three chapters. I was nevertheless impressed with how much could be done with only the secondary sources. In a seminal article on comparative history written forty years ago, the eminent economic historian Fritz Redlich described very cogently the special relationship between primary and secondary sources in comparative historical work:

> Comparative historiography's main sources are by necessity historical monographs, i.e. the results of preceding generations of historians. While up to now a historical work to be recognized had to be based on primary sources . . . comparative historiography demands as its source material a welter of monographs. It would go to the archives to fill gaps in our knowledge and check to see if the monograph writers really saw those aspects of historical fact or development in which we are interested. One might put it this way: while traditional monographic historiography begins in the archives, comparative historiography ends it there.[13]

Of course some types of comparative history can and should rely more heavily on primary sources than others. *Black Liberation,* essentially a work of intellectual history, was based mainly on the actual discourse of black protest in the two societies, rather than what historians had written about it. The texts I relied upon were primary sources, even if many of them could be found in published books at any good research library rather than in archival collections. The history of ideas and ideologies requires less digging and scurrying about than the history of institutions or patterns of behavior; it can be done comparatively without a heavy reliance on monographic literature. Comparative social history can also be based mainly on primary sources if the units being treated are small enough. There is a trend in comparative historiography, as some of the work discussed in chapter 3 would suggest, to focus on selected local experiences in two societies rather than a nationwide phenomenon. Cross-national comparisons of two cities or two organizations, for example, make it feasible to do extensive archival research on each case. But knowledge of the relevant secondary literature on each nation is still necessary to establish the broader contexts that give shape and meaning to the local experiences being treated in detail.

Besides reading the relevant works in their original language, the comparative historian would be well advised to establish direct contacts with historians working on the other, exotic case. Connections that I established with historians of South Africa in Britain, the United States, and South Africa itself during the 1970s alerted me to a major shift in historiography that surfaced initially in seminar papers and articles in relatively obscure journals rather than in widely distributed books and periodicals. I was able to learn from, and respond to, this emerging historiography in *White Supremacy* because correspondents and people I met on my travels informed me of what was going on.

My final word of advice to would-be comparativists concerns how the findings should be presented, once the basic research and analysis have been completed. To my way of thinking, it is much more effective—and genuinely comparative—to have topical chapters dealing interactively with both countries rather than separate chapters on each country. An argument against three-way comparisons is that it becomes very difficult to use this format without making excessive demands on the reader, who tends to feel like an inept juggler. The worst organization in my view is the one that has a long chapter on each case and then a last chapter that does the actual comparison. My two books on the United States and South Africa, as well as chapters 10 and 11 of this volume (shortened and recast versions of the last two chapters of *Black Liberation*), show how one can develop comparisons within each topical chapter without (I hope) giving the reader a headache. Separate treatment tends to result in parallel histories rather than genuinely comparative ones. Two narratives can be presented in such a way that the reader is always aware of both and senses that they are, as it were, constantly commenting on each other. Comparative history of this type is an extended conversation between two national histories in search of common themes and an understanding of the variations on them. It might be viewed as one aspect of the wider search of international or world historians and other scholars with cosmopolitan interests for a common language and a common set of concerns that cross international frontiers.

To the extent that it is a cosmopolitan or universalizing enterprise, however, comparative history may seem to many in the late 1990s to be intellectually problematic (or at least unfashionable) in light of the postmodernist stress on the particular and unique—in other words the incomparable or incommensurate. Can comparative history of the kind I practice, or any other kind for that matter, survive in the world as defined by postmodernists? Is it necessary to choose between comparative studies and what appears to be the dominant intellectual trend of the age? These questions are not confronted directly in the essays that follow (although "Understanding Racism" appropriates for my own purposes some of the language usually associated with postmodernism). But they have to be faced if the essays in this book are to be taken seriously.

The historical profession contains within it a strong trend that is consistent in some ways with the general thrust of postmodernism, without, in most cases, revealing much awareness of the affinity. This is the "revival of narrative history"—the growing emphasis on discrete storytelling at the expense of analysis and generalization. Most historians of course believe that their stories are factually based and not just fiction in another form, as some postmodern theorists do, but a heavy stress on the particularity or singularity of the human experiences that we treat and on the color and drama that our narratives about them can convey tends to aestheticize history, just as postmodernism often aestheticizes politics and philosophy.[14]

I believe that narrative is an essential aspect of historical writing but that is not its be-all and end-all. Discrete narratives of particular events that eschew the extraction of larger meanings are the antithesis of comparative history or any other kind of history that seeks to generalize beyond the immediate facts of the case at hand. If telling a good story in vivid detail becomes the sole or even the paramount aim of historians, if history becomes exclusively an art rather than a science, comparative history has no future. But we have not reached that point, if we ever will, and the desire to find a middle ground between narrative and analytical history remains the dominant aspiration of most working historians.

The treatment of change over time—the essence of historical scholarship—must in some basic sense take the form of storytelling. But the best storytellers have also been moralists. If the moral is not explicit, as in Aesop's fables, it is usually implicit and evident to the perceptive reader. Besides telling a good story, most great novels reveal something about human motivation and often make judgments on the social values and practices found in particular times and places. Historians' narratives are not, of course, freely invented but are based on sources that other historians can examine. The moral or meaning cannot be simply illustrated or personified, as in the case of fiction. It must be supported by a body of evidence.

Both history and fiction aim to be truthful in some sense, but the historian's truth is subject to evaluation by a community of inquirers who have established rules to determine reliability, quality, and persuasiveness. Besides seeing if the historian has been true to her sources, a critic can evaluate a given narrative by seeing to what extent it is consistent with the stories that other historians have told about the same or similar events. The process can be compared to a jury's evaluation of the testimony of a number of witnesses to the same crime. Cross-national history takes two stories in two different contexts that are presumptively true by the normal standards of historical evaluation and juxtaposes them in the hope of finding a deeper meaning for each narrative and beyond that, if possible, a larger meaning that applies to both.

The revival of narrative history can have a salutary effect on comparative work by encouraging the idea that two stories are being compared, not simply two structures or conditions. Comparing the institution of slavery in what is taken to be its normal or typical form in two societies, for example, suspends time and is basically ahistorical. Comparing the process of enslavement, or the story of how the bonds of servitude were created and strengthened—or weakened—is a better way of conceiving the project. Radical historicity, the belief that time changes everything and that nothing is truly permanent or "essential," is a characteristic of postmodernist thought that is congenial to the instincts of many historians.

But the comparative historian needs to know what slavery is in order to justify treating its evolution in two or more societies. One culture's word that translates into English as "slavery" may refer to something quite different from another's term for a state of servitude and extreme dependency. It is at this point that comparative history seems to clash directly with postmodernism. Is it justifiable to construct a general category or ideal type and then view two specific stories as examples of its presence? Pauline Marie Rosenau, a Canadian political scientist who has studied the implications of postmodernism for social science, argues that this new way of thinking invalidates all comparisons. After describing postmodernism's characteristic denial of the connection between the "signifier" and the "signified," its rejection of the possibility of representation, she goes on to show the devastating effect of this premise on comparative studies:

> Dismissing the possibility of representations undermines social science methods in general, but its questioning of comparative analysis is particularly thoroughgoing. The very act of comparing, in an effort to uncover differences and similarities, is a meaningless activity because postmodern epistemology holds it impossible ever to define adequately the elements to be contrasted or likened.[15]

If this is what postmodernists are really saying, and all that they are saying, then the comparative historian might be sorely tempted to join the ranks of those currently denouncing it as a form of nihilism that is threatening to undermine morality, rationality, and civilization as we know it. Some of the thinkers identified with postmodernism have undeniably espoused a radical skepticism of all claims to the establishment of truth, except of course their own claim that all truth is relative. The inherent contradiction of unqualified relativism, as its philosophical critics have often pointed out, is that its own assertion is either absolutely true or no more valid than various claims of a reality beyond language. In either case the result is incoherence.[16]

But postmodern thought, restrained by a modicum of common sense and respect for what most human beings have taken to be good and true, may have something to offer the comparative historian. Some forms of social-scientific comparison, those inferring structures that can be diagramed from quantifiable data, may indeed be open to criticism for detaching the signifier from the signified. Do they in fact refer to any reality other than one that exists on hard disks or in hyperspace? What is real for human beings must be present in their consciousness. To argue, for example, that southern slaveholders defended their peculiar institution to the death because modern economists have determined that it was profitable is not a convincing historical argument if the evidence shows that the slaveholders themselves believed it was unprofitable. The relationship between what historical actors firmly believed and an external set of facts that contradicts their beliefs is one of the most difficult problems of historical interpretation. I am not one of those who would endorse a purely subjectivist history by claiming that realities external to human consciousness are of no historical significance or (in the extreme postmodernist formulation) do not even exist. In the long run, brute reality can kill us whether we believe in it or not. The good news is that people do learn from experience. If patients die often enough from a particular illness, a traditional remedy once deemed efficacious is likely to be abandoned. The belief of American settlers of the Great Plains that rain followed the plow did not survive a decade-long drought. Truth, as William James and John Dewey taught us, is what works: when it no longer works, it is no longer true.

One pragmatic test of new historical truth is the perception by the community of historians that the work has enriched our sense of the past and has raised new questions that are worthy of further investigation. No absolute truth can ever be attained, at least not until the end of the universe, but provisional truths that work for us here and now are within our grasp. Comparative historians may construct a working definition, or what Max Weber called an "ideal type," of whatever recurring category of human thought and action they want to compare. This abstract model or categorization is obviously an intellectual construction and not the direct representation of something that actually exists. But it is informed by knowledge of a range of conditions, institutions, ideologies, and other factors that share some defining features with the model or ideal type. The defining conception works if the cases to which it is applied manifest these characteristics. Once a basic and abstract resemblance has been established, it is possible to isolate some important differences and ask what accounts for them. This approach "works" if the differences can be correlated with other differences between the two societies, in which case a causal argument can be developed.

Nothing about this procedure necessarily involves a belief in the possibility of finding an absolute and final truth about anything significant.

The historian's representation of past human experience is provisional and subject to correction by fellow inquirers. It is also filtered through the historian's own consciousness and made to serve the historian's own purposes. The results are published and their significance is determined by how well they suit the purposes of an audience. Such an enterprise contributes to truth in the pragmatic sense to the degree that it is useful. Usefulness can be purely intellectual: it may stimulate and guide further inquiries that an intellectual community finds to be interesting and potentially rewarding. It may also be useful in a social and political sense by contributing to the construction of ideologies and the development of policies that provide more effective ways to deal with contemporary manifestations of whatever has been studied historically. Comparative history has a special ability to suggest new ways of thinking about old problems by calling our attention to alternative approaches to their management or solution. Understanding how another society has confronted challenges similar to our own can be a stimulus to social and political creativity.

My comparative work on race and racism in the United States and South Africa is therefore truthful to the degree that it stimulates inquiry and constructive debate within the community of historians and social scientists. It would become even more valid in a pragmatic sense if it added some wisdom or insight to efforts of concerned citizens and policy makers to respond in a just and equitable manner to the demands of formerly enslaved and disenfranchised people for equality of rights, status, and opportunity.

The pragmatic test of truth, as I conceive it, does not sanction amorality or a nonjudgmental relativism. What is useful should accord with some sense of how human beings deserve to be treated by virtue of being human. Phrases like "human rights" and "human dignity" may be hard to define precisely, but they obviously refer to a universal entitlement that we are bound to respect if we hope to make a world in which everyone will have a chance at happiness and self-fulfillment. An ethics based on utility or practicality in the broadest sense requires a conception of what is best for humanity as a whole. If we could ask every person in the world what would be of most practical value for him or her, we would receive many answers. But common to most of them, I imagine, would be the desire to be treated with respect, to be protected from torture and other forms of brutality whether administered by the state or by private parties, to be assured of the wherewithal to sustain physical existence with some degree of comfort and security, and to be provided the opportunity to develop one's individual talent or genius freely to the full extent of one's abilities, as long as doing so does not impede the chances of others to do the same. To the degree that postmodernism is compatible with a pragmatic humanism of this type, I would welcome it. To the degree that it is not, I would resist it. Drawing a balance sheet is difficult and beyond the scope of this introduction. It is, however, both clear and incontestable that an intellectual encounter with postmodernism can stimulate new thought even if we end up modifying or rejecting some of its precepts.

These philosophical reflections may not seem necessary to conventional historians, but postmodernism is not going to go away, and it behooves historians, comparative and otherwise, to come to terms with it. David Harvey has recently made a strong case that postmodernity and the thinking that goes with it are the products of profound economic and social developments presently transforming world capitalism. From a pragmatic point of view, its assumptions are therefore becoming "true" for many people. But believers in human freedom and rationality have the right and the obligation to criticize many of these tendencies in the name of more humane and inclusive conceptions of practical truth. Scholars who value the legacy of the Enlightenment on whatever epistemological grounds should be prepared to explain and defend their work against the radical skeptics, but if they are true to the essence of the Enlightenment heritage, they must do so by reasoned argument rather than dogmatic assertions of absolute or revealed truth.[17]

I have made some effort in this introduction to conform to one of the healthier tendencies of postmodernism, the call for historians and other scholars to be more candid about where they are coming from, autobiographically and ideologically, rather than assuming an Olympian objectivity. One does not have to give up the hope for a common discourse, or what Jürgen Habermas called "communicative rationality," to be willing to reveal one's particular route to the public space available for the discussion of ideas. I could not, however, continue to do my work if I believed that my ascribed peculiarities—race, ethnicity, gender, and sexual orientation—predetermined what I had to say and provided sufficient grounds for accepting or rejecting it. I would not deny that being a heterosexual white male of Swedish-American ancestry has some effect on my view of the world. But I firmly believe that a willingness to participate in rational discussion and debate with others committed to the process—including some who might share none of the above attributes—can lead to transcendent perspectives and the staking out of common ground. My conception of the character and function of comparative history will not be everybody's, but I hope that my version of it will stimulate or provoke those who see potential value in such an enterprise to understand my formulation, debate its merits, and try to provide better alternatives. This is the way that truth is made.

PART ONE

Historiographical Explorations

CHAPTER ONE

The Status of Comparative History (1980)

Surveying recent comparative work by American historians is not an easy task; for there is no firm agreement on what comparative history is or how it should be done.[1] All history that aims at explanation or interpretation involves some type of explicit or implicit comparison, but to isolate "comparative history" as a special trend within the profession requires a reasonably precise and restrictive definition. One can, first of all, distinguish comparative history from history that uses the "comparative method" in a relatively brief or casual fashion, more as a heuristic device than as a sustained method or approach. The limited use of a generalized "comparative perspective" or exotic analogy as a way of shedding additional light on some phenomenon in a single nation or society is not comparative history in the full sense.[2] Neither is the type of study—so important in the "new social history"—that closely examines a particular community or social action in terms of conceptual schemes or categories that are applicable to the study of similar entities in other contexts.[3] If "microcosmic" studies with comparative implications are ruled out, so are "macrocosmic" works that attempt to describe international developments of some kind without a prime concern for analyzing and comparing the variable responses of particular societies.[4]

What remains is a relatively small but significant body of scholarship that has *as its main objective* the systematic comparison of some process or institution in two or more societies that are not usually conjoined within one of the traditional geographical areas of historical specialization.[5] It is only in work of this sort that comparison per se is consistently at the core of the enterprise. In other types of history sometimes described as comparative, the main concern is placing some local phenomenon in a broader geographical context, revealing the general trends prevailing in a given region or throughout the world, tracing some idea or influence across national or cultural boundaries, or describing a particular case in terms that may lend themselves to comparison.

The object of comparative history in the strict sense is clearly a dual one: it can be valuable as a way of illuminating the special features or particularities of the individual societies being examined—each may look different in light of the other or others—and also useful in enlarging our theoretical understanding of the kinds of institutions or processes being compared, thereby making a contribution to the development of social-scientific theories and generalizations. But the practitioners of comparative history may differ on the priority that they assign to these two aims. Those in the humanistic "historicist" tradition will normally give preference to the former, while those who consider history as nothing more than contemporary social science applied to the past will tend to favor the latter.[6] To some extent, although not consistently, this difference of priorities follows disciplinary lines. It is impossible to discuss comparative history without recognizing the contribution of historically oriented sociologists, political scientists, anthropologists, and economists. But their work tends to differ from that of those who are squarely in the historical profession by its greater concern for generating and testing theories or models that are either of potentially universal application or at least readily transferable to a number of social situations other than those being directly examined.

Unfortunately, the body of work that qualifies as comparative history in the strict sense is characterized both by its relative sparseness and by its fragmentation. Comparative history does not really exist yet as an established field within history or even as a well-defined method of studying history. Unlike "the new social history" or even psychohistory, it does not possess a self-conscious community of inquirers who are aware of each other's work and build on it or react critically to it. Most of those who do comparative history do not define themselves as comparative historians in any general or inclusive sense. Those interested in the comparison of one kind of institution or process often seem unaware of the cross-cultural work being done on other kinds of phenomena. Scholars working on particular topics in the comparative history of certain traditionally juxtaposed areas, such as the United States and Latin America, often make no reference to relevant work being done on other parts of the world.

Because of the sparseness and fragmentation of comparative studies, it is difficult to describe general trends over such a relatively short period as a decade. To gain a coherent view, it is necessary to consider works published in the 1960s as well as the 1970s and view them in relation to special lines or traditions of comparative inquiry. To grasp one important tendency, it is useful to go back to 1966, a year that saw the publication of two unusually ambitious studies in comparative history—C.E. Black's *Dynamics of Modernization*[7] and Barrington Moore's *Social Origins of Dictatorship and Democracy*.[8] These two books provided competing paradigms for doing comparative history in the grand manner, which is nothing less than an attempt to compare the essential dynamics of entire societies. Black's work was rooted in modernization theory, which, according to him, described "the process by which historically evolved institutions are adapted to the rapidly changing functions that reflect the unprecedented increase in man's knowledge, permitting control over his environment, that accompanied the industrial revolution."[9] In this initial study, he looked at the process worldwide, and, concentrating on the political dimension, identified seven distinct patterns of "political modernization." Black has remained a dedicated promoter and practitioner of "comparative modernization" studies.[10] In 1975 he collaborated with seven other authors, three of whom were fellow historians, to produce *The Modernization of Japan and Russia*, a magisterial product of integrated team scholarship which combined richness of historical detail with a consistent theoretical framework.[11] The work was genuinely interdisciplinary— the other contributors were two economists and two sociologists— and relentlessly comparative; at no time is the reader so absorbed in one society that he is unaware of the other. It is the most successful example to date of the social-scientific approach to comparative history and suggests that the wave of the future for this kind of work may well be joint efforts by historians and comparative sociologists or economists.

Moore's *Social Origins* provided a quite different model. It was also concerned with "modernization" as a comparable process occurring throughout the world, but the important variable for Moore was the role of social classes, especially the peasantry, and not the interrelation of state formation, cultural traditions, and technological development that is central for Black and his collaborators. In comparing the agrarian sources of modernity in England, France, the United States, China, Japan, and India, Moore distinguished three different paths to the modern world: one leads to capitalist democracy by way of bourgeois revolution, a second to fascism ("revolution from above"), and a third to communism through the revolutionary mobilization of the peasantry. Moore's neo-Marxian class analysis offered a clear alternative to the conventional modernization paradigm as a theoretical scheme for comparing the transition from preindustrial to industrial society in various parts of the world. No other work comparable to his in scope and incisiveness has appeared, but in the same neo-Marxian vein were Eric R. Wolf's *Peasant Wars of the Twentieth Century*[12] and Immanuel Wallerstein's *Modern World-System*. Strictly speaking, however, Wallerstein's influential study was not comparative at all, because its frame of reference was a single "European world-economy" that had its origins in the sixteenth century. But its distinction between "core," "semi-peripheral," "peripheral," and "external" areas and its discussion of the kinds of processes that occur in each offered a provocative set of hypotheses to guide the work of comparative historians with a Marxian orientation.[13]

Most of the comparative history that has been done by Americans since the 1960s has not had the grand scope and commitment to a single overarching theory that characterizes the work of Black, Moore, and Wallerstein. It has been concerned less with the dynamics of entire societies than with the role and character of particular ideas, institutions, modes of social and political action, or environmental challenges in a small number of national settings, most often only two. It has tended to be eclectic, ad hoc, or casual in its use of social theory and usually retains as its main purpose the better comprehension of particular societies or groups of related societies rather than the discovery of universal laws of social development or the driving forces of world history. Hence it is closer than the work of the "grand manner" comparativists to the conventional tendency of historians to look for particularity, complexity, and ambiguity. Yet the very act of comparison requires categories that are comparable and some presuppositions about what is constant and predictable in human motivation or behavior. Without such assumptions, one could write parallel histories but not comparative ones. Hence comparative historians with more modest ambitions than Black, Moore, and Wallerstein are inevitably driven to a kind of "middle range" social theorizing that is generally more defensible when it is made explicit. Some of the questions that comparativists have difficulty evading are the extent to which people in comparable circumstances are impelled by "idealist" or "materialist" motives; the appropriateness of such concepts as class, caste, race, ethnic group, and status group to describe particular forms of social stratification; and the cross-cultural meaning of such terms as equality, democracy, fascism, racism, and capitalism. One of the great values of comparative history is that it forces such issues to the forefront of consciousness and demands that they be resolved in some fashion that is neither parochial not culture-bound.

It must be conceded, however, that the usual impulse that has led Americans to do comparative history has not been so much a desire for cosmopolitan detachment or conceptual clarity as the hope that they can learn something new about American history by comparing some aspect of it with an analogous phenomenon in another society. The subjects of comparative historical study which have aroused the greatest interest and stimulated the most work in the United States are clearly those that arise from a sense that some central feature of the American experience has an obvious parallel elsewhere. The fact that other societies have arisen out of a process of settlement and geographic expansion has spawned comparative colonization and frontier studies; the existence elsewhere in the Americas of black servitude has led to a substantial outpouring of comparative work on slavery and race relations; and, most recently, the awareness that the struggle for women's rights and equality with men has not been unique to the United States has resulted in the first signs of a comparative historiography of women and sex roles. An efficient way to sum up the most characteristic manifestations of comparative history in the United States is to deal with each of these subareas individually before taking note of a small amount of work that deals with other subjects and suggests additional comparative possibilities.

The comparative study of colonization and frontier expansion derives from a post–World War II reaction against dominant traditions in American historiography which viewed the United States in isolation from the rest of the world and asserted a uniqueness that was never verified—as any claim to uniqueness must be—by a sustained use of the comparative method. Fredrick Jackson Turner's celebrated hypothesis that "the American way of life," and more specifically its legacy of democracy and individualism, resulted from the frontier experience and not from the transplantation of European culture and ideologies was reexamined in a cross-cultural perspective. Frontier historians and historical geographers have produced a literature, mostly in the form of articles or essays, juxtaposing the westward movement in the United States with frontier expansion in Canada, Australia, South Africa, Argentina, and Brazil; some have looked even farther afield and examined Roman, medieval European, Russian, and Chinese frontiers in light of the Turner thesis.[14] What has emerged is a distinct impression that frontier expansions have varied so greatly in their causes and consequences that it is questionable whether one can speak of "the frontier" as a distinctive historical process with predictable results. In 1968, however, Ray Allen Billington attempted to resurrect a neo-Turnerian claim for American uniqueness by arguing that many of the differences between frontiers can be accounted for by varying physical conditions. The American frontier differed from all others in its consequences, he asserted, because nowhere else was "the physical environment conducive to exploitation by propertyless individuals *and* the invading pioneers equipped by tradition to capitalize fully on that environment."[15]

This cross-cultural testing of the Turner thesis has led to some suggestive comparative insights about the effect of physical environments and preexisting institutions or values on the establishment of new settler communities, but it has not resulted in book-length studies of historiographic significance. A major reason for this lack of development beyond the essay has been a widespread tendency among American historians in general to repudiate Turner's thesis that the frontier had a decisive effect on American society, politics, or "national character." In 1968, Seymour Martin Lipset concluded after a brief review of comparative frontier studies that doubt had been cast on Turner's contention that "the frontier experience was the main determinant of American egalitarianism." What happened on other frontiers pointed to the importance in the American case of "values derived from the revolutionary political origins and the Calvinist work ethos."[16] As frontier history moved to the periphery of American historiography, the impulse to do comparative frontier studies waned. But the recent vogue of American Indian history and a tendency to redefine the frontier as "an intergroup situation"[17] (Turner and his followers had conceived of the frontier as "open land" and had grossly neglected the Native American side of the process) has inspired renewed interest in comparative frontier history as a way of making sense of the interactions of the white settlers and indigenous peoples in a variety of contexts, especially the North American, South African, and Latin American.[18]

A serious attempt has also been made to develop a comparative perspective on European settlement in North America and elsewhere based on premises radically different from those of the frontier school. In *The Founding of New Societies* (1964) Louis Hartz sought to substitute a kind of cultural and ideological determinism for Turner's environmentalism to explain why the United States had become a unique kind of "liberal" society.[19] Collaborating with specialists on the history of settlement in Latin America, South Africa, Canada, and Australia, Hartz further developed the thesis, anticipated in his *Liberal Tradition in America*,[20] that European colonists and the societies they founded were shaped less by frontier processes and experiences than by their European antecedents. He argued that each settler society represented a particular "fragment" of an evolving European civilization, the nature of which was predetermined by the mindset and social background of the original colonists. Since each "new society" contained at the outset only one element of a European dialectic that included "feudalism," "liberalism," and "radicalism," it lost "the impetus for change that the whole provides."[21] Latin American civilization, therefore, represented an immobilized feudalism, the United States an ossified liberalism, and Australia an atrophied form of the proletarian radicalism of the early industrial revolution. The grand schema that Hartz set out in his introduction and in his essay on the United States was only partly sustained by the other contributors. Although they made an effort to remain within the framework that he had laid down, they were not entirely successful, suggesting that the scheme may have been too rigid and deterministic to do justice to complex historical situations. Although the "fragment" theory provoked considerable discussion for a time, it did not in fact become a guiding paradigm for subsequent comparative history.

The ideas and actions of colonizers nevertheless remain viable subjects for comparative study. James Lang's *Conquest and Commerce* juxtaposed and contrasted the political structures and economies of the colonial systems or empires established by Spain and England in the New World from the beginnings of settlement until the end of the eighteenth century.[22] After giving a detailed portrait of each pattern, Lang concluded with a comparison that threw into sharp relief the major differences accounting for the divergent outcomes of simultaneous efforts at imperial reorganization in the late eighteenth century. By focusing on the view from the metropole rather than on the internal development of colonial societies, he provided a useful perspective for understanding the degree to which politically dependent "frontier" societies were in fact influenced or manipulated by outside or metropolitan forces.

The most highly developed subject of comparative historical study in the United States is the character and consequences of a single institution that developed initially within the colonial systems treated by Lang—Afro-American slavery. More than the study of frontiers or "the founding of new societies," comparative work on slavery and race relations has resulted in a substantial body of literature that has developed its own set of issues and stimulated an ongoing debate. Among the reasons that comparative history "took off" in this field rather than others are (1) the assumption that slavery as a concept is relatively easy to define, at least when compared with "frontier"; (2) the great public preoccupation in the 1960s and early 1970s with the race issue in the United States; and (3) the stimulus of a well-formulated thesis about the differences between slaves societies and their legacies in Anglo and Iberian America around which the discussion could revolve. The Tannenbaum-Elkins thesis, developed in the 1940s and 1950s, postulated a Latin American pattern of mild slavery and "open" race relations that was ascribed mainly to the persistence and enforcement of Catholic-hierarchical traditions. This pattern was contrasted with that in British America, where, it was argued, Protestantism, capitalistic individualism, and a high degree of local autonomy for slaveholders resulted in a peculiarly harsh and closed system of servitude that left behind it a heritage of blatant discrimination against all those of African ancestry.[23] Herbert S. Klein's *Slavery in the Americas* attempted to confirm this basic view of differences between the two patterns through a detailed comparison of slavery in Cuba and Virginia.[24]

David Brion Davis presented the first really substantial challenge to the Tannenbaum-Elkins thesis in *The Problem of Slavery in Western Culture*.[25] Although this work was mainly a history of ideas about slavery within an international context rather than a comparative history in the strict sense, it contained a long section showing the basic similarities of slave institutions in British and Latin America. Arguing that slavery necessarily involved some kind of tension or compromise between the conception of the bondsman as property or thing and the recognition of his essential humanity, Davis suggested that Tannenbaum and Elkins had exaggerated the extent to which the legal systems of British and Iberian America stressed different sides of this inescapable duality. He also cast doubt on the assumption that Latin American slaves were treated less harshly by their masters. In a later essay summarizing his argument, Davis conceded that "American slavery took a great variety of forms," but attributed the differences less to the cultural-legal traditions stressed by Tannenbaum and Elkins than to "economic pressures and such derivative factors as the nature of employment, the number of slaves owned by a typical master, and the proportion of slaves in a given society."[26] The stage of economic development in particular regions, he concluded, was probably more important for distinguishing slave regimes than was the national or cultural background of the slave owners. Subsequent comparative studies of slave conditions have tended to sustain Davis's position. The work of Franklin Knight, Carl Degler, and others has deepened our sense of how economic and demographic conditions shaped the treatment and governance of slaves in fairly predictable ways that were to a great extent independent of cultural and legal traditions.[27]

But Davis had left open an avenue for cross-cultural contrast by acknowledging the validity of Tannenbaum's contention that manumission was easier to obtain and much more extensive in Iberian America than in British settlements and that subsequent distinctions between freedmen and whites were less rigid. What he was questioning was the extent to which this difference resulted from "the character of slavery."[28] In an essay entitled "The Treatment of Slaves in Different Countries" Eugene Genovese helped to clarify the issue and pointed toward a possible synthesis by distinguishing among various kinds of "treatment." Where Tannenbaum's followers went wrong, he suggested, was in contending that slaves were better treated on a day-to-day basis in Latin America than in the United States and then using this alleged contrast to explain the readier access of "the black slave as a black man" to "freedom and citizenship."[29] There was in fact no necessary causal relationship and hence no contradiction between studies showing that physical treatment was dependent on material conditions and those claiming a significant cross-cultural difference between patterns of racial mobility and differentiation.

In the early 1970s, therefore, day-to-day conditions of slave life were less and less taken as a basis for contrasting British American and Latin American slave societies. The generalization that slavery in this sense was milder in Latin America than in the United States appeared to be almost totally discredited. But the difference that Tannenbaum had also found in the racial attitudes and policies arising first during the slave era in relation to manumission and free people of color and then persisting after emancipation now came to the forefront as something that needed to be explained independently of the harshness or mildness of plantation regimes. The most important and successful study that clearly distinguished the determinants of slave conditions from those of race relations was Carl Degler's *Neither Black nor White: Slavery and Race Relations in Brazil and the United States* (1971). Degler argued that demographic factors, particularly the persistence of an international slave trade that provided relatively inexpensive bondsmen, actually made slavery a harsher institution in Brazil than in the United States. In the latter case, the earlier closing of the trade and the need for domestic reproduction of the slave force resulted in better material conditions and less flagrant cruelty. At the same time, however, the American system produced a more restrictive attitude toward manumission and imposed a racial caste system on freedmen and their descendants that had no real analogue in Brazil. Although he documented a tradition of color prejudice and discrimination in Brazil, Degler found that a "mulatto escape hatch" provided a chance for upward mobility for many Brazilians of African descent. He explained this difference from the more rigid American form of racial stratification in terms of larger differences between Brazilian and American social and cultural development. The contrast between a rapidly modernizing, politically democratic, and formally egalitarian society and one that has been characterized by underdevelopment and the persistence of a hierarchical social order provided a contextual basis for understanding why race relations have differed in the two countries.

Despite its extremely favorable reception, *Neither Black nor White* has not been followed by similarly ambitious and detailed comparisons of the historical origin or background of race patterns in two or more New World societies. An important article by Donald L. Horowitz, published in 1973, drew attention to the circumstances surrounding early miscegenation and to the security needs of various slave societies as key variables in determining whether or not an intermediate mulatto or "colored" group emerged.[30] For the most part, however, the trend in the 1970s has been away from the direct comparison of slave societies and the racial systems associated with them. As evidenced by volumes emanating from "comparative" conferences, the scholars of various disciplines who are interested in New World slavery and race relations have been devoting themselves mainly to applying new and more sophisticated approaches and techniques, particularly those involving quantification, to the study of individual cases.[31] Explicit comparison has been left largely in the hands of editors and reviewers, who have

been understandably reluctant to draw sweeping comparative generalizations from such a complex mass of new data. In the long run, this
particularism may lead to better and more subtle comparisons; but for
the moment its stress on the shaping effect of local economic, demographic, and ecological contexts makes cross-cultural contrast more
difficult and problematic than it has been in the past.

Somewhat distinct from the mainstream of interdisciplinary comparative slavery and race-relations studies are efforts to deal cross-culturally
with slaveholding classes, antislavery movements, and the causes and
consequences of emancipation. Instead of focusing on the enduring
structural features of multiracial slave societies, this body of work has
concentrated on historical processes and transformations with a crucial
political dimension. The landmark study of this kind was the first long
essay in Eugene Genovese's *World the Slaveholders Made,* which differ-
entiated between slaveholding classes in various parts of the Americas
and tried to account for their divergent responses to the threat of abolition.[32] The important variable for Genovese was the nature of class consciousness among planter groups as determined by their relations both
with dominant classes in a metropole and with their own slaves.
Although not systematically comparative, Robert Brent Toplin's
Abolition of Slavery in Brazil frequently referred to analogous developments in the United States and lent support to some of Genovese's arguments.[33] In a 1972 article, Toplin made direct comparisons between
slaveholder reactions to abolitionism in the two contexts.[34] David Brion
Davis's *Problem of Slavery in the Age of Revolution* dealt with antislavery movements on both sides of the Atlantic in the late eighteenth and
early nineteenth centuries.[35] Like his earlier work, this study was more
in the genre of "international history" than an example of sustained
comparative analysis, but it did provide considerable insight into how
the hegemonies of social class could influence antislavery attitudes and
actions in various settings. In 1978 C. Vann Woodward and I both published essays pointing beyond slavery itself and comparing emancipa-
tions and the subsequent establishment of new racial orders in a variety
of situations.[36]

My use of the Cape Colony of South Africa as one of three cases may
be part of a new trend to look beyond the Americas for forced-labor or
racial situations suitable for comparison with those in the United States.
William Wilson's sociohistorical analysis of race relations in the United
States and South Africa in *Power, Racism, and Privilege*[37] and Kenneth
P. Vickery's 1974 article "Herrenvolk Democracy and Egalitarianism in

South Africa and the U.S. South"[38] suggested the potentialities of a comparative approach to the development of patterns of racial inequality in North America and South Africa.[39] The introduction to the volume edited by Suzanne Miers and Igor Kopytoff, *Slavery in Africa*,[40] and the comparative essay that provides the conceptual framework for Fredrick Cooper's *Plantation Slavery on the East Coast of Africa*[41] have begun the process of integrating indigenous African slave systems into the universe of cross-cultural slavery studies. Work is also in progress comparing American slavery and Russian serfdom.[42] A pioneer effort to extend the comparative study of race relations into modern urban situations on both sides of the Atlantic is Ira Katznelson's *Black Men, White Cities: Race, Politics, and Migration in the United States, 1900–1930, and Britain, 1948–1968*.[43]

If the civil rights movement of the 1960s gave an impetus to the comparative study of slavery and race relations, something similar is now beginning to occur in the new field of women's history that is associated with the recent revival of feminism in the United States. The role and status of women are obviously subjects readily accessible to cross-cultural analysis. As yet, however, comparative women's history has not produced any major hypotheses that lend themselves to testing in a variety of situations. All we have, in fact, are a small number of isolated studies that do not bear any clear and direct relationship to each other. The most important of these are Ross Evans Paulson's *Women's Suffrage and Prohibition*,[44] an analysis of the interaction between feminist and temperance movements in the United States, England, and the Scandinavian countries (with asides on France, Australia, and New Zealand); Roger Thompson's *Women in Stuart England and America*,[45] an attempt to explain why women were apparently better off in the colonies than in the mother country; and, most recently, Leila Rupp's *Mobilizing Women for War*,[46] an ingenious comparison of the nature and success of propaganda directed at increasing female participation in World War II in the United States and Germany. Because this body of work lacks a common focus, theme, or set of theoretical assumptions, it is clearly premature to speak of a comparative historiography of women and sex roles in the same sense that one can point to a tradition of comparative slavery or frontier studies.

During the past decade or so, there have also been a small number of "one-shot" comparative works that have not as yet been followed up. Perhaps the most significant of these was Robert Kelley's *Transatlantic*

Persuasion, a study of liberal-democratic ideologies and spokesmen in the United States, England, and Canada in the mid- to late-Victorian period.[47] But Kelley's pursuit of uniformities and his conviction that he was really dealing with a single transatlantic phenomenon inhibited his use of comparative analysis. Another kind of comparativist would have been more alert to differences that would require explanation. Some of the essays in C. Vann Woodward's *Comparative Approach to American History* suggested some excellent possibilities for comparative history that have still not been pursued systematically. John Higham's short but provocative discussion of how American immigration looks in relation to the experience of "other immigrant receiving countries," such as Canada, Argentina, Brazil, and Australia, provided an open invitation for detailed comparisons of immigration and ethnicity.[48] David Shannon's fine essay "Socialism and Labor" revived the old question of why socialism failed to develop in the United States in the way it did in other industrial nations.[49] The current vogue of labor history should eventually inspire some brave scholars to attempt sustained comparisons of the political role of labor in the history of the United States and other modern societies. The possible rise of a new focus of comparative historical interest—the maintenance of public order—may be heralded by two books published in 1977, one comparing police activity in New York and London in the mid–nineteenth century[50] and the other analyzing problems of public security in Ireland during the era of World War I and in Palestine in the late 1930s.[51]

When all is said and done, however, the dominant impression that is bound to arise from any survey of recent comparative work by American historians is not how much has been done but rather how little.[52] What we have been considering is in fact a very small fraction of the total output of American historians. The percentage would shrink even further were we to limit our attention to the work of those who are historians in the strict disciplinary sense. Such notable comparativists as Moore, Wolf, Wallerstein, Hartz, Lang, Wilson, and Katznelson have in fact been trained in other disciplines. A main reason for what was earlier referred to as the "sparseness" of comparative work is the way the historical profession is organized in the United States. Historians receive most of their predoctoral training in the history of a single nation or cultural area. Teaching and publication are similarly specialized. There are, to my knowledge, no professorships of comparative history at major institutions.[53] There is no journal devoted exclusively to comparative history, although *Comparative Studies in*

Society and History provides a forum for historians along with comparativists from other disciplines. The absence of doctoral programs,
professorships, and journals devoted to comparative history per se has
clearly had an inhibiting effect on the development of this mode of historical analysis. Since reputations and successful careers are the products of intense geographical specialization, young historians launch
into comparative work at some risk to their future prospects.
Established scholars can afford the luxury of a foray into cross-cultural
analysis, but are reluctant to go too far lest they lose touch with the
main lines of development in their own field of specialization. This is
especially true because historians are more uncomfortable than sociologists, for example, with generalizations that are not based on detailed
knowledge and some immersion in primary sources. It thus becomes
necessary for would-be comparativists to develop what amounts to a
second or even a third field of specialization, almost equivalent to their
original area of expertise, if they wish to go beyond "comparative perspective" and do sustained comparative history that will be respected
by experts on each of the societies that they are examining.
Understandably, therefore, few historians are willing to devote the time
and energy that such an enterprise involves. Unless comparative history
becomes a distinct field or recognized subdiscipline within history, in
the manner of comparative sociology, politics, or literature, it is unlikely that it will become a major trend within the profession. Perhaps
the decision to make comparative history the theme of the 1978 convention of the American Historical Association reflected some tentative
movement in this direction. But for the moment, most comparative history is done by scholars who are either based in another discipline or
taking an extended holiday from their normal role as historians of a
single nation or cultural area.

CHAPTER TWO

The Frontier in South African and American History

The frontier experience still looms large in popular descriptions and explanations of the "American character." Pioneers hewing new communities out of the wilderness are revered as the archetypal American democrats and individualists, a notion that received historical respectability in the writings of Frederick Jackson Turner and his disciples. Other nations have also had frontiers and frontier interpretations of their history, and one of the most conspicuous is the Republic of South Africa. Afrikaner nationalism—the ideology of the dominant segment of the ruling white minority—draws strength and determination from a romanticized image of the Great Trek, a mass migration of Dutch-speaking stock farmers into the interior of South Africa during the 1830s and 1840s.

For Afrikaners the Great Trek combines elements of our revolution and the westward movement; for the migrants known as Voortrekkers were not merely seeking new pastures for their cattle and sheep but were also making a conscious effort to escape from the mildly autocratic rule that the British had established over the Cape of Good Hope earlier in the century. The republics they founded in the Orange Free State and the Transvaal did not survive the Anglo-Boer War of 1899–1902, but Afrikaner nationalists regard them as prototypes for the modern South African state.

The American and South African frontier myths differ somewhat in the kind of nationalism they project. According to Turner, the West was a great melting pot for various white ethnic and sectional groups—out of the mixture came a common American nationality. The Voortrekker experience, on the other hand, is the exclusive property of only one of the two major white ethnic groups in South Africa. English speakers— about 40 percent of the present-day white population—have inherited some of the stigma attached to their ancestors for opposing Afrikaner independence.

But in another respect the two mythologies are quite similar: both necessarily deny the right of indigenous populations to the land that people of European origins settled in the course of frontier expansion. They do this in part by making it appear that native peoples were very thin on the ground in all or most of the territory now occupied by whites. Turner and his followers virtually ignored the American Indian and generally referred to the areas settled by pioneers as "free land." Low estimates of Indian population at the time of Columbus—now believed to be a small fraction of the actual numbers—reinforced the myth that America was scarcely peopled at all before the whites came.

Popular Afrikaner historiography makes the similarly misleading claim that Europeans occupied most of South Africa before Bantu-speaking Africans, migrating from the north, had arrived. The fact is that Bantu-speakers were thickly settled almost everywhere except in the present-day Cape Province before the first white settlement in 1652, and other indigenous peoples occupied the Cape itself. Because of the historical accident that many of the Voortrekkers migrated into areas recently depopulated by wars among Africans, even the great interior plain known as *highveld* is portrayed as a kind of demographic vacuum into which whites could move without really dispossessing anybody.

Yet the histories of both America and South Africa are filled with wars between white settlers and indigenous groups fighting to maintain their territory. Celebrants of white expansionism have thus been unable to ignore entirely the historical record of conquest and dispossession. To justify the forcible displacement and subjugation of American Indians or indigenous Africans, they have resorted to the ethnocentric—and at times downright racist—argument that the encroaching white civilization was so vastly superior to the way of life of "savages" who got in its way that human progress or the will of God was served by its triumphant march.

This one-sided, self-serving, and stereotypical view of the frontier process remains deeply embedded in the popular consciousness of contemporary white Americans and South Africans. But, because of the enormous difference in the numbers and relative importance of surviving indigenous groups, it is a mythology that has much more resonance in the South African case. American Indians were so decisively outnumbered, defeated, and dispossessed in the course of American history that they have been relegated to the margins of American life and consciousness—objects of neglect or paternalism rather than fear and systematic repression.

In South Africa, of course, the descendants of those on the "other side" of the frontier remain the overwhelming majority of the total population. There is a genuine and plausible fear among whites that the frontier will, in a sense, reopen and that the European dominance achieved by violence in the late nineteenth century will be violently overthrown in the late twentieth. It is inconceivable that American Indians will ever regain their original domain, but it seems highly probable that Africans will some day win back theirs. Hence the legendary exploits of the Voortrekkers in their wars with the Zulus or Ndebeles retain a deadly contemporary relevance. White American children can casually divide up to play "cowboys and Indians," but it is hard to imagine Afrikaner youngsters playing "Voortrekkers and Zulus." Traditional enemies who remain dangerous are not romanticized and made into heroes with whom children can identify.

The books under review seek to dispel ethnocentric mythologies by viewing frontier phases of South African or American history in their full complexity, and from the indigenous as well as white perspective.[1] All three are collections of essays by several authors, and this of course makes it impossible to do justice to most of the individual contributions or to the full range of issues explored. Only one of them—*The Frontier in History*—focuses exclusively on the frontier per se and attempts a comparison of the American and South African experiences by juxtaposing essays that treat similar aspects of each.

The others—*The Shaping of South African Society* and *Economy and Society in Pre-Industrial South Africa*—bring together the work of a new generation of scholars (British, American, and South African) concerned with various aspects of South African history between the beginnings of settlement in the seventeenth century and the consolidation of white rule by the British at the beginning of the twentieth. But several of the contributors address the nature of frontiers and the role they have played in the rise of a white-supremacist nation-state.

In the introductory essay to *The Frontier in History,* a path-breaking work of comparative history, Howard Lamar and Leonard Thompson

define a frontier "not as a boundary line, but as a territory or zone of in-
terpenetration between two previously distinct societies. Usually, one of
the societies is indigenous to the region, or at least has occupied it for
many generations; the other is intrusive."[2] To understand fully what is
going on in a given frontier zone, they maintain, the historian has to look
at the process from the indigenous as well as the "intrusive" side. In
contrast to earlier frontier historians, who concentrated on the actions
and attitudes of European colonists and pioneers, most of the contributors to *The Frontier in History* devote at least as much attention to the
outlook and responses of Indians or Africans. Indeed, the essays on the
American frontier tend to go to the opposite extreme by dealing much
more extensively with the Indian reactions or adjustments than with the
causes, motivations, and long-term consequences of white expansionism.

Unlike Turner's, the Lamar-Thompson frontier is more a phase of
race relations than a wilderness where settlers were free to build new
societies. But it does retain one feature of Turner's theory: it "opens"
and "closes" in predictable ways. According to the essay by Hermann
Giliomee, a leading South African historian, a frontier is open so long
as neither the intruders nor the original inhabitants have exclusive political control and must, for some purposes at least, deal with each
other as equals. It closes when the whites have effectively conquered
and subordinated the indigenous peoples. For Turner the closing of the
frontier meant that there was no more free or empty land for settlement; for Giliomee and other contributors to *The Frontier in History*,
the frontier phase is over when there are no more independent sources
of opposition to white political dominance.

There is a teleology at work here that raises questions about the relationship of frontiers to broader patterns of historical development. If
one asks why whites in the United States and South Africa bothered to
open frontiers in the first place and what they had achieved once they
had closed them, the inquiry has gone beyond the usual bounds of frontier history. Most of the writers on South African frontiers in Lamar
and Thompson (and also in the other two anthologies) explicitly or implicitly reduce the frontier to a phase or chapter in some larger, continuing process. Their counterparts among American historians—with
their stress on how the white triumph irrevocably destroyed the Indian
way of life—are less likely to achieve this broader kind of perspective.

The work of the South Africanists suggests that it is not enough to
counter ethnocentrism by looking at the frontier from the "other
side." It is also necessary to expose the underlying forces or ideologies

that affected both sides, determined the outcome, and shaped the "postfrontier" society. But these historians are not of one mind on the nature of these deeper influences. One school of thought stresses material or economic forces. According to Robert Ross in Lamar and Thompson's book and Martin Legassick and other contributors to the book edited by Marks and Atmore, frontier interaction can best be interpreted as an episode in the growth of capitalism. The long-term development that preoccupies them is the transformation of members of independent tribes into oppressed proletarians.

There are differences of opinion on exactly how or when this occurred. According to several writers in Marks and Atmore, the commercial capitalism of the frontier and immediate postfrontier periods offered substantial opportunities for indigenous black "peasants" to produce for the new markets created by white expansionism. It was not, in their view, until the triumph of industrial capitalism in the early twentieth century that Africans were turned en masse into an economically exploited class, a process rationalized by racism rather than caused by it. From this perspective the frontier stage itself begins to look surprisingly benign.

South African settlers, we are told, not only fought against black Africans but also traded with them, formed alliances with them against other whites, and sometimes even married them. It appears that there was much more racial tolerance and mutually advantageous give-and-take than in the brutally repressive society that emerged after the frontier closed. Robert Ross, on the other hand, seeks to qualify this image of a preindustrial age of racial accommodation and African opportunity by arguing that the extension of capitalistic relationships which began in the seventeenth century had always tended to undermine native economies, deprive Africans of access to the means of production, and force them to do menial work for whites. During the two and a half centuries of white expansion, there were recurrent opportunities for independent native producers to feed off the white economy, but they were invariably squeezed out as soon as Europeans were in a position to do their own hunting, livestock raising, or farming. The industrial revolution, one might conclude, did not bring a decisive change in attitudes and policies; it merely offered a new arena for traditional forms of exploitation.

Several of the writers in *The Frontier in History* as well as in *The Shaping of South African Society* resist the notion that economics and

the rise of capitalism were at the root of all major frontier developments. For them, culture and ethnicity have a life of their own that is
not completely reducible to the pursuit of profits, markets, and labor.
From the beginnings of settlement white colonists manifested a strong
sense of cultural or racial superiority over their indigenous rivals. A
major theme of *The Shaping of South African Society* is the early rise
of color prejudice and discrimination in South Africa—not as a result
of the frontier itself, as an earlier generation of historians had claimed,
but mainly because of preconceptions brought from Europe and the
subsequent opportunity to identify race with social status. While the
frontier was still "open," conditions on the outer fringe of settlement
actually worked to leaven or modify these racist attitudes, because survival often required cooperation with, and sometimes even dependence
on, indigenous groups. But when white rule was firmly established, the
discriminatory ethos already rooted in the more settled areas rapidly
took over. These historians see in the larger setting for frontier history
the early emergence of white supremacy as an ideology with deeper
roots than economic determinists will acknowledge.

Whatever the extent and depth of early white racism—and this is a
debatable issue—it is clear that Africans did not think so readily of the
difference between "us" and "them" as Europeans were capable of
doing when the chips were down. English and Afrikaners quarreled and
even fought with each other, but when the European presence was
clearly threatened by African resistance, they generally found some way
to collaborate. Africans, on the other hand, tended to place loyalty to
tribe or nation above the need for a common front against the intruder.
There were few "native wars" in South African history that did not find
indigenous blacks joining forces with whites as a way of revenging
themselves on some traditional enemy.

American Indians also failed to match the white invaders' racial solidarity, and some of the essays in Lamar and Thompson's book shed additional light on this weakness and help to explain why the white "side"
prevailed on both frontiers. Here, too, purely economic pressures are
played down and stress is placed on cultural differences that gave greater
cohesion to the intruders. In his fine essay on "The North American
Frontier as Process and Context," Robert Berkhofer notices the incompatibility between Anglo-American and Indian economies, but he emphasizes differences in political culture as determining the nature of the
conflict and its outcome. Crucial for him is the fact that whites belonged
to nation-states while Indians were members of "stateless societies."

This meant that conquering the Indians was a slow and piecemeal process, but it also ultimately gave whites the upper hand, because they were capable of mobilizing and commanding the loyalty of larger populations while at the same time exploiting the differences among many autonomous and weakly governed Indian groups. This insight is not entirely applicable to South Africa; for there *were* indigenous nation-states in southern Africa—most notably the centralized Zulu kingdom. But there, as in the United States, the comparatively broader and more inclusive national, ethnic, and racial identities of whites usually gave them the edge in confrontations with indigenous peoples.

In another perceptive essay, James Axtell compares Anglo-American and Amerindian religion during the colonial period. The former was militant, aggressive, and intolerant; the latter was pluralistic, pragmatic, and capable of borrowing and synthesizing the usable elements of other faiths. In a good companion piece, Richard Elphick describes the great energy and dedication that characterized white missionary activity in South Africa during the nineteenth century. The missionaries were successful in converting Africans because their message seemed more appropriate to the circumstances of colonized blacks than indigenous religions that had worked well enough before the great disruptions brought by the European invasion. Although they differ somewhat in tone and interpretation, the two essays suggest that aggressive Christianity was a powerful weapon in the white arsenal, because it could sow doubts about traditional world-views and create serious cultural divisions which whites could sometimes exploit. (It could also backfire in the form of millenarian protests inspired in part by Christian eschatology.)

Making the frontier primarily a zone of cultural or ideological conflict in which whites had most of the advantages runs the risk of overlooking some of the more mundane reasons why the whites won out. If an ideological or cultural interpretation is a useful corrective to materialist explanations, the reverse is also true. Would Indians and Africans have been so culturally vulnerable if they had not already been weakened or outgunned by purely physical factors?

The physical vulnerabilities of American Indians are well described in Ramsay Cook's essay, in *The Frontier in History,* on the Canadian fur trade. Initially, Cook points out, the trade "provided the framework for a mutually profitable partnership" between whites and Indians. Tribes involved in this commerce retained their cultural integrity and independence for extended periods. But inexorably the trade created dependence on Europeans and induced native Americans to exhaust their capital of fur-bearing animals. Furthermore, "the same trade routes that brought buyer and seller together also brought epidemic diseases." Cook then summarizes the recent work suggesting that "the most significant consequence of early contact was biological." It is now estimated that there were perhaps 4.5 million Indians north of Mexico in 1492; by 1900 the figure had fallen to approximately 350,000. The main cause of this demographic disaster was the introduction of European diseases—smallpox and many others—for which native Americans had no immunity. Germs and viruses actually did more to ensure white conquest than settlers or armies. Besides merely reducing the numbers of Indians capable of resisting the white advance, epidemics caused "a breakdown of traditional values and beliefs"; for Indian medicine and religion "were totally ineffective when faced with these foreign contagions."[3]

Again the parallel with South Africa is inexact. Differences in the degree of indigenous susceptibility to the diseases brought by Europeans assume enormous comparative significance. In the early phases of white settlement at the Cape of Good Hope, as described in Elphick and Giliomee, the Dutch intruders confronted a native population with a relatively limited immunity to European microbes. As a result, the Khoikhoi—aboriginal herders known to Europeans as "Hottentots"— were decimated by a series of epidemics and greatly weakened in their capacity to resist Dutch encroachment and eventual reduction to semi-slavery. But the Bantu-speaking Africans whom settlers encountered for the first time on the eastern Cape frontier late in the eighteenth century were more resistant to epidemiological disaster. They not only kept their numbers but maintained a high rate of natural increase throughout the period of frontier contact and afterward. This demographic vitality is one of the main historical reasons why white domination of native populations remains fragile and reversible in South Africa.

It also helps to explain the differing situations of indigenous peoples after the frontier was closed. The most obvious contrast between the fate of the original inhabitants of the two places is that Africans became the principal source of labor for a white-dominated capitalistic economy while Indians were simply shunted aside to make way for plantations worked by African slaves and factories relying heavily on the labor of European immigrants. There are several reasons why Indians never became a significant part of the agricultural or industrial labor force in the United States, but the most important is the sheer lack of numbers resulting from the ravages of disease.

That the Euro-American triumph in the United States was so complete makes understandable the reluctance of historians interested primarily in the Indian experience to investigate the legacy of the frontier as a force in contemporary American life. Their concern is with a tragedy that is essentially over and irreversible, although Indian claims to land and self-government remain a live issue and a burden on the conscience of Americans committed to minority rights. But the questions Frederick Jackson Turner raised about the lasting impact of the westward movement on Euro-American culture and society deserve reconsideration from a new perspective that would be less given to emphasis on triumphs of the frontier settlers. To what extent is the careless and wasteful exploitation of natural resources in the United States an inheritance from the frontier scramble for seemingly limitless wealth? Does the resurgent American ethic of "looking out for number one" in any way represent a carryover of frontier individualism? Are we bellicose and moralistic in international relations partly because of habits of mind acquired during the conquest of North America? Do liberal fears of "a cowboy in the White House" represent more than a loose metaphor?

The historians in Lamar and Thompson's book shed little light on such questions because they assume that the frontier ended when the Indians were defeated. But some other recent writers on Indian-white relations have tried to see the process of Indian expropriation as a formative episode in the history of American capitalism.[4] If we look upon the frontier as a place where the spirit of capitalistic accumulation could flower without restraint, we can perhaps begin to recapture its significance for American history in general.

The extent to which the South African frontier prepared the way for what came later, namely the modern apartheid regime, remains a burning question for the Afrikanist contributors to these volumes. But virtually all of them conclude that the frontier experience per se was not a principal cause of contemporary racism, despite the popular metaphor of the "*laager* mentality" for Afrikaner attitudes. The historians of early white attitudes in Elphick and Giliomee are inclined to trace apartheid back to traditions established in the early postfrontier society of the western Cape (essentially Cape Town and its hinterland). The Marxist scholars writing in Marks and Atmore tend to attribute the theory and practice of apartheid to the rise of industrial capitalism after the closing of the last nineteenth-century frontier. It is not possible here to assess the particular strengths and weaknesses of these arguments. But it seems to me that these historical revisionists, in their zeal to refute an earlier and oversimplified view of the frontier as the determining factor in contemporary race relations, are in danger of forgetting some real contributions that the frontier made to the shaping of the South African brand of white supremacy.

A clear foreshadowing of modern apartheid policies can be found in the Afrikaner republics and the British colony of Natal in the mid-nineteenth century. In the former, the principle was established for the first time that only those of white ancestry were eligible for citizenship rights; in the latter, policies of territorial segregation and separate governance for Africans and Europeans were first devised. Hence two key elements of apartheid—a white monopoly on political power and the designation of separate living areas or "homelands"—were set out in preindustrial frontier polities still struggling with independent African nations on their borders.

Settlers in these areas had two urgent needs—physical security from the masses of Africans who either remained independent or were under only a loose form of white control, and an adequate supply of agricultural labor. In other words, they both feared and needed blacks. Efforts to exploit Africans as workers without giving them power and citizenship in white-dominated states or colonies not only antedated the migratory labor system and occupational "color bar" that developed in the gold mines at the end of the nineteenth century but also helped to provide a precedent for them.

Thus some of the attitudes and policies associated with contemporary apartheid were rooted in that phase of the frontier experience involving the initial establishment of white settler states in the interior of South Africa. Inherited prejudices may have influenced these pioneers, and the rise of industrial capitalism obviously suggested new and modified applications for the basic devices that they had developed for racial control and exploitation. But their contribution was important enough, in my view, to raise doubts about the emerging consensus that the frontier was not a significant source of the apartheid mentality.

CHAPTER THREE

From Exceptionalism to Variability

Recent Developments in Cross-National Comparative History

Seventeen years ago, I attempted to sum up the state of comparative history in the United States and concluded that "the body of work that qualifies as comparative history in the strict sense is characterized both by its relative sparseness and by its fragmentation." In 1997, work of this kind is no longer sparse, but it remains fragmented.[1]

The sheer volume of cross-national comparative work has increased markedly, but there is little commitment to comparative history as a primary specialization within history or even within sociology (where it is subsumed under the rubric of historical sociology). In both disciplines, cross-national comparative work exists primarily as a vehicle for the exploration of a particular problem or topic. Historians normally start with concerns arising from a particular problem or topic. Historians normally start with concerns arising from a particular national history and then seek to gain insights by examining an analogous phenomenon elsewhere. For historians of the United States, the anticipated payoff—at the outset, at least—is likely to be a better understanding of something American.

For sociologists and political scientists, the trigger is interest in a transnational process or recurring condition, such as class formation, ethnicity, state building, or revolution. For most historians and social scientists, comparative history is a way of isolating the critical factors or independent variables that account for national differences. But the former usually value the discovery and explanation of differences primarily as a stimulus to the reinterpretation of national histories; the latter value their

contribution to the development of a better model or theoretical understanding of the process, structure, or condition being studied.

It follows from such topical specializations—whether nationally specific or international and theoretical—that those who do cross-national
comparative history do not usually have a strong awareness of, or interest in, comparative work on other themes or topics. The two topics
that have generated the most intensive and sustained comparative interest in recent years are slavery and race relations and the growth of
welfare states (with special attention to the role of women and gender).
But comparative historians of race and those of welfare do not normally interact or comment on each other's work. Cross-disciplinary fertilization is most likely to occur in work on similar topics. To increase
the chances for such fertilization, to make more historians aware of the
potential gains from comparative studies, we need to transcend the existing fragmentation.

This essay attempts to do that by surveying and classifying recent comparative studies of interest to Americanists. I have tried to show the connections among comparative studies by scholars in different disciplines
and those on different topics. I offer the survey in the hope of stimulat-
ing awareness, because the prospects for the development of comparative history seem brighter than in 1980—indeed, than ever before.

What should comparative historians compare? How should nation-
states figure in their work? There is a lively debate on this issue. Like
other fields in modern history, comparative history has traditionally focused on nation-states. But some historians are now skeptical about the
value of cross-national comparisons, those that examine similar developments in two or more nations, discussing each case in roughly equal
depth and detail. Instead they advocate international or comparative
perspectives that do not juxtapose nations as such. In a thoughtful
essay criticizing historians of the United States for their failure to adopt
comparative perspectives, Raymond Grew argued that "the tendency to
make the nation (and the nation as defined by the state) the ultimate
unit of analysis" is "the single most important inhibition on comparative study." "Whole nations," he maintains, "usually prove too grand,
too comprehensive for the kind of fruitful comparison that uses dis-
criminating logic to make a discovery or establish a point not visible before." Ian Tyrrell echoed these concerns in an appeal for "international," as opposed to what is here described as cross-national
comparative history. "The critical failure" of American historians with

cosmopolitan ambitions, he contended, "has not been comparative and international perspectives themselves but rather the failure of comparative history to transcend the boundaries of nationalist historiography." Although they did not supply examples, Grew and Tyrrell implied that historians of the United States who do comparative work are likely to use other cases to buttress an exceptionalist view of the American past.[2]

American exceptionalism is in ill repute among contemporary historians for good reasons. The history of every nation has distinctive features, but the notion that the United States has exhibited radical peculiarities that have made its experience categorically different from that of other modern or modernizing countries has encouraged an oversimplified and often idealized view of the American past. Recent historians have shown that the United States was not immune to the tensions and conflicts that have occurred in other nations at similar stages of social and economic development. To the extent that cross-national comparative history involving the United States inevitably promotes radical exceptionalism, any claims that it contributes significantly to historical understanding would be highly suspect.

A distinction needs to be made between two ways of doing cross-national comparisons. Efforts to compare the entire history of one country with that of another—for precisely the reasons that Grew pointed out—have rarely been attempted. *Continental Divide,* by sociologist Seymour Martin Lipset, is the closest approximation that comes to mind, but this contrast of "the values and institutions of the United States and Canada" focuses on the present and makes brief forays into history in search of the origins of differences revealed by contemporary observations and opinion surveys. (Lipset, an unreconstructed American exceptionalist, argues that the Revolution bequeathed to the United States an enduring pattern of liberal individualism that to this day contrasts with a Canadian culture and institutional life that retain significant traces of Tory conservatism and collectivism.[3]) More commonly, cross-national historians compare a specific ideology, institution, or historical process in one society with its analogue in another and then explore the respective national contexts in order to uncover the sources of the similarities and differences that they have found.

Comparative historical sociologists, now major practitioners of comparative history, generally endorse the nation-state as a unit of analysis. According to the historical sociologist Aristide R. Zolberg, for example, "throughout modern history, national variations in economic organization and development determined different patterns of social stratification, and these in turn contributed to varied outcomes in state and nation formation." There is nothing sacred or primordial about nation-states, but in the West during the past two or three centuries and everywhere during the past fifty years, they are the largest units that provide an adequate context for most social, political, and cultural phenomena. Use of the nation-state—or of the semiautonomous colony or possession of an imperial power—as a unit of analysis does not by itself commit the historian to historiographic nationalism or to a belief in national exceptionalism. As Zolberg points out, the recognition that every nation is the unique product of its particular history does not necessarily mean that one nation departs from a general pattern manifested by all the others. A historian studying some comparable phenomenon in two nations would have no reason a priori to consider one of his cases the exception and the other the rule. That even the most localized comparative studies can benefit from a cross-national perspective is demonstrated by Norbert MacDonald's *Distant Neighbors: A Comparative Study of Seattle and Vancouver.* MacDonald argues convincingly that the most important source of difference in the way these similarly situated cities have developed is that one is in Canada and the other in the United States.[4]

The case for the nation-state as a basic unit of analysis in comparative historical studies gains additional credibility from the recent trend away from depoliticized social history and toward a recognition of the state or the polity as having a life of its own and an ability to shape, as well as be shaped by, economy and society.[5] Patterns of social and economic development in different national settings may seem similar, and invocation of such rubrics as advanced industrial capitalism can give an illusion of homogeneity. But differing governmental and political structures may produce widely divergent social movements and policies.

The interest in national differences is not limited to political sociologists and historians of the state. A competing paradigm emerges from the work of cultural sociologists such as Liah Greenfield. Her recent comparative study posits enduring cultural and ideological differences as the source of the diverse forms of nationalism that emerged in England, France, Russia, Germany, and the United States.[6] Whether one chooses political structure or political culture, national differences remain crucial to recent efforts to understand modern world history.

Those who favor international history over cross-national comparative history, such as Ian Tyrrell, are doing important work on efforts to transcend nationalism and national consciousness by affirming identities and developing organizations based on something other than national origin—in his work, gender or international sisterhood. But, despite Tyrrell's intentions to the contrary, his study of the international activities of the Women's Christian Temperance Union movement between 1880 and 1930 implicitly affirms the importance of national differences and identities. The women from various countries did not succeed in creating enduring solidarities based on gender. National differences got in the way and led to a fragmentation of interests and priorities.[7]

One might wish that it were otherwise. but historians have to confront the world as it has actually existed rather than as they would like it to have been. Nations and national identities are not facts of nature; they were socially and historically constructed, but they have become potent forces—probably the most salient sources of modern authority and consciousness. Historians, comparative or otherwise, can scarcely afford to ignore them.

To treat international and cross-national history as mutually exclusive would be a mistake. Nations are affected by international movements as well as by their own internal dynamics. In their practice historians recognize this. Such studies as David Brion Davis's two volumes on the problem of slavery effectively combine international and cross-national perspectives. My work on the comparative history of black ideologies in the United States and South Africa necessarily employs two distinct frames of reference—the national contexts and the international movements for liberation that inspired blacks in both countries.[8] Nations have their peculiarities that should never be forgotten, but they do not exist in isolation. There may be (as there were in the United States and South Africa) nations within nations—distinctive population groups that identify with an imagined community that transcends state boundaries and is very different from the polity in which they are forced to live.

Acknowledging the international context does not mean disregarding the nation as a unit of analysis. The most profound insights may come from showing how the national and international dimensions interact and modify each other. It might be argued, for example, that the living conditions of slaves were affected more by international economic imperatives than by specific national or colonial cultures and polities but that the racial ideas and practices that emerged from slavery and outlasted it were more variable and culturally specific.[9]

Although the logic of cross-national history does not require an exceptionalist perspective, the focus on the nation may at times give rise to the distortions of exceptionalism. A historian's preoccupation with the single nation that he habitually studies may contribute to the problem. It may be hard to avoid treating that nation as the foreground and creating a generalized image of others as background. But whatever its roots in habits of mind and in concerns about a particular nation, the chief source of the problem is a faulty method, resting on unexamined assumptions. It may be, as Grew and Tyrrell suggest, that historians of the United States who view their work as comparative find it difficult to avoid concluding that American history has been singular in some fundamental respect. If the other case or cases are assumed to represent an international norm from which the United States deviates radically, cross-national studies are likely to strengthen, rather than weaken, the notion of American exceptionalism. To skirt the trap, the comparative historian needs to begin with the assumption that each of her cases may be equally distinctive, equally likely to embody a transnational pattern or to depart from it. Notions of exceptionalism have long been woven into the fabric of comparative history involving the United States, but some comparative works of recent decades offer salutary models of nonexceptionalist history.

It was a contrast between the United States and certain European nations that gave rise to the exceptionalist historiographic tradition. Contrary to what is often alleged, that contrast was not always an unthinking one based on a vague notion of Europe; at times, it was rooted in a detailed knowledge of European history and culture.

The godfather of cross-national comparative history involving the United States, and the unwitting godfather of a certain view of American exceptionalism, was Alexis de Tocqueville. Although he never set out systematically to compare the two countries, his work, as the French scholar Jean-Claude Lamberti has pointed out, was "from beginning to end based on comparison of France and the United States" and was driven primarily by a desire to understand the legacy of the French Revolution. Yet Tocqueville did not intend to examine the United States as an exception. As Lamberti observed:

> To argue that the lessons of *Democracy in America* are relevant only to the United States is to encourage belief in American exceptionalism while discouraging the use of comparative method in political science. It is also to neglect the fact that the unique features of democratic liberalism in the United States are due to the absence of a great revolution in its origin.[10]

If France was the norm, the United States was indeed exceptional, but Tocqueville was keenly aware of the singularities of French history even within a European context (as compared with English history, for example). For the most part, he took American, rather than French, democracy to represent the normal path for egalitarian societies.

When Tocqueville was rediscovered by American historians in the 1940s and 1950s, they ignored his larger comparative framework and made his insights the basis of the "liberal consensus" view of the American past. But most neo-Tocquevillians did not do cross-national comparisons to sustain their view that the United States was exceptional because of its lack of both a feudal tradition and an antifeudal democratic revolution. They simply took for granted the notion that the United States had been spared the ideological and social cleavages that characterized West European history. The political scientist Louis Hartz was a partial exception. Hartz, who taught European as well as American political thought at Harvard University, combined Tocqueville's view that the United States was a liberal or democratic society virtually from its beginnings with a Marxian conception of the ideological history of Europe. *The Liberal Tradition in America* (1955) is actually a comparative work.[11] Although it focuses on American liberal thought, it makes innumerable references to European, especially French and British, thinkers. Had Hartz made his view of West European ideological development more explicit—rather than simply referring continually to European theorists and ideas (mostly to show how unimaginable they would have been in an American setting)—his work would have had greater weight.

In 1964, Hartz and several other scholars produced *The Founding of New Societies,* a pioneering comparative examination of the "settler societies" produced by European expansion. This work compares the United States as a *liberal* "fragment" of Europe with other fragments— Latin America, Canada, Australia, and South Africa—each exceptional in its own way. Hartz can be criticized for his relatively static conception of the fragments—only Europe, it seems, had an intellectual history, while its extensions and dependencies failed to evolve ideologically—but he cannot be accused of making the United States *more* "exceptional" than, say, South Africa. Rather than portraying a United States that departs from a general pattern, the book conveys the impression that the "new societies" presented a range of peculiarities. But Europe, the source of settlement, continues to serve as the standard from which all deviations are measured. The greatest significance of *The Founding of New Societies* was that it encouraged comparison between the United States and other settler societies and that it suggested a new and more sinister kind of American exceptionalism—the peculiarly rigid and intense racism that results when liberal democracy and the subjugation and exploitation of nonwhites are combined.[12]

Attempts to explain that kind of exceptionalism—and the habit of comparing the United States with the other settler societies—played a major role in the practice of comparative history involving the United States in the 1960s and 1970s. The most significant work in the genre avoided explicit contrasts with Europe and focused on slavery and race relations in the Americas. It debated the thesis developed earlier by Frank Tannenbaum and Stanley Elkins that North American slavery was peculiarly harsh mainly because of cultural differences between English and Iberian colonizers. At the root of this comparison, therefore, was an intra-European cross-national contrast. The United States became peculiar in its race relations partly because of its English Protestant derivation. As Elkins developed the thesis, a lack of Catholic hierarchicalism and organicism permitted the growth of an intensely capitalistic and individualistic society that produced an especially dehumanizing form of slavery and a uniquely rigid color line.[13]

In the 1960s and early 1970s, critics of the Tannenbaum-Elkins hypothesis—Marvin Harris, David Brion Davis, Carl Degler, and others—rejected or qualified this cultural explanation for variations in the treatment of slaves and questioned the notion that the slave regime in English North America was peculiarly harsh. They maintained that the treatment of slaves depended on economic and demographic variables that sometimes made for *better* living conditions for slaves in the United States South than elsewhere. But Harris and Degler also acknowledged that demographic variables (early race or sex ratios) produced something like the rigid color line and peculiar categorization that Tannenbaum and Elkins had attributed to an individualist Protestant heritage.[14]

Only one revisionist study published in those decades took the form of a direct cross-national comparison: Degler's *Neither Black nor White: Slavery and Race Relations in Brazil and the United States,* which won the Pulitzer Prize in 1972. While denying the national uniqueness of slavery in the southern states, Degler implied that race relations in the United States had exceptional features. If Brazil's "mulatto escape hatch," or something like it, existed in other Latin American societies, the North American two-category pattern of race relations with its "descent rule" (meaning that anyone with known African ancestry was categorized as black) could scarcely have developed.[15]

By the 1970s, therefore, comparative studies had given rise to a new and more malevolent conception of American uniqueness. In an era of racial conflict and of calls for Black Power, historians concluded that the United States was exceptional because of its intense and exacting racism.

There was a subtle continuity between the new and old versions of exceptionalism. The liberal-democratic tradition that the consensus historians had emphasized figured in the comparative work on American race relations done by Degler and other historians of the 1970s (as it had in Hartz's *Founding of New Societies*). The norms of equality and democracy that set the United States apart from other New World societies with quasi-feudal or patrimonial traditions now explained the rigidities of the color line. White prejudice that denied blacks in the United States social and political equality set them apart and denied their humanity more thoroughly than would the means of enforcing subordination in a less professedly democratic and more consistently hierarchical society. As Degler recognized, Tocqueville had first made the connection between American democracy and American racism when he asserted that "the freer [that is, the more democratic] the white population of the United States becomes, the more isolated [from other races] it will remain."[16] The case for exceptional racism was therefore linked to the Tocquevillian argument for liberal-democratic exceptionalism that had inspired the consensus historians. It was the other and uglier side of the same coin. Now, however, the American egalitarian tradition, in its racially exclusive form, became a cause for conflict and dissension rather than for social peace and unity.

In the 1970s exploratory studies in comparative women's history suggested the potentiality of cross-national examinations of feminism and gender issues. Ross Evans Paulson's *Women's Suffrage and Prohibition* and Richard J. Evan's *The Feminists* surveyed and compared the growth of feminist consciousness and women's movements in the United States and several other countries.[17] In these works, the sense of a shared international context was strong, and the United States evinced no radical peculiarities. By dealing with several countries even-handedly, without privileging one case or establishing a normative framework, they demonstrated how to do a comparative history in a nonexceptionalist way. They depicted a range of variations on a common theme, rather than a sharp contrast between the American case and the others. Giving rise to women's rights movements in a variety of nations were the growth of middle-class liberalism and the extension of its conception of individual rights to include the right of women to be free of male domination over their persons and property. Besides agitating for legal equality, women promoted social reforms designed to prohibit or control male behavior considered detrimental to women; thus there was a close association between feminist movements and campaigns against alcohol and prostitution. Nineteenth- and early twentieth-century feminism culminated in successful campaigns for woman suffrage that were based on an expectation that the empowerment of women would purify politics and society. Variations in this general pattern resulted form differing local conditions, but they were in the end less significant than the similarities, unless one extended the comparison (as Evans did) to include Catholic countries. Not surprisingly, women's rights movements were stronger and had greater success in Protestant cultures than in those where Catholicism predominated.

These works had relatively little impact, because they most often confirmed what historians of feminism in individual nations had already discovered. Unlike comparative studies of slavery and race relations, they did not uncover unsuspected variations that generated new explanatory hypotheses. They did not, for example, follow up on evidence suggesting that American women were more likely than women elsewhere to form independent organizations and movements, rather than working in close cooperation with liberal or socialist movements dominated by men. Had these studies done so, they would have raised questions that generated a deeper consideration of how the character and consequences of women's movements were affected by differing cultures, political systems, and economies. Part of their problem was that they dealt with too many cases to go deeply into any of them. Works such as those of Paulson and Evans brought cosmopolitanism to women's history, but they did not convince many historians that important new insights could be learned from cross-national comparisons. As a consequence, before the late 1980s, cross-national women's history remained relatively underdeveloped despite a significant growth in feminist scholarship.

In the 1980s the most widely noticed comparative work continued to be devoted to the history of slavery and race relations. Between 1980 and 1982 books on white supremacy by Stanley Greenberg, John Cell, and myself broadened the frame of reference beyond the Americas to include South Africa and transcended the exceptionalist paradigm. Despite differences in emphasis and interpretation, these works all found major commonalities in the ways that racism developed and manifested itself in the United States and South Africa. Since white South Africans, and especially Afrikaners, were formally democratic and egalitarian in their relations with each other, no stark contrast between aristocratic-hierarchical and liberal-egalitarian cultures could be invoked to explain differences. (My interpretation, unlike the others, attributed some explanatory power to the universalist and potentially nonracial character of the American equal rights tradition.) More significant and calculable were variations in the rate and character of economic development and state formation. Greenberg examined the relationships among business interests, labor systems, and government race policies in Alabama and South Africa in the twentieth century, Cell emphasized the nexus between urbanization and the rise of legalized segregation in South Africa and the American South, and I attempted to correlate the development of racist ideologies and programs with changing patterns of white economic and political activity throughout the histories of the two countries.[18]

What most distinguished my work from that of the others was the importance that I attributed to one American peculiarity—the enduring ideological and constitutional consequences of the Civil War and emancipation.[19] If the history of race relations in the United States remains truly exceptional, I would maintain, it is because slavery was abolished through a massive internal bloodletting without analogue in any comparable society and was followed by a Reconstruction that affirmed—prematurely and inadequately, as it turned out—what contemporary South Africans would call a "nonracial" citizenship. It opened the way for an extension of the limits of democratic inclusion beyond what Tocqueville thought was possible, although it did not make racial equality easy to attain or inevitable. I now realize, however, that this breakthrough was not, as national exceptionalists might argue, simply a logical outgrowth of the abstract commitment to equal rights contained in the Declaration of Independence. As historians are increasingly discovering, it took the courageous initiative of African Americans, then and later, to move the nation slowly and tortuously toward racial democracy, just as it took the black antiapartheid movement of the 1980s to deracialize South Africa.[20] A recent development in the cross-national study of slavery and race is the appearance of two major works that compare slave society in the Old South with aristocratic agrarian regimes in

Europe. Peter Kolchin's *Unfree Labor: American Slavery and Russian Serfdom* and Shearer Davis Bowman's *Masters and Lords: Mid-Nineteenth Century U.S. Planters and Prussian Junkers* draw our attention away from the similarities and differences in the circumstances of black people in the United States and in other multiracial societies and focus it on patterns of agrarian domination and resistance to modernization in the United States and parts of Europe in the early to mid-nineteenth century.[21]

In general the work of the eighties and early nineties on comparative slavery and race relations makes every society distinctive, but none truly exceptional. There is a potential debate on whether race—as manifested in such societies as the United States and South Africa, where subordinate status had traditionally been based on skin color and descent from nonwhite ancestors—functions differently from ascriptive inequalities based on other criteria, as in Russia and Prussia. But there seems little warrant in this work for maintaining that the United States can be categorically distinguished from all other societies through the possession of some unique basic and enduring trait.

Another focus for cross-national comparative history developed during the 1980s and is now producing sophisticated and significant work. Interest in the emergence of modern social insurance and welfare policies in the United States and Western Europe has generated a substantial literature, to which sociologists, political scientists, and historians have all contributed. The historical sociologists Theda Skocpol and Ann Shola Orloff took the lead in a 1984 article contrasting policies of social spending in Britain and the United States in the early twentieth century. Their work came to fruition in the early nineties when Orloff published a major study comparing "the politics of pensions" in Britain, Canada, and the United States between 1880 and 1940, and Skocpol applied a broad comparative perspective in her notable work on "the political origins of social policy in the United States."[22]

Skocpol and Orloff explain the failure of the United States to establish a system of publicly administered old-age pensions in the early twentieth century, when Britain was doing so, by the American experience with its Civil War pension system. That experience created among the middle class of the Progressive Era a distrust of government action in this sphere. Underlying this distrust was an awareness that the United States, then in transition from a patronage-based popular politics to a system that relied heavily on independent commissions, lacked the professionalized civil service and "administrative capacities" that existed in Britain. But, as Skocpol's work shows, "maternalist" welfare policies that aided mothers and children developed early and extensively in the United States because of the political influence that women's voluntary groups could exert in a relatively weak state, even though women were still denied the right to vote and hold office.

Reflecting an approach to comparative history known as "macro-causal analysis," Skocpol and Orloff first demonstrate the basic similarities between their cases.[23] They maintain that there are no essential differences in ideology and social structure between the English-speaking democracies that they are comparing. The causal variable is therefore political, rather than cultural or socioeconomic. The failure of the American state to overcome fully the reliance on courts and patronage-based parties that had historically limited its administrative capacities explains, more than anything else, the failure to adopt "paternalist" welfare policies such as pensions and unemployment insurance in the early twentieth century.[24] This argument comes close to advocating a new version of American exceptionalism—what made the United States unique, at least in the period under consideration, was the absence of a "normal" state apparatus.

An alternative way to view variations in the growth of welfare and social insurance in Western nations is found in Daniel Levine's *Poverty and Society*. Levine attributes the differences he finds to national cultures. Refusing to isolate structural variables and single causes, he develops what is essentially a national character contrast. The basic attitude toward poverty engendered by a particular nation's historical experience and cultural heritage explains the differing social policies. Levine's cultural or historicist approach makes every case exceptional, or at least unique; it is diametrically opposed in spirit and method to the structural or social-scientific analysis of Orloff and Skocpol.[25]

There are problems with both orientations. Levine's radical nominalism, which treats each case as simply a unique constellation of special features, comes close to rendering comparison superfluous. But Skocpol and Orloff's approach impoverishes historical explanation by giving so much weight to the effect of formal political arrangements that little room is left for intellectual and cultural agency. What is needed is a comparative method that takes both culture and structure seriously but makes neither deterministic. A good general statement of such an approach can be found in Liah Greenfield's recent comparative study of nationalism. According to Greenfield:

Neither "structuralism" nor idealism recognizes the significance of human agency, in which structure and culture are brought together, in which each of them is every day modified and recreated, and only by—not through—which both are moved and shaped and given the ability to exert their influence.[26]

But structure and culture do not always make roughly equal contributions to historical outcomes. The historical sociologist Jack Goldstone argues in a comparative study of early modern European revolts and revolutions that whether "material" or "ideological" factors dominate in a particular case should be resolved by empirical investigation. "To assume that it is *always* material factors (or conflicts) or *always* ideological factors (or consensus), or always both that provide the key to social dynamics is to theorize historical variation out of existence."[27]

Approaches that take seriously both cultural and structural factors and that (without deterministic preconceptions) probe their interactions may help counter the tendency of cross-national comparative historians to endorse national exceptionalism. Each nation has a distinctive culture, but each confronts similar structural problems or conditions during modernization. The strength and salience of both the culture and the physical circumstances are variable and in flux. Ideology might be viewed as a group's mobilization of cultural resources to deal with structural opportunities or challenges. Ideologies themselves have both nationally specific and cross-cultural aspects. They often represent ideas with international currency that are modified and adapted to fit local cultural and structural circumstances.

The most important political and social ideologies of the modern world—liberalism, socialism, and fascism—can be studied as international movements of thought that took on special characteristics in particular national settings. One can imagine, for example, a comparative study of British and American socialism that would acknowledge common sources of socialist ideas (Karl Marx and the First and Second Internationals), as well as similarities in economic and social conditions resulting from massive industrialization, and then examine how differing cultural traditions modified the basic doctrines and influenced courses of action. In the British case, there was tension between antimodernist traditions stemming from the craft heritage of the medieval guilds and from the "moral economy" of early modern village life—as reflected in the thought of William Morris, G. D. H. Cole, and Raymond Williams—and the modernist ideal of bureaucratic centralization advanced by Beatrice and Sidney Webb and other Fabians. In the United States, a comparable tension may have existed between the residue of nineteenth-century democratic republicanism or "producerism" that influenced Eugene Debs and the technocratic utopianism advocated by Edward Bellamy or Thorstein Veblen. The comparativist would analyze how these socialist or protosocialist currents of thought were synthesized in each country before comparing the resulting mix with the one found in the other country. To explain the differing success of the socialist movements in the United States and Great Britain, the historian would need to assess the strength within broader national cultures of the strands that favored socialism and to consider how the institutional setting for political action favored or hindered leftist movements.

Comparing the way that similar ideologies vary with the situation, serve differing purposes, and contribute to divergent policy outcomes can bring the general and particular into balance. The general and the particular can coexist when one studies, for example, how Pan-Africanist ideology was used—and with what results—in the struggles of black people against white supremacy in the United States and South Africa.[28]

Within comparative welfare history, where a disagreement between structuralists and culturalists has been especially sharp, important recent work on "maternalist" ideologies and policies in various national settings has begun to bridge the gap. Following the lead of Skocpol and Orloff, that work places major emphasis on variations in political structures and "administrative capacities." But the first full-scale cross-national history of maternal and infant policies in two countries—a study of the United States and France by the historian Alisa Klaus—argues that differences in ideology and culture also mattered. "While female activists in the United States and France shared a legacy of domestic ideology and a sense of the special role women were destined to play in social reform," Klaus maintains, "the nature of their reform activities and their influence on the development of welfare-state policies differed strikingly. . . . These differences were the result of both structural and ideological factors." The prime mover in French maternalist legislation in the early twentieth century was the government, which regarded the declining French birthrate as a threat to national security. The state inaugurated pronatalist policies primarily to provide soldiers for future wars. Although women contributed to the development and implementation of governmental efforts to protect the health of mothers and children, men played the dominant role.[29]

In the United States, the problem was defined differently—it was the quality, not the quantity, of the population that mattered. Fears of the "race suicide" of old-stock Americans because of the higher birthrate of recent immigrants focused anxieties about the health of women and children on the native-born white segment of the population and called forth racist and eugenicist arguments for government intervention. Women took the lead in the movement and in staffing the state and federal agencies that resulted because of the relative strength of autonomous women's organizations in the United States and because of the space for female political activism in a decentralized state without a strong tradition of public bureaucracy. In the United States, established male political leaders were more reluctant than their counterparts in France to sanction a permanent and far-reaching increase in the welfare responsibilities of government, but they were willing, under maternalist pressure, to make a limited exception for programs serving women and children. The differences also meant that American maternalist policies had a weaker foundation than did the French; most of them did not survive the 1920s, making it necessary to reinvent an American version of the welfare state during the New Deal.

Klaus's work provides a good model for a cross-national comparative history that does justice to culture and ideology as well as structure, draws attention to the most significant causal variables, and shows the peculiarities of each case without making one of them the exception to a general pattern represented by the others. It suggests that other bilateral studies of gender-based ideologies in the United States and comparable countries would be valuable. The earlier attempts in this genre have been disappointing. Olive Banks's *Faces of Feminism* deals with women's movements in the United States and Great Britain, but it is not a comparative study sensitive to national differences. It is instead an effort to treat what happened in the two countries as a single narrative.[30] (For some inquiries in cultural and intellectual history, such a homogenization of the two great "Anglo-Saxon" nations is legitimate.) Donald Meyer's *Sex and Power* contrasts women's experiences and movements in the United States, Russia, Sweden, and Italy without clearly specifying the critical causal factors, because, like Levine's study of welfare policy, it makes variation simply the product of the cultural peculiarities of each country.[31] Those undertaking cross-national gender studies would, in my opinion, be well advised to follow Klaus rather than Banks or Meyer.

Greenfield's *Nationalism,* an erudite comparison of the rise of national consciousness in five countries, offers a methodological prescription to mediate between structuralism and idealism, but it does not consistently follow it. Although the book analyzes the structural conditions that contributed to the origins of each national consciousness, it fails to specify how changing circumstances subsequently altered the national consciousness in England, France, Russia, Germany, and the United States. Once implanted, it seems, a nationalist ideology becomes a virtually autonomous and unchanging mind-set that acts but is not acted upon. To a historian of American race relations, it also seems curious, if not perverse, to view American nationalism as simply and straightforwardly a democratic individualism of British origin. If recent historiography on the formation of white American racial or ethnic identities has taught us anything, it is that American nationalism has often been circumscribed by implicit or explicit racial limitations that belied its universalistic promises—thus it has had some covert affinities with the "ethnic nationalisms" of Germany and Russia. Emphasis on the exclusionary aspect of white American national identity undermines Greenfield's stark contrast between the "civic" and "ethnic" varieties of nationalism.

A recent cross-national study that shows the racist potentialities of American nationalism is John Dower's *War without Mercy,* a penetrating comparison of the role of race in American and Japanese propaganda during World War II. But Dower's cross-cultural perspective permits him to avoid the version of American exceptionalism that makes intense racism a peculiarly American trait. He shows that the Japanese were quite capable of racially stereotyping their American antagonists and proclaiming their own innate superiority to the Yankee "devils."[32]

The phrase "American exceptionalism" originated within the Marxist tradition in response to the perception that the United States, unlike other industrial societies, failed to develop a strong socialist movement because of its inability to generate a proletarian class consciousness. But recent labor historians have generally eschewed American exceptionalism, arguing that the early industrial United States had a tradition of class consciousness and working-class activism, albeit one that was normally based on "radical republican" or "producerite," rather than socialist or Marxist, principles.[33]

It thus seems curious that there have been no book-length cross-national studies by American labor historians to see if working classes in other nations also expressed their opposition to industrial capitalism in other particular, culturally conditioned ways that depart from the classic Marxist view of class conflict. The lesson that such was the case, and that varying cultural and structural conditions made each working-class movement equally "exceptional," can be drawn from the work by historical sociologists and social historians of Europe that was brought together in 1986 in a notable volume, *Working-Class Formation.*[34] Close attention by American labor historians to labor protest and politics in other nations might raise new issues for analysis and interpretation. Why, for example, did American strikes tend to be more violent than those in Britain? Why were American and French workers, but not those in Britain and Germany, attracted to anarcho-syndicalist ideologies and organizations in the early twentieth century?

Historical sociologist Jeffrey Haydu's comparative study of "skilled workers and factory politics" in the United States and Britain between the 1890s and the 1920s shows the similarities and differences in the fate of craft radicalism and movements for workers' control in the two countries. Closely examining workers' control movements among machinists or engineers in Bridgeport, Connecticut, and Coventry, England (placing each in the context of labor relations in its nation), Haydu discovers that the efforts of skilled craftsmen to retain control over the work process were undermined during the era of World War I in two quite different ways. In Britain, where organized labor was relatively strong, employers worked with national union officials to limit radical factory politics, but this accommodation restrained employers from adopting technological innovations and management techniques that diluted skills and reduced workers to a common level. In the States, with its weak unions, the "open shop" permitted employers to establish company unions that posed no obstacles to "scientific management" and the deskilling that went with it. Haydu's work suggests the value of additional comparative studies of workers in the same crafts or industries in different countries.[35]

Why have historians of American labor and class relations not become as cross-cultural and as systematically comparative as those interested in gender, race, and nationality? Perhaps that failure reflects the recent propensity of American social historians to avoid macrosocial analysis, or efforts to deal with the forces shaping society as a whole, in favor of localistic and subcultural phenomena that do not lend themselves readily to cross-national comparison. Comparative work may require greater efforts at synthesis and generalization than many labor and social historians are inclined to make. Social historians are often among those who would deemphasize the nation-state as a unit of analysis and comparison. But surely the governmental structures and national cultural traditions that helped determine the fate of race- and gender-based movements also affected those deriving from class or occupational consciousness. And, as this essay has tried to show, using the American nation as a unit of comparison does not require endorsing American exceptionalism.

Cross-national comparative history can undermine two contrary but equally damaging presuppositions—the illusion of total regularity and that of absolute uniqueness. Cross-national history, by acquainting one with what goes on elsewhere, may inspire a critical awareness of what is taken for granted in one's own country, but it also promotes a recognition that similar functions may be performed by differing means. For example, the notion that the United States has had a peculiarly weak or inactive central state during much of its history is true and important. But it is also significant that private or semiprivate bureaucracies, including nonprofit corporations, charitable and philanthropic organizations, professional associations, and self-regulating business federations and exchanges, developed in the late-nineteenth-century United States to perform many tasks assumed by government in other modernizing societies. A comparative perspective might therefore spur historians to investigate the causes and consequences of differing relations between government and civil society in the United States and in comparable industrializing nations.

Finally, cross-national history encourages interdisciplinary perspectives. Contact with the comparative work by sociologists and political scientists can help historians cultivate methodological awareness and rigor. At a bare minimum, historians' efforts to define what they are comparing will require theoretical attention to the meanings of such analytical categories as slavery, race, class, gender, urbanization, government, nationalism, and social movements. The cautious rapprochement of historical sociology and comparative history that can be perceived in studies of welfare states, patterns of race, and varieties of nationalism results not only from the interest of some historians in social theory but also from the fact that social scientists are learning from historians how to use primary sources and to recognize the complexity and multiplicity of historical causation.

Now, far more than when I reviewed work in comparative cross-national history seventeen years ago, it is possible to imagine the field as a coherent cooperative enterprise. It is not yet a single community of inquirers, but it is not too much to hope that it can someday become one.

CHAPTER FOUR

Planters, Junkers, and *Pomeschiki*

Cross-cultural comparative history in the fullest and strictest sense—sustained comparisons in which equal attention is paid to the exotic cases—remains relatively rare. An obvious reason for this state of affairs is that historians of the United States, or any other nation state, are not normally prepared by their training, or encouraged by the nature of their professional responsibilities, to undertake sophisticated, in-depth work on other societies and cultures.

I suspect that there are also doubts in some quarters as to whether the results of cross-national comparisons are worth all the effort. Often the more ambitious and systematic comparative works appear at first glance to do little more than confirm what is already known from studies focusing on a single nation. It can scarcely be denied that the bold hypotheses of broad-gauged and freewheeling works of comparative history or historical sociology like Frank Tannenbaum's *Slave and Citizen* (1947), Barrington Moore's *Social Origins of Dictatorship and Democracy* (1966), and Theda Skocpol's *States and Social Revolution* (1979) have generated new questions and stimulated inquiry. But careful historical examination of particular cases has usually led to the modification or even the discrediting of some of the bold claims made by such works. The books by historians of the United States that have systematically compared some American phenomenon with its analogue in another society have nurtured the growing cosmopolitanism in their fellow Americanists, added some weight to one side or the other in current historiographic debates, and, crossing disciplinary lines, helped to improve the historical sensitivities of comparative sociologists and political scientists. But, up to now, they have not had a major impact on the main lines of historical interpretation established by historians whose work may employ comparative perspectives for heuristic purposes but does not go deeply into exotic cases.

What cannot be known to most Americanists is the extent to which bilateral studies have raised new questions or even suggested new interpretations in the other historiography on which they impinge. It may be significant that two of the most influential and provocative comparative studies involving the United States were actually written by historians specializing in the other case—the Latin Americanist Frank Tannenbaum and the Africanist John Cell, whose *The Highest Stage of White Supremacy* (1982) shed new light on American segregation but had no discernible impact on the historiography of South Africa. It would not be surprising if fresh insights came most readily from looking at another history from the vantage point of the one that is more familiar, but to reach its full potentiality, comparative study should jolt historians out of accustomed ways of thinking about their original areas of specialization and enable them to look at the familiar in a new way. The Balkanization of the historical profession is an obstacle to the appreciation, as well as the practice, of cross-national comparative history. Too few of the readers and evaluators of such works are knowledgeable about, or even strongly interested in, both sides of the comparison.

The two most ambitious recent examples of bilateral comparison by historians of the United States are Peter Kolchin's *Unfree Labor* and Shearer Davis Bowman's *Masters and Lords*.[1] It is not surprising that both of them involve aspects of the social history of the antebellum South. Slavery and slave society is the single aspect of American history that has inspired the most extensive and sophisticated comparative literature. But whereas most previous work has focused on slavery in the Americas, these studies broaden the frame of reference to include parts of Europe where, by the mid–nineteenth century, landed gentries with unfree or quasi-free labor systems were confronting pressures and challenges comparable in some ways to those faced by the slaveholders of the Old South at roughly the same time. One virtue of extending the comparison to Russia and Prussia is that it sharply poses the question of what difference, if any, arose from the fact that southern slavery was based on distinctions of "race"—meaning that masters and unfree workers differed in pigmentation and geographical origins—whereas the European patterns of agrarian dominance and dependency were not, or at least not to nearly the same extent. (This variable is of course lacking in inter-American studies or in comparisons of the United States and South Africa.)

There are, however, significant differences in the nature of the two works. Kolchin's study is broader in scope and more ambitious than Bowman's. It treats the entire history of American slavery and Russian serfdom up to the point of emancipation (which will be the subject of a second volume), and it attempts to compare the experiences of slaves and serfs as well as those of slaveowners and serfholders (*pomeschiki*). Bowman, on the other hand, limits his attention mainly to the nineteenth century and to dominant classes of planters and Junkers. He makes no effort to compare the lot of southern slaves with that of peasant workers on the Prussian estates. Another difference is that Bowman gives prominence to theoretical and historiographical issues, addressing them at length in his text, while Kolchin is, for the most part, content to state his conclusions without ruminating on their relevance to current debates among historians and sociologists. The books differ in substance as well as in approach: in fact their respective comparisons are used to support contrasting views of slave society in the Old South and especially of the character of its dominant class.

Kolchin's massively erudite and elegantly crafted study begins by establishing a fundamental similarity between American slavery and Russian serfdom. He persuasively demonstrates that by the eighteenth century the legal status of the serfs differed little, if at all, from that of slaves in the Americas. Contradicting what is theoretically the defining characteristic of serfdom—that workers were tied to the soil—he shows that they could be, and sometimes were, moved about and even bought and sold at the whim of their masters. This finding is meant to persuade the reader that he is not merely comparing the apple of slavery with the orange of serfdom, but he does not fully put to rest the suspicion that his study is the predictable contrast between too inherently dissimilar institutions. In fact the differences that he finds end up being more or less what one would expect from a comparison of classic slavery and classic serfdom. Unlike slaves, the serfs lived in partially self-governing village communities and spent at least part of their time working for themselves on lands assigned for their communal use. One class of serfs were also required to work as laborers in their masters' fields, but others were permitted to discharge all of their obligations to noble landlords by paying rent. Kolchin argues that traditions of lord-peasant relations originating in the time before serfdom became legally transformed into a form of slavery that helped to maintain this pattern. One could just as well say that although eighteenth- and nineteenth-century Russia may have had de jure slavery, or something close to it, it had a de facto or customary system of serfdom. If practice rather than law is taken as the defining characteristic of this system, then much of Kolchin's comparison merely validates and elaborates the predictable differences between categorically different systems of unfree labor. His somewhat contentious argument that the relatively rich communal experience of the serfs shows how "rudimentary" the organization of the slave community really was (p. 200), implying that historians need to rethink recent efforts to celebrate the way the slaves came together and made a collective life for themselves, may simply follow from the axiom that a society of lords and peasants offers greater opportunities for bottom-up community organization than one of master and slaves.

But one major difference that Kolchin finds between slavery and serfdom is more historically specific and does not seem to follow quite so inevitably from a typological contrast of the two systems. Relying heavily on the work of Eugene Genovese, he argues that American slavery was more "paternalistic" than Russian serfdom. By this he does not mean that southern slaveowners were necessarily kinder than Russian *pomeschiki*, but they felt a greater responsibility for the moral and physical condition of their unfree workers. "The essence of this paternalism," he contends, "was to treat the slaves as permanent children, who on the one hand needed constant protection, but on the other needed constant direction and correction" (p. 134). The *pomeschiki*, by contrast, normally felt few paternal obligations and left their serfs to shift for themselves so long as they discharged their formal obligations. Kolchin explains this difference in much the same way that Genovese explains the paternalism that he takes to be the major divergence between southern slavery and that in many other parts of the Americas: slaveholdings were comparatively small in the United States and masters were much less likely to be absentees than their Russian counterparts.

To explain the fact that slaveholders militantly defended their peculiar institution and ultimately went to war to protect it, while serfowners acceded to the authority of the czar to determine the fate of their labor system, Kolchin points to four characteristics present in the United States but absent in Russia: "a racial distinction between owner and owned, a democratic political system, freedom of the press, and the sectional nature of servitude," and then adds a fifth "which subsumes the other four and is the most basic of all, the independence of the master class and the strength of its civilization" (p. 182). Although acknowledging a role for American race consciousness, he does not in the end give it a very significant one. He presents much evidence to show that the *pomeschiki* regarded the serfs as so radically and unalterably inferior to themselves that their social attitudes and practices become difficult to distinguish, functionally or even ideologically, from the racism of southern whites.

Bowman contends that his comparison of southern planters and Prussian Junkers is based on a stronger analogy than Kolchin's. He can scarcely claim, as Kolchin does, that the labor systems were roughly equivalent—there is obviously a substantial difference between a quasi-feudalism evolving into a system of agricultural wage labor and chattel slavery—but his choice of a landed gentry to compare with that of the Old South eliminates most of the variables that Kolchin uses to distinguish between slaveholders and *pomeschiki*. Like southern planters, the Junkers were a regional elite, residing in most cases on relatively small estates, and generally businesslike in their orientation toward market production. (Kolchin pays little attention to the fact that slaveholders had to be more entrepreneurial in their outlook than *pomeschiki*, who tended to have so much land and so many inherited "souls" that they did not need to be very efficient and calculating in order to maintain their position.)

The theoretical basis of Bowman's claim of comparability between Junkers and planters is a distinction between capitalism and modernity. Departing from the neo-Marxist synthesis of Eugene Genovese and his followers, Bowman argues that southern planters (and also Prussian Junkers) were capitalistic and antimodern at the same time. (His conception of modernization relies heavily on the neo-Weberian theories of Reinhold Bendix.) What made these agrarian elites antimodern and reactionary, in Bowman's view, was not some repudiation of the market and capitalist enterprise but their opposition to the political and legal principles that were associated with the growth of representative democracy and equality under the law. Differing intellectual traditions shaped Prussian and southern defenses of authority and hierarchy—the former drew on nineteenth-century German romanticism and idealism, while the latter harked back to Edmund Burke's more matter-of-fact critique of Enlightenment rationality and reformism—but the result in both cases was the promulgation of a conservative ideology at odds with nineteenth-century conceptions of political and legal progress. But

Bowman does not assume that most planters and Junkers were conservative intellectuals or ideologues. He makes a distinction between the "idealists," who were ready to live and die for their beliefs, and the larger number of "pragmatists," who put their practical interests ahead of ideological rigor or consistency and were willing to bend or compromise if they saw some immediate advantage in it.

The differences that Bowman finds between planters and Junkers are nevertheless substantial, and they stem for the most part from the peculiar conjunction of racism and republicanism in the southern case. Following the lead of a number of recent historians, Bowman describes how the racist subordination of blacks enabled the southern elite to accept and even on occasion to celebrate the republican citizenship of all white males, without at the same time surrendering to the liberal principle of equal rights for all and thereby undermining their defense of slavery. The Junkers, on the other hand, were monarchists and defenders of a multitiered hierarchy of legally constituted status groups or orders. Whether one prefers to characterize the Old South as a "*Herrenvolk* democracy," calling attention to its de jure equality for all white males, or "an aristocracy of race," which underlines the undemocratic features of this society when viewed from a nonracist perspective, it is clear that it differed from the kind of corporate hierarchy that the Prussian Junkers were defending. As we have seen, Kolchin acknowledges the role of racism in differentiating the American case from the Russian, but he raises doubts about the sharpness of the contrast and accords less weight to racism than to other variables. Perhaps if Bowman had examined more closely the attitudes of Junkers toward the peasants on their estates, he would have found the same kind of quasi-racism that Kolchin detected among the *pomeschiki*. But regarding subaltern people as hopelessly inferior is not the same thing as consciously and deliberately basing a social order and a polity squarely on the alleged fact that one large population group is radically and permanently inferior to another.

The other main contrast between the two books is in their treatment of the capitalism/paternalism issue. For almost forty years historians of the American South have been debating the question of whether or not southern slavery can be persuasively described as a paternalistic institution. Since paternalistic social and economic relationships were assumed to be characteristic of precapitalist society, neo-Marxist historians, led by Eugene Genovese, have argued further that the South was a precapitalist society and that the world view of its ruling class was antithetical to that of the bourgeois North. From this vantage point, the Civil War becomes comparable to European struggles between the rising bourgeoisie and the old order of landed aristocracies and their peasant retainers.

Kolchin does not explicitly invoke the dichotomy of a capitalist North and a precapitalist South, but he has no doubts about the paternalistic character of the master-slave relationship. His assurance on this issue is surprising given the serious attacks that have been mounted recently on this view of slaveholders' mentality. But since his book was published in 1987, he could not have had the benefit of such works as Michael Tadman's *Speculators and Slaves* (1989) and Norrece Jones's *Born a Child of Freedom, Yet a Slave* (1990). These studies focus on the crass commercialization of slave labor and the callous attitudes that must have been associated with it. The heavy dependence of most masters on the internal slave trade for purposes of speculative profit and for the leverage that the threat of sale gave them over their unfree workers strongly suggest that paternalism was more myth and ideology than social reality. If Kolchin had compared the slave trade to the more incidental and marginal trade in Russian serfs, he might have come to a different conclusion as to which system was more paternalistic. Parental neglect may be a poor form of paternalism, but a willingness to sell one's "children" cannot be reconciled with any conception of familial governance; it clearly represents the triumph of the capitalistic marketplace over any conceivable ethic of paternal responsibility.

Bowman's treatment of the capitalism/paternalism issue is, to my mind, more persuasive than Kolchin's. "Although slavery manifested some paternalistic features," he concludes, "positing the paternalistic character of the institution is more problematic than portraying planters as 'capitalist in every sense of the word.' Even plantation labor itself was capital, in the literal sense of a productive asset used to create more wealth" (p. 183). Bowman argues that nineteenth-century planters and Junkers were essentially market-oriented capitalist producers and that their professions of paternalism revealed more about their reactionary political ideas than it did about their relations with their unfree or semifree laborers. He thus comes down decisively on one side in the debate that has divided historians and sociologists over the essential features of capitalism. For him capitalism means private property and the pursuit of profit through market activity; he agrees with Jean Baecher that "There is no necessary or essential link between the capitalist system and free labor" (p. 100). There is also in his view no essential link between capitalism and political democracy. Agrarian capitalists dependent on legalized hierarchies of race or status will tend to be fierce opponents of the equalization of status and citizenship when they confront liberal reformers. The difference between the planters and Junkers was that the former could use the racism that they shared with most nonelite southern whites to avoid a direct conflict with the American republicanism that they had embraced when they supported the American Revolution. The monarchism and (in most cases) the legally sanctioned aristocratic status of the latter permitted a more comprehensive and straightforward defense of inequality. Such a comparison makes a great deal of sense and may help to dispel some persistent but misleading notions about "the world that the slaveholders made."

Although narrower and not as well-written as *Unfree Labor,* *Masters and Lords* comes closer to achieving the full promise of comparative history. Southern planters look different to me than they did before Bowman had compared them to the Junkers, whereas the southern slavery of Kolchin's study seems on the whole relatively familiar. Perhaps the greatest potential contribution of *Unfree Labor,* and it is a valuable one, is to convey an understanding of Russian serfdom that will make it, along with the slave societies of the Americas and white supremacist regime in South Africa, an unavoidable point of reference in the search for perspective on the enigmatic history of the American South.

PART TWO

Race and Racism in Comparative Perspective

CHAPTER FIVE

Understanding Racism

Reflections of a Comparative Historian

Historians of black-white relations in the United States often refer to "racism," but only rarely do they define the term precisely and explore its theoretical implications. Compared with the explanatory power associated with the economic and political variables operating in a specific historical situation, the cultural predisposition to stigmatize and abuse the racial "Other" is likely to be treated as a secondary phenomenon—the by-product of something else—or, alternatively, as one ingredient in an eclectic stew, the effect of which is impossible to isolate. Sometimes the term is used narrowly to refer to a set of doctrines that rose and fell in the United States between the late eighteenth century and the mid-to-late twentieth. Often, however, it is a catchall that refers to whatever was thought and done to the disadvantage of African Americans from the sixteenth century to the present. For some purposes, perhaps, nothing much is lost by inattention or lack of analytical rigor. But comparative historians need sharper tools and stronger conceptualizations; otherwise they are likely to find implicit, attitudinal racism in most times and places—a given of any situation that appears to involve "races"—or an explicit ideological racism in only a few places and for limited periods. It is high time that historians devoted the same effort to understanding "race" as a transnational social and historical phenomenon that they have sometimes applied to class, gender, and nationalism.

Postmodernists have contributed some useful new vocabulary to this effort—especially the description of race as "a social construction" rather than an objective fact. Substantively speaking, this formulation is not so radically new as some of its proponents suggest. The concept of race as a "social fiction" rather than a biological fact has been a staple of the sociological literature on "race relations" for half a century. But the new formulation puts an emphasis on process—how and why the fiction was created—that the older language permits but does not require. Furthermore, postmodernist thought has put gender, nation, and even class in the same category of ideologically constructed fictions that race already occupied in the thought of antiracist scholars. It invites us, therefore, to probe the connections between race and other social constructions of human identity rather than making race a secondary or derived category—the mere reflection of some deeper and more fundamental reality.

Perhaps, it has been suggested, we should no longer use the term "race" at all, because to do so gives credence to the idea that there is a physical reality to which it refers. Human beings do of course differ in physical appearance, but variations in skin color have no more intrinsic or scientific significance than differences in hair color. It is the associations that people make between such visible phenomena and their entire range of interests, beliefs, and attitudes that determine whether or not "race" comes into play. My own view is that we can continue to use the term if we recognize that it refers to an ideology rather than an objective reality. The recently coined verb "to racialize" (in the noun form "racialization") is useful in referring to the process of constructing race rather than to its results.

Like some other notable ways of construing human diversity, racism has enormous historical consequences—on the same order of importance as nationalism, sexism, class consciousness, and sectarian religious zeal. Unless one is prepared to take one of these great signifiers of human diversity and make it the root of all the others—class is the most popular candidate, although gender has its advocates—the historian faces the task of showing how a number of social and cultural constructions interact rather than proving that one is more "real" or fundamental than the others.

Merely recognizing that something is socially, culturally, or ideologically constructed does not fully explain it—indeed it scarcely explains it at all. We need to know how and why it was constructed in the way that it was. Furthermore, only the most radical postmodernists would claim that something can be constructed out of nothing. What raw materials were used, where did they come from, and how well do they serve the aims of the builders? One can use wood to make a house or a warship. The materials do not determine the function of the thing that has been constructed, but they may help to determine how well it fulfills the purposes for which it was designed. Wooden houses burn more easily than those made of brick, and wooden ships were more vulnerable to enemy cannon fire than the steel-hulled vessels that took their place in the world's navies. Science-based concepts of race may lose credibility as the result of new discoveries and shifting paradigms, but concepts of race based on the cultural differences associated with descent groups may have greater durability. The notion that race or anything else is a social and cultural construction is the beginning of an inquiry rather than the end of it.

When sociologists and historians first wrote about racism in the period between World War II and the 1960s, they generally meant an explicit ideology based on the putative scientific truth that population groups distinguishable from each other in physical appearance or ancestry were different and unequal in genetically determined mental and behavioral capabilities. As recently as 1967, for example, the British sociologist Michael Banton defined racism as "the doctrine that a man's behavior is determined by stable inherited characteristics deriving from separate racial stocks having distinctive attributes and usually considered to stand to one another in relations of superiority and inferiority." In that same year, an American sociologist, Pierre van den Berghe, described it as an ideology based on the belief that "organic, genetically transmitted differences (real or imagined), are intrinsically associated with the presence or absence of certain socially relevant abilities or characteristics."[1]

Such a doctrine or ideology was used to justify or rationalize a range of policies, depending on the circumstances and aims of the racializing group. The principal possibilities were the subordination and unequal segregation of the Other, exclusion or expulsion from a community or nation, or in the most extreme case physical annihilation. Hitler's view of the Jews and what should be done with them and the southern white supremacist's conception of the African American's place in nature and society were obvious and unambiguous examples of racism in this strict sense.

Since the late 1960s, however, scholars and activists in the United States have tended to apply the term to attitudes and practices viewed as objectively harmful to the interests and aspirations of people previously designated as racially inferior, even though an explicit doctrine of innate racial differences is no longer invoked as a rationale. The discovery of "institutional"—as opposed to "attitudinal"—racism has broadened the concept to include the discrimination that persists because institutions operate on the basis of seemingly color-blind rules and procedures that in fact deny equal opportunity to members of minority groups. But to maintain that such discrimination is truly unintentional and does not involve individual attitudes would undermine the conception of racism as an ideological construction and make it synonymous with the statistical inequality and apparent social inefficiency of any group with a sense of racial or ethnic identity, whatever the actual causes of its situation might be.

The concept of racism remains relevant in such cases only if it can be established that members of one identifiable group falsely assume that the members of another such group perform less well than themselves because of their inherent or deep-seated inadequacies rather than their disadvantages in an unjust social system. This standard would still cover most of what has been described as institutional or structural racism. Whites who oppose programs that seek to secure equal opportunities for blacks may deny with varying degrees of sincerity that they consider blacks to be genetically inferior to themselves, but can anyone really doubt that if the inhabitants of our inner cities were white rather than black or Latino, more would be done to alleviate the conditions that breed gang warfare, crime and a variety of other social problems? It also seems likely that support for the death penalty would not be as strong as it is in the United States today if a disproportionate number of those on death rows did not happen to be black.

Evidence in fact abounds that actual prejudice continues to operate on all levels of American society. The persistence of white supremacist attitudes is manifested in a toleration of police brutality against minorities, black-white disparities in judicial punishments for the same crimes, housing and mortgage discrimination, and glass ceilings in corporate personnel policies. It is therefore premature and misleading to maintain that attitudes and ideologies are no longer the problem. If American institutions operated in the way they are supposed to operate, we would still have class and status inequality, but racism would no longer be the appropriate diagnosis for such conditions.

Racism is not the only form of injustice and inequality in the world, and if we wish to think about it in useful and productive ways, we have to be able to distinguish it from other varieties of human nastiness. Rather than enlarge the concept of racism to include structural inequalities that are independent of racialization, it would be more fruitful to expand the concept to include modes of thought and behavior that we do not usually think of as racist because they do not involve the classic racist doctrine of biological logical inferiority signified by color.

Two recent books illustrate the difference between the old and new versions of racist ideology. *The Bell Curve* by Charles Murray and Richard Herrnstein is an effort to revive old fashioned biological racism. In their view blacks are simply less well-endowed intellectually than whites. Dinesh D'Souza's *The End of Racism* eschews the genetic determinism of abilities in favor of a cultural determinism that does much the same work. D'Souza attributes African American "failure" to a "dysfunctional" group culture and then uses this judgment to support a contention that racism is not the source of black underachievement. Stereotyping and stigmatizing a racialized group on the basis of cultural rather than biological inferiority provides a new rationale for discrimination rather than a basis for combating it. This "new racism" is not really unprecedented. Cultural rather than biological determinism was the official justification for apartheid in South Africa. Furthermore, D'Souza's line of argument recalls the rationale for black enslavement and subordination that preceded the growth of scientific racist doctrines in the late eighteenth and nineteenth centuries.[2]

According to sociologists and historians who draw a sharp distinction between racism and ethnocentrism, it is anachronistic to describe as racist the prejudice and discrimination against the Other that emerged *before* Western ethnological thinkers articulated naturalistic conceptions of human diversity and inequality. In an early effort to grapple with the relationship between the ideologies rationalizing slavery in the early colonial period and those employed in the nineteenth century, I made a distinction between ideological and "societal" racism. In the latter category, I included practices that treated a subaltern group as if it were inherently inferior to the socially dominant group even though an explicit doctrine of innate racial differences had not yet been promulgated and widely accepted. But there was of course an ideological basis for such discrimination. An alternative to identifying racism by its effects rather than by the consciousness that produced it is to seek the common element in the differing ideological formulations that have sustained white or European domination over people of color. If the term racism is to apply, I now believe, its association with the specific form of biological determinism that justified slavery and segregation in the nineteenth and twentieth centuries must be regarded as fortuitous rather than essential.[3]

What we need for comparative historical analysis is a theoretical understanding of racism that is broad enough to take account of contemporary ideologies that stigmatize the Other without appealing to racist science as well as attitudes that preceded the elaboration of classic racist doctrine. But in seeking such breadth we must be careful to avoid giving credence to the view that racism is an essential or primordial human response to diversity, something that inevitably takes place when groups that we would define as racially different come into contact. It must be remembered that we are doing the defining and that, as the historical record shows, the categories we use did not always exist and were in fact constructed or invented by our ancestors. There is a strong, and perhaps unavoidable, tendency in any society to disparage those defined as Other or alien. Such negative stereotyping may be an inescapable component of identity and boundary maintenance. But who the outsiders are and how much or in what ways they are despised and mistreated are the products of history, not of basic human instincts.

I therefore agree with historian Barbara Fields that "race" and all the ideas and attitudes associated with it are shaped and sustained by social contexts that change over time and are not therefore the reflection of some "transhistorical" impulse that is rooted in objective human differences. But Fields and other historians who argue that "class" is real and "race" is not are captives of a theory of social relationships that privileges one form of social inequality over others in a manner that does violence to the actual history of human inequality. If class is defined very loosely as "the inequality of human beings from the standpoint of social power," there is no disagreement, although it is hard to make analytical use of such an all-encompassing passing concept. Problems emerge when Fields goes on to invoke "the more rigorous Marxian definition involving social relations of production." Is it really true, as she claims, that class in this sense "can assert itself independently of people's consciousness" while race cannot? People certainly do differ in economic power and position, but such differences have literally no meaning until they enter people's consciousness and are interpreted in some fashion. The specifically Marxist conception of two essential and perpetually antagonistic classes is not a necessary deduction from the existence of economic inequality in a capitalist society. There could be more than two essential classes, and classes do not have to be viewed as inevitably at war. Class in my view is as much a historical and social construct as race, which also builds on differences that actually exist but are not meaningful until constructed into an ideology of differences that serves the purposes of a social group.[4]

Besides differing in their relation to the means of production or to the market, people really do differ in physical characteristics that are subject to classification, immediate or remote ancestry, and cultural traits associated with belonging to a historically defined community. It is my contention that race and racism derive from the act of interpreting or construing such noneconomic differences to create a sense of group solidarity or peoplehood that becomes the basis for assertions of dominance or privileged status over those considered outside of the group. (If the process stopped at group identity and solidarity, we would have ethnocentrism but not racism.) This way of grounding group power and inequality is not simply a variation on the larger theme of class domination. It has independent roots and consequences. Class refers to the fact that every developed society has an economy and that some people have more access to its fruits than others. Race arises from the equally pervasive fact that all human beings have some sense of family or kinship, a way of differentiating those with whom one has real or fictive "blood ties" from those who are unrelated. Ethnicity can be viewed as extended kinship, and race can be seen as an inflation and elaboration of the notion that my "family" not only is better than yours but also has special rights and privileges as a consequence.

Although race and class are both historical inventions—creative interpretations or ideological constructions based on two ways of conceiving human diversity—it would be a mistake to infer that, once invented, they do not become durable and enormously influential ways of perceiving the world. The construction of class may lead to class conflict, revolution, and socialist societies. The construction of race may lead to secession in defense of racial slavery, the creation of social orders based on racial caste, or to gas chambers for stigmatized peoples.

A useful way of comprehending the relationship of race and class is Max Weber's writings on social hierarchy as a general phenomenon and stratification based on ethnicity or race as a special case. For Weber, "status," or the unequal assignment of honor and prestige to individuals or groups, may vary independently from "class," which he defines as the economic advantage or disadvantage that comes from objective relationships to a capitalistic market. Status may be based on aristocratic descent or the ability to maintain a prestigious life-style, but in multiethnic societies it can also be derived simply from membership in an ethnic or racial group that has a history of dominance over other groups and seeks to preserve that relationship.[5]

Using Weber's concept of "ethnic status" to get at the nature of racism allows us to sidestep an unprofitable debate on the difference between race and ethnicity. As Donald L. Horowitz has argued persuasively in a broad-ranging comparative study of "ethnic conflict," the designation of people by skin color and the mistreatment of them on that basis has no special features that would distinguish it in any definitive theoretical way from group domination based on religion, culture, or the simple belief that some people have defective ancestry. It is only because modern Western liberalism often assumes that it is relatively easy for people to change their religion or culture and be assimilated into a group other than the one in which they were born that the distinction has become important.[6]

Even in the West the de facto ascription of ethnic status has often been derived from something other than skin color or reputed nonwhite ancestry. Northern Ireland, for example, has the essential characteristics of what sociologist John Rex calls a "race relations situation." A Catholic could certainly convert to Protestantism; however, it is not only extremely unlikely that one would do so but also doubtful whether one could thereby win full acceptance into the Protestant community. Racial consciousness is also what what makes the Palestinian-Israeli conflict so difficult to resolve, despite the lack of clear physical differences between the antagonistic ethnic communities. A large proportion of the population of Israel are Jews who found themselves increasingly oppressed in various Arab societies, and the Arab minority in Israel, despite having the right to vote, is not eligible for full citizenship in a Jewish ethnic state.[7]

The key element in ethnicity is descent, and ethnic status emerges when a group of people with a real or fictive common ancestry assert their dominance over those who are believed to be of a different and inferior ancestry. The Burakhumin of Japan are descended from a caste that once engaged in occupations considered unclean or impure. Although they differ scarcely at all in phenotype or general culture from other Japanese, the discrimination against them, on grounds of descent alone, closely resembles the color discrimination of Western societies. One might conclude, therefore, that racism, or something virtually indistinguishable from it, has no essential relation to skin color or other obvious physical characteristics and need not even be based on significant cultural differences. The essential element is the belief, however justified or rationalized, in the critical importance of differing lines of descent and the use of that belief to establish or validate social inequality.[8]

Ethnic status—the sense of being top dog because of one's ancestry—may come from the conquest or earlier enslavement of other ethnic groups or simply from being the original inhabitants of an immigrant-receiving society. To a degree that Weber did not anticipate, such a sense of social superiority could also develop in societies that considered themselves ethnically homogeneous, placed great value on this lack of diversity, and were therefore unwilling to receive ethnic strangers into their national community—one thinks of the history of Australia and Japan, for example. Lest we fall into essentialism, however, we have to bear in mind that the operative group definitions and boundaries are not fixed but are in fact constructed or reconstructed in response to changing historical circumstances. At the same time, we must avoid going to the opposite extreme and overestimating how easily they change or how directly responsive they are to short-term historical developments. Constructed racial categorizations may endure for very long periods, as the career of the patently illogical "one-drop rule" for defining African American ethnicity clearly exemplifies.[9]

Racism, then, can be defined as an ethnic group's assertion or maintenance of a privileged and protected status vis à vis members of another group or groups who are thought, because of defective ancestry, to possess a set of socially relevant characteristics that disqualify them from full membership in a community or citizenship in a nation-state. A racist society functions like a private club in which the membership conceives of itself in a certain way and excludes those who do not fit in. (This analogy is especially apt, because under the "black ball" system not all members have to be strongly prejudiced against an applicant for membership; they merely have to defer to the prejudices of others.) Such a sense of ascribed identity and entitlement naturally inclines its beneficiaries to defend their group position if they believe it to be threatened. Many years ago the Weberian sociologist Herbert Blumer caught the essence of racism when he described race prejudice as an anxious sense of "group position."[10]

In contrast to traditional ways of defining racism, this definition puts less emphasis on how the alleged deficiencies of the Other are described and explained and more on how a group defines itself and its prerogatives. The essence of racism is caught by such old American expressions as "give him a white man's chance" or "she's white, free, and twenty one." Historian David Roediger has recently suggested that the key to racism in the United States is an understanding of the meaning of "whiteness" rather than blackness. If we examine the concept of whiteness, we find that it has no specific cultural content, but exists solely as an indicator of higher status than those designated as black or colored.[11]

I would simply add that an ascribed status of whiteness signifies that the bearer comes from preferred stock, whereas one of blackness or brownness implies a debased and unworthy ancestry. Whites may find it natural that blacks are underrepresented in positions of prominence because such roles have always been occupied by people like themselves and are therefore legitimately inherited from their ancestors—even if they have no firm basis for believing that blacks would not perform as well as their own "kin." This sense of inherited entitlement may be the hard core of racism. When combined, as it usually is, with motives of a more mundane and material kind, it becomes a powerful source of social and cultural identity.

Racism as a general phenomenon is not therefore defined by any specific set of beliefs about what makes a given minority undeserving of equal treatment. We know from the history of anti-Semitism and anti-Japanese discrimination in the United States that racism of a virulent sort can be directed at groups believed to be *superior,* at least in their competitive efficiency, to an in-group seeking to protect its position. Using this definition, we would have no problem in considering the South African regime of the late 1980s to be racist even though it was edging toward a willingness to "share" power with Africans and refrained from invoking innate racial superiority to justify its presumption that whites must retain de facto social and economic dominance in a reformed, "multiracial" South Africa. Similarly, those opponents of antidiscrimination or affirmative action programs in the United States who, implicitly or explicitly, base their resistance on fears of losing something to which they feel entitled by ethnicity or ancestry can be described as racists despite the fact that they talk about acquired culture or competence rather than genetics. Even Brazil, that allegedly most nonracist of color-differentiated societies, displays an element of status consciousness based on ancestry, as is clearly evident when a person of dark complexion finds that he or she must have more money or education than a white to attain a comparable social position.

If Weber's concept of ethnic status helps us to understand racism in a general and theoretical way, it is not sufficient in itself to make sense of the history of racism in different societies. The contribution of ethnic consciousness to the grounding of social hierarchies is a variable and not a constant. Weber acknowledged that in modern capitalist societies class can overwhelm or subsume status, and some of his followers took this to mean that "modernization" meant the decline of "ascription" based on race or ethnicity in favor of a social hierarchy determined purely by "achievement." But it is obvious to anyone reading the newspapers or watching television that domineering and even genocidal ethnicities persist and flourish in the modern world. The analysis of particular cases often reveals that the material and political interests of an elite are responsible for arousing the latent ethnic consciousness of the masses. Hence it is not a matter of differentiating sharply between "class" and "race" situations. All that Weber's theory really requires is that one make an analytical distinction and not reduce one tendency to the other. Demagogues may encourage racism for their own ulterior ends, but they could hardly succeed in doing so unless the attitudes of the people they sought to influence provided fertile ground for sowing the seeds of ethnic hatred.

The histories of the United States, Brazil, and South Africa suggest that the color-coded variety of racism varies significantly in intensity and in function within specific social structures, economies, and cultures. What accounts for differences in the nature, strength, and consequences of racism in these societies? How do we explain the growth or decline of racist attitudes and policies within a nation's history? Anyone who has lived in the United States for the past four or five decades should realize that racism—or status consciousness based on race—changes over time in its strength and capacity to shape a social order. Blacks are far from equal in American society, but their status has improved in significant ways, and white racism, while still very much alive, has declined in power and intensity. Recent signs of retrogression have led some frustrated proponents of full racial equality to charge that "nothing has changed," but few African Americans who grew up in the South before the 1960s would find it of little significance that they are no longer disfranchised, segregated in public places, and exposed to lynch law. How do we account for such changes?

Variability and change in the salience of ethnic status and consciousness depend to a considerable extent, it would appear, on variations or changes in the power relationship among ethnic groups. To the degree that an oppressed and stigmatized group can somehow gain in physical resources, political power, and cultural recognition or prestige, it can induce or force a dominant group to share some of its rights and privileges. This in turn can gradually erode the material and even the psychological foundations for the sense of a *Herrenvolk,* or dominant race, that it has clearly defined borders and a collective sense of entitlement. Unfortunately, the process is reversible; loss of power, for whatever reason, normally entails a loss of status or prestige. Emancipation from slavery or other forms of directly coerced labor does not by itself empower a group to challenge its subordinate status and the stigma that continues to be associated with servile ancestry, but it does unsettle the power equation by opening new possibilities for action to challenge the racial order as well as new dangers of marginalization, expulsion, or even extermination.

Many historical examples can be offered from the history of the United States, Brazil, and South Africa to show how political or economic power affects ethnic status. One of the most important reasons why free people of color in Brazil had greater opportunities for upward mobility than their American counterparts in the era of slavery, and were thus in a position to win a greater degree of social acceptance, was the vital role that they played in the plantation economy as growers of foodstuffs, herders of livestock, and catchers of escaped slaves. The "free Negroes" of the Old South could not play such a role because there was a large population of nonslaveholding whites to service the plantation economy. But the acquisition of political power by southern African Americans during the Reconstruction era gave them, during the relatively brief period when they could exercise their right to suffrage, an influence over public policy greater than that enjoyed by freedpeople in Brazil after *their* emancipation, which was completed in 1889. (Since the right to vote in the Brazilian republic depended on literacy until quite recently, most ex-slaves and their descendants have been prevented from exercising it.) In the Reconstruction period in the South, laborers' lien laws, giving the worker priority over the merchant in the division of the planter's crop after the harvest, were a tangible result of this temporary gain in political leverage.[12]

But nothing is more dangerous for a racialized caste fighting for equality than a partial and precarious accession of power. Caste consciousness dies hard, as the example of India's tortuous efforts to elevate the status of Untouchables demonstrates. Consequently, the new order must be firmly and consistently enforced over a long period if a successful backlash is to be prevented. Such persistence might require a national government acting resolutely in the name of an egalitarian ide-

ology that has the capacity to override the racist attitudes of the majority. Otherwise, popular resistance to minority rights can readily erase
most of the gains made under an earlier dispensation of national power.
The decline and fall of Radical Reconstruction in the southern states is
the prime example of such a retreat in the face of resurgent racism. The
assertion of federal power on behalf of equal rights was inadequate and
short lived, partly because the ideology available to sanction the effort
was not rooted firmly in the kind of radical democratic values needed
to sustain it.

The subsequent disfranchisement of southern blacks after white supremacists regained control was congruent with efforts to place them
at the mercy of employers or landlords and restrict their opportunities
to acquire wealth and property or to follow occupations other than
sharecropper, laborer, or servant. The partial success of this effort made
it possible for whites to stereotype turn-of-the century blacks as radically and irremediably inferior. Only when blacks migrated in great
numbers to the relatively freer atmosphere of the North after 1914 did
they begin to acquire the resources and political influence to challenge
the Jim Crow system and begin to elevate their ethnic status in ways
that eventually impelled whites to abandon their claims to a racial hierarchy sustained by law.

Recent developments in South Africa also reflect changes in the
racial power equation that have culminated in the presidency of Nelson
Mandela and the achievement of one-person one-vote, a process that
began with the government's decision in 1989–1990 to negotiate with
the African National Congress. These advances are due in large part to
the leverage that black protesters gained in the 1980s over the South
African economy—internationally through the antiapartheid movement's promotion of sanctions and disinvestment, and domestically
through their growing influence as organized workers or consumers
and their resistance to white rule, which made the country virtually un-
governable and thus undermined the security and prosperity of the
white minority.

Such examples show that racism, however tenacious, is not a constant and unalterable influence on public action in ethnically divided
societies. For Weber, status was only one of three analytically distinguishable but overlapping and interacting sources of social power and
inequality. Others were "class" as determined by objective relationships
to the market and "party," meaning ability to influence public decisions
through political organization and access to suffrage and officeholding.

As Weberian social scientists have demonstrated, inequalities of class, status, and party do not exactly coincide. A main historical dynamic is the interaction among these forms of social power—that is, the manner in which social stratification of one kind conflicts with the others or reinforces them, as the case may be.[13]

Under a system of racial slavery, there is of course little or no contradiction; the three Weberian categories coincide almost perfectly. Blacks in the Old South had almost no access to social prestige, government, or the marketplace. After emancipation, however, the three types of inequality could vary independently. At the turn of the century, the Jim Crow era reached its height—almost, but not quite, approximating the early pattern of total subordination. Because there was now an emerging black middle class, albeit restricted to a segregated economy, there was no longer such a close fit between class and racial caste as during the slave era. Furthermore, as we have seen, the exclusion of southern blacks from American politics was mitigated to some extent by accelerating migration to the North where the right to vote and hold office persisted.

But the ethnic status of blacks in the nation as a whole may have been at a low point in the period between 1910 and the Great Depression, as reflected in the generally unfavorable or derogatory stereotypes projected by the dominant culture and in the pervasiveness of social segregation and discrimination. In 1913, the federal civil service was segregated. Also in that period the blatantly racist film *Birth of a Nation* achieved great popularity; the United States officially admonished French authorities during World War I to discourage fraternization between French civilians—especially women—and black soldiers out of deference to the belief of most white Americans in black inferiority and social unacceptability; and bloody race riots and a resurgent Ku Klux Klan characterized the immediate postwar years. But this was also the period when the NAACP won its first court victories and came close to getting antilynching legislation through Congress. In addition to limited political leverage, black migration to the North brought greater access to industrial jobs and better educational facilities.

The persistence of a sharply defined ethnic status hierarchy in the United States between World War I and the 1940s—a time when blacks were making some economic and political advances—does not prove that ethnic status is unaffected by changes in political and economic empowerment. In the long term, as developments in the 1950s and

1960s demonstrated, substantial and durable gains in one respect can
be translated into gains in the others. Racism gains much of its strength
and legitimacy from ingrained cultural attitudes, which of course
change more slowly than the social and economic structures with which
they were once directly and transparently associated. Furthermore, the
extent to which racism is rooted in associational preferences derived
from an expanded notion of family and kinship probably means that
racist thought and behavior is to some degree inevitable in any ethnically diverse society. Racism can, however, be made generally disrep-
utable, thus eliminating most of its socioeconomic effects and transforming its traditional targets into quasi-kin—or even actual kin to the
extent that intermarriage becomes acceptable.

The salience and social power of racism clearly vary over time and
may decrease significantly in response to changing historical circumstances. It is difficult to maintain at the core of one's identity a culturally sanctioned sense of status in the face of substantial changes in the
class, prestige, and power position of a subordinate group. Racism does
have a life of its own, but it cannot persist without changing its character and gradually losing some of its force in the face of dramatic and
durable improvements in the economic and political strength of a disadvantaged ethnic group. Some might argue that this is getting the cart
before the horse, that the empowerment of an oppressed minority requires a radical change in the status-affirming attitudes of a dominant
group. But what I am in fact advancing is a kind of interactionist or
feedback model of change. Increases in power affect attitudes, and
changing attitudes open access to power.

How, one might ask, does such a process get started? Studies of the
history of race relations in several societies suggest that something ex-
traneous to the racial order may occur, some larger economic, political,
or ideological development that calls for adjustment by the society as a
whole in ways that have accidental or unintended advantages for subordinated status groups. The independent effect of nationalism, especially when loyalty to a nation in peril can be construed as requiring an
inclusive rather than an exclusive sense of the national community, may
be of prime importance.[14]

Major wars or intense international competition among nations can
have such a catalytic effect on race relations. The Paraguayan war of
1865–1870 speeded Brazil on the path to slave emancipation because it
became necessary to use thousands of slaves as soldiers and to reward
them for their participation by freeing them. Black Americans were of

course freed from bondage as the result of a Civil War that was fought primarily for the preservation of the federal union and not for their liberation. As a result of the necessities and opportunities of war, emancipation and the use of black troops became a means to the end of national integrity. The victories of the civil rights movement a century later were aided, perhaps decisively, by the belief of influential and powerful whites that Jim Crow was a serious liability in America's competition with the Soviet Union for the "hearts and minds" of Africa and Asia. White South Africa became serious about dismantling apartheid and negotiating with African nationalists because black resistance and the threat of international sanctions raised fears that, unless something was done to accommodate blacks within a capitalistic framework, a future South Africa would have no place at all for an affluent and acquisitive white minority.

These examples suggest that in times of national peril or catastrophe, inclusive forms of nationalism, sometimes encouraged by a belief that survival on any terms available requires a redefinition of citizenship, may prove stronger than ethnic status consciousness and open the way to lowering or even eliminating barriers to the participation and empowerment of oppressed racial groups. Such a stretching of the boundaries of national solidarity is not an unambiguous victory over prejudice against the Other, however. It can be a concomitant of intensified international conflict, in which case the burden of Otherness is shifted to some extent from the shoulders of the usual domestic scapegoats to those of foreign nationals.

A more fundamental and less contingent force that undermines traditional racial hierarchies and the status claims they engender are long-term trends in the structure and value systems of modern societies away from "ascription" and toward "achievement" as a basis for status and power. We need not adopt the naive view that these trends are irresistible or that industrial capitalism is a direct and automatic solvent of ethnic stratification; the long career of apartheid in South Africa and of group conflict in Northern Ireland show that this is not the case. Yet we can, nonetheless, recognize that ethnic hierarchies become more problematic and vulnerable when they are the only form of ascribed status that persists in an open and publicly sanctioned way. A key function of explicit racist ideology, in its heyday between the mid–nineteenth century and the Second World War, was to rationalize the conspicuous exceptions to the prevailing Western norm of a liberal, open-class society that could be found in places like South Africa, the American South, and various European colonies.

But the period since World War II has seen an international revulsion against racism, inspired in large part by the increasing role in international affairs and organizations played by the emerging nations of Asia and Africa. Another important impetus for changing attitudes is the internationalization of capitalist enterprise, a development that has made overt racial prejudices a liability for those who would seek to compete with the Japanese and other Asians for world markets. Vast international inequalities that correlate roughly with color persist, but the current tendency to talk of the resulting conflict as pitting rich nations or parts of the world against poor ones may reflect the nature of this struggle better than the language of race that would have been more appropriate in the age of conquest and colonization.

The trend toward a worldwide struggle based on "class" in the Weberian sense, or between those who have a favored access to markets and scarce resources and those who do not, is to some extent paralleled within industrialized nations with strong traditions of racial or ethnic inequality. It is clear to many observers of contemporary Brazil that the central issue is the vast differential between a rich minority and an impoverished majority. The fact that people of darker skin are disproportionately represented among the poor is evidence of a long history of slavery and racial prejudice but may not be the most productive way to think about the current situation. Emancipating the poor as such would seem to be the main challenge, despite the exposure of subtle but persistent forms of discrimination that has recently compelled Brazilians to recognize that they do not in fact have a "racial democracy."[15]

Even in South Africa an assessment of the prospects for class conflict or accommodation may give a better sense of the forces currently at work than an exclusively racial or ethnic view of the struggle. Racism gave this version of capitalist industrialization its peculiarly segmented quality. But two theoretically color-blind ideologies, free market capitalism and Marxian socialism, came to dominate the two sides in the conflict by the 1980s, gaining in strength at the expense of a statist and corporatist doctrine of white supremacy on the one hand and a racially defined black nationalism on the other. Workers and employers alike seemed increasingly ready to view the struggle in class terms. Contrary to what one might expect from Marxist-Leninist theory, such a redefinition or reconstruction of the situation increased the prospects for a peaceful transition of power; for history shows that class adjustments and compromises are easier to bring off than the reconciliation of groups that view their differences as primarily ethnic or racial. But South Africa has a long way to go before the dream of "nonracial democracy" is fully achieved. Whites continue to dominate economic life, and many undoubtedly believe that their European ancestry still brings certain entitlements. They may cling to the hope that they can keep the substance of white power and privilege by giving up the trappings and allowing a middle-class black minority to share their advantages.[16]

What of current black-white relations in the United States? Historically speaking, racism—in Weberian terms, Euro-American status consciousness—has tended to predominate over any consciousness of class that transcends racial categories. The inability of the southern Populist movement of the late nineteenth century to build an interracial political coalition in the face of its opponents' appeals to racial solidarity is a well-known example of this tendency. Another is the notorious difficulty of uniting white and black workers in a collective struggle for class interests, as reflected in the long history of antiblack discrimination by organized labor and the failure of socialist movements to attract substantial black support. During the height of the great depression, when it appeared to many that there were unprecedented opportunities for class action across racial lines, W. E. B. Du Bois was driven, despite his sympathy for Marxism, to espouse the economic self-segregation of blacks, because he despaired of the capacity of white workers to overcome their cultural racism. Three decades later, after the civil rights movement had freed southern blacks from de jure segregation and de facto disfranchisement, advocates of black power and black nationalism came to a similarly pessimistic assessment of American society's ability to overcome racial segmentation. The Kerner Report's 1968 description of the nation as "moving toward two societies, one black and one white—separate and unequal" reflected a general sense in the late 1960s that the United States was still a society stratified by race or ethnic status and not merely by economic or class differences.[17]

Ten years later, however, a leading black sociologist, William Julius Wilson, argued that race was declining in significance and that the situation of blacks in American society could now best be approached in terms of class. Wilson, who refined and elaborated his argument in a later work on the black "underclass," based his case primarily on the growth of a substantial black middle class that he believed was being successfully integrated into the larger American middle class. This was in sharp contrast to the earlier situation of black elites who had been condemned by racism to seek higher status exclusively within the segregated African American community. But the price of this desegregation of elites was that blacks who could not qualify for middle-class opportunities because they lacked skills, education, and employment possibilities were stranded in the ghettos without middle-class leadership or behavioral examples. Consequently, their condition had worsened, and the nation faced the major social problem summed up in the phrase "black underclass." Underclass disabilities, Wilson concluded, were primarily a matter of class rather than race and needed to be addressed as such, mainly through social democratic or New Deal–type policies.[18]

Wilson's theories are controversial and have been sharply criticized by sociologists and historians who believe that racism is not only alive and well but perhaps even stronger than ever. My own opinion is that the class-based, social democratic policies Wilson recommends would do much to alleviate inner-city poverty and demoralization. Also his distinction between race and class as variable determinants of black inequality is a valuable clarification of the theoretical issues involved in the study of American inequality. But Wilson overstated his case for the decline of racism, at least in his original formulations, and has not always made it sufficiently clear that he has identified an uneven and reversible trend rather than an accomplished reality.

It is certainly true that the black middle class suffers less than in the past from specifically racial discrimination, but the affirmative action policies that made such advancement possible are now in grave danger. Black achievers and aspirants for middle-class status on our campuses sometimes face harassment from white students who resent what they view as special privileges or unfair advantages for African Americans, and subtle but effective forms of discrimination persist in access to skilled jobs and white-collar employment, the competition for status and influence within corporate bureaucracies, housing opportunities, and the treatment of black customers in stores, restaurants, and other places of public access. A majority of white Americans still regard interracial marriage as undesirable and a substantial minority would like to outlaw it. Middle-class assimilation, in other words, is not as complete or as certain as Wilson sometimes implies.

Furthermore, it would be hard to deny that the black underclass is feared and despised by many whites not merely for its poverty and statistical propensity to commit crimes or use drugs but also for reasons of race. The Willie Horton stereotype, as employed by the Bush campaign in 1988, was racially charged and not merely the product of class anxieties. What has changed is the ability of education and wealth to compensate to some extent for the stigma of African appearance and ancestry. (Although it might be hard to convince a middle-class African American trying to hail a taxicab in a big city of this fact.) But to be both poor and black is to be doubly disadvantaged. Until this changes, it cannot truly be said that race is no longer significant and that the United States can confront its inequalities exclusively in terms of class.

Wilson's problematic interpretation of current race relations may, however, have some value as prophecy. The deepening economic deprivation and insecurity that relatively large numbers of blacks share with somewhat smaller proportions of other racial and ethnic groups make it conceivable that a sense of class division could eventually eclipse race consciousness as the main source of public conflict in American society. Status based on race and the politics of status protection stubbornly persist and may even increase in hard times—as recent events suggest—but they lack ideological legitimacy and no longer, as in the past, clearly sustain a functional segmentation of labor based on race. Opportunities for the construction of class and the deconstruction of race may now exist to an unprecedented degree, because blacks are no longer consistently and categorically relegated to lower-caste occupations, a development that may change basic social alignments and make class-based responses to the growth of social and economic inequality more likely.

But a sense of racial status or caste is very difficult to eradicate, and the opposite extreme of a homegrown fascism based on a heightened Euro-American status consciousness could also result from the struggle over a shrinking economic pie. Working- and lower-middle-class whites who are struggling to make ends meet or to find and keep a decent job have a tendency, especially when nudged in this direction by right-wing politicians, to blame their hardships on blacks and other racialized groups—which are allegedly benefiting unfairly from affirmative action or being supported in idleness and immorality by the welfare system—rather than on the behavior of large corporations and the operations of the market economy. But it may not be too much to hope that such appeals to ethnic status consciousness will eventually wear thin in the face of growing evidence that blacks have nothing to do with declining wages and emigrating jobs.

A comparative historical perspective permits the hope, if not the confident expectation, that a plausible combination of circumstances and initiatives could lead to the end of racism as a significant determinant of inequality in the United States. Antiracists should be prepared to capitalize on the opportunities for class-based progressive action that will undoubtedly present themselves. To paraphrase Martin Luther King, Jr., Will it matter so much what kind of ship our ancestors came over in, when we realize that we are all in the same boat now?

CHAPTER SIX

Race and Empire in Liberal Thought

The Legacy of Tocqueville

A recent French intellectual "turn" that has aroused less interest in the United States than some other Paris fashions of the past thirty years is the reevaluation and heightened appreciation of Alexis de Tocqueville as a political and social theorist. The repudiation of Marx that followed the belated French discovery of the Soviet gulag has triggered a growing respect for the kind of liberalism espoused by the author of *Democracy in America* and *L'Ancien Régime*.[1]

In the United States, of course, Marxism never dominated social, political, and historical thought to anything like the extent it did in France between the 1930s and the 1970s. Tocqueville's prestige was at its high point among American historians and social scientists during the 1940s and 1950s, when his writings on the United States helped to buttress the concept of American exceptionalism—the belief that the United States differed from other Western nations in its lack of deep and persistent social and ideological divisions. During the 1970s, when Tocqueville's claim that there were significant continuities between the French Revolution and the ancien régime was being rediscovered and validated in France, his putative thesis that American history was shaped by a nonrevolutionary liberal consensus was coming under sustained attack from historians of the United States, who were discovering more conflict and change than this paradigm could account for.[2]

Jean-Claude Lamberti has recently tried to bring together the classic interpreter of the French Revolution with the author of the most influential book on America ever published. In *Tocqueville and the Two Democracies,* he has explored the connections between Tocqueville's observations on America and his reflections on the prospects for democracy in France. According to Lamberti, Tocqueville's point of departure was a specifically French concern: "how to defend the values of 1789 against the revolutionary spirit," or, in other words, how to affirm the Rights of Man without unleashing the Terror. Tocqueville was a liberal in the basic sense that his highest priorities were the encouragement and protection of individual freedom and self-development: "Because of his great faith in liberty, Tocqueville argued that the purpose of any political association must be to perfect the individual." This commitment to the individual meant that he could endorse neither the organicism of the traditionalist right nor the class-based collectivism of the socialist left, both of which subordinated the needs of the individual to those of the group.[3]

Democracy, the subject of the great works inspired by Tocqueville's visit to America, might serve the cause of liberty, or it might not, depending on the historical circumstances and culture of the people seeking to rule themselves. Tocqueville's main project in *Democracy in America* was not so much the study of the United States for its own sake as the comparative analysis of democracy and liberty in the United States and France. In America, he informed his French readers, the democratic spirit had been made relatively safe for liberty by such factors as the absence of a persistent thirst for revolution, the strength of voluntary associations, the broad participation of the citizenry in local government, the check on majoritarianism provided by legalism and lawyers, and the moral discipline supplied by religion. But America was not a perfect model. The weight of public opinion—the "tyranny of the majority"—was a constant threat to individual independence and to the creative use of personal freedom; for this was a society without the sublimated aristocratic traditions that Tocqueville believed were necessary to breed a respect for intellectual and cultural distinction.[4]

In France, very different historical and cultural conditions prevailed. Threats to liberal democracy came from two sides: a bourgeoisie with a narrow conception of personal freedom as the pursuit of individual wealth and comfort and a lower class with a penchant for revolutionary action. The bourgeoisie, unlike its American counterpart, tended to retreat from public life and leave governance to a central bureaucratic state. In times of popular insurgency, the bourgeoisie was all too willing to put its trust in a strongman or dictator who promised to control the masses. What needed to be learned from America was the value of administrative decentralization, voluntary associations, and the rule of law, as well as an understanding of the positive role that religion could play as a basis for public morality when church and state are separated. In modern parlance, Tocqueville was saying that liberal democracy required a strong civil society, and France, because of its traditions of statism and revolution, did not as yet possess one.[5]

Tocqueville's comparative insights were based on a political philosophy that departs in certain respects from the usual representations of nineteenth-century liberalism. As Roger Boesche has pointed out, it was a "strange liberalism" that comes close to being sui generis. Tocqueville did share with a number of other liberals the desire to moderate or discipline the leveling tendencies of the age in order to retain some of the virtues associated with the aristocratic past. Alan S. Kahan has recently identified an important strain of European social and political thought, well exemplified by Tocqueville, that he calls "aristocratic liberalism."[6]

Nevertheless, Tocqueville was especially, if not uniquely, insistent on the need to maintain aristocratic conceptions of honor, public service, and respect for personal distinction in the face of the apparently irresistible trends of world history that favored democracy, equality, and the ascendancy of the middle class. Although he saw no practical or preferable alternative to a market economy, he viewed the untrammeled pursuit of economic self-interest that it encouraged as dangerous to liberty rather than expressive of it. He did not believe for a moment that public and private interests were automatically reconciled by the operation of a laissez-faire economy. For him, liberty in the fullest sense required that citizens participate regularly and creatively in public affairs out of a patriotic devotion to the common good or the national interest.

The distinction that historians of American political thought sometimes make between classical republicanism and liberalism is difficult to apply to Tocqueville because of the way he synthesized elements of both traditions. Classical republicans feared declension from the standards of virtuous citizenship exemplified by the small republics of ancient Greece or early Renaissance Italy, while liberals normally celebrated modernity as moral and material progress. Tocqueville believed that modernity in the form of large nation-states, commercial-industrial development, and mass politics was irresistible, but it might or might not mean progress. Progress for him, as for Condorcet and other thinkers of the Enlightenment, meant the growth of truth and virtue through the exercise of freedom. But he departed from the optimism of the Enlightenment and many of its nineteenth-century liberal successors by making true progress a possibility or hope—something to be striven for—rather than an inevitability. Retrogression to barbarism and tyranny was also possible. The tension in his thinking between progressive hopes and declensionist fears—his belief that human beings were naturally capable of becoming more virtuous and rational but were also corruptible and subject to destructive passions—invites us to characterize him as a republican liberal or a liberal republican. And it raises the possibility that there is no necessary or essential contradiction between these two political philosophies.

For the most part, Tocqueville disdained deterministic theories of historical development. He maintained that the choices made by human beings and the actions that resulted from them would determine the future—not race, geography, or impersonal economic forces. He also believed, however, that national or ethnic cultures—a given people's "mores"—changed very slowly and that their persistence restricted the range of available choices. The tension between the voluntarism of his liberal hopes and the quasi-determinism of his cultural anthropology was a key element in the thought about race and empire to be found in *Democracy in America* and in his writings on French colonialism.

Tocqueville lived at a time when Europeans or people of European descent were acutely aware of the "Otherness" of Africans, Asians, and American Indians. Most of those who defined themselves as white believed strongly in their own superiority to those they designated as black, brown, yellow, and red. But they disagreed as to the causes and nature of white or European superiority and its implications for the kinds of relationships that were justified and desirable between Europeans and non-Europeans. Ideological racists, like Tocqueville's friend and correspondent Joseph-Arthur de Gobineau and some of the defenders of slavery in the southern United States, were beginning to advance the theory that racial differences in competence and capacities were innate or biologically determined and that existing hierarchies in power and privilege were in accordance with the laws of nature. From their perspective the efforts of humanitarians to liberate and uplift non-European peoples was sentimental folly. But the vast missionary enterprise of the Christian churches, which was burgeoning in the early-to-mid–nineteenth century, was based on the presumption that the "heathens" of Africa, Asia, and the Americas could be converted and "civilized." Existing European superiority was not in dispute, but there were serious disagreements on whether the inferiority of non-Europeans was the irremediable verdict of science or a temporary condition subject to amelioration through programs of reform and education that might in the future raise them to the level of civilization currently manifested by the West.

The specific question that brought these issues to the fore between the 1830s and the 1850s—the period when Tocqueville was writing—was the future of black slavery in the Americas. Those abolitionists who professed religious and humanitarian motives subscribed to the missionary logic. Their opponents, as well as some of those who opposed slavery on purely pragmatic or economic grounds, were increasingly influenced by the arguments of naturalistic racists. Because it combined the Christian humanitarian impulse and a growing commitment to capitalistic free labor, the antislavery movement proved to be irresistible during the middle decades of the nineteenth century—first in British colonies, then in those of France, and finally (although only after great bloodletting) in the United States.

But the hegemony of Europeans over other races or ethnic groups was not limited to the enslavement of blacks. This was also an era of Western imperial expansion in Africa, Asia, and North America. The United States participated in this process without fully acknowledging it by enlarging its domain through the conquest and dispossession of American Indian societies and the acquisition of new territories with Mestizo and Indian populations as a result of the war with Mexico. For the French, the 1830s and 1840s saw the beginnings of the colonization of Algeria. The question of race and the Otherness of non-European peoples played a role in white or European discourse about empire, but with somewhat different ideological alignments than in the debates over slavery. Missionaries and Christian philanthropists were likely to favor imperial expansion because it brought more people within the reach of the gospel. (In the United States, however, the entanglement of the slavery question with the expansionist program made many northern missionaries less than enthusiastic about Manifest Destiny.) Naturalistic racists, on the other hand, could have qualms about assuming any direct responsibility for people who had such limited capacities for improvement unless, as in the case of American Indians, they were viewed as on the path to extinction. An example of racist opposition to territorial expansion was the ideological resistance to a proposed annexation of all of "mongrel" Mexico by the United States when it seemingly had the power to do so after its victory in the war of 1846–1847.[7]

European and Euro-American estimates of the problems or opportunities associated with the imperial domination or colonization of particular societies or regions inhabited by non-Europeans depended to a great extent on how they evaluated the current social and cultural state of the people to be dominated. Scientific racists differed on how many "Great Races" there were—the number ranged from three to five depending on whether Malay-Polynesians and American Indians were subsumed under Mongolians or regarded as distinctive. But every European or American effort to rank the races of the world put Caucasians on top and Negroes at the bottom.

Another way of ranking peoples encountered in the expansion of Europe was derived from eighteenth-century conceptions of social and cultural evolution. The idea that humanity in general had progressed from savagery to barbarism to civilization provided a guide to non-European societies and to the use that European colonizers could make of them. "Savages"—essentially nomadic hunter-gatherers—were difficult to domesticate and civilize (they did not even make good slaves), but if they were relatively thin on the ground, as they usually were, they could be expected to die off to make way for white colonists, as appeared to be happening in Australia and North America. Barbarous peoples—herders of livestock and subsistence farmers such as many of the peoples of sub-Saharan Africa—might be utilized for agricultural labor or for work in mines. The most problematic category were those sometimes designated as "semicivilized" because they had cities and developed commercial economies, written languages, and religions that competed with Christianity in their intellectual and institutional sophistication. India, China, and the Arab-dominated societies of North Africa and the Middle East were the "semicivilized" areas of most interest to European imperialists in the period between the 1830s and the 1850s. Missionaries found such peoples difficult to convert because of the depth and strength of their commitment to Islam, Hinduism, Confucianism, or Buddhism. The path of least resistance for Europeans who wished to dominate and exploit societies of this type was some form of indirect rule through the cooptation of traditional rulers that necessarily entailed a willingness to tolerate non-Christian religious beliefs and practices. When they possessed large and thickly settled indigenous populations, such areas were regarded as unpromising receptacles for white emigrants or colonists.

This necessarily crude and oversimplified sketch of white or European attitudes toward race and empire between the 1830s and the

1850s provides a context for describing and analyzing Tocqueville's reflections on "Otherness" and how to deal with it. As a man of his own time and place, the author of *Democracy in America* (as well as an important series of reports on French prospects in Algeria) could hardly have failed to be influenced by the ethnocentrism and imperialism that pervaded current thought about the relationship between Europeans and non-Europeans. The ultimate question for those who wish to assess the legacy of Tocqueville's republican liberalism is whether his Eurocentric biases—and his willingness to tolerate, and sometimes to defend, brutal and unscrupulous uses of power to subjugate non-Europeans—were essential or incidental features of his political thought. Can one be a Tocquevillian without being a white or European chauvinist?

If racism is defined as a belief in the innate inferiority of the Other, then Tocqueville was not a racist, and his thought shows how strict biological determinism conflicts with the kind of liberalism he espoused. His most famous and categorical rejection of biological racism came in two letters that he wrote to Joseph-Arthur de Gobineau in the 1850s objecting to the latter's racial theories. Gobineau's conception of a natural racial hierarchy and his warnings against the degeneracy that supposedly resulted from miscegenation between higher and lower races (even among European or white populations of differing ethnic origins) were to have enormous influence on the growth of the ultimately genocidal doctrine that Aryans were superior to Semites as well as to Africans and Asians and must maintain their racial purity at all costs.[8]

Tocqueville wrote to Gobineau in 1853 objecting to such theories as "probably wrong and very certainly pernicious." He regarded them as a materialist equivalent of the religious doctrine of predestination and charged that they resulted in "a very great contradiction, if not a complete abolition, of human liberty." "What interest can there be," he asked, "in persuading the base people who live in barbarism, in indolence, or in servitude, that since they exist in such a state by virtue of the nature of their race, there is nothing they can do to ameliorate their condition, change their mores, or modify their government?" From the perspective of Tocqueville's liberal ideology, "the destiny of man, either as an individual or as a nation, is what he wants to make of it." As he made clear in a letter of 1857, Tocqueville's Christian faith also testified against biological racism and affirmed that all human beings could be educated and civilized. Anyone who believed in the biblical doctrine of the unity of mankind and accepted the underlying assumptions of the campaign to spread the gospel throughout the world had to reject Gobineau's racial determinism.[9]

It is clear from this correspondence that Tocqueville and Gobineau agreed on the existing abject inferiority of non-European and non-Christian peoples or nations. They differed only on the causes of this "base" condition and its possibility for change. For Gobineau the condition of non-Europeans was a reflection of their physical or biological makeup and was therefore unchangeable; whereas Tocqueville, who attributed it to culture and circumstances, believed that it could be ameliorated through missionary work, education, and the imposition of a civilizing discipline. It also may be noteworthy that Tocqueville was more convinced that Gobineau's theories were "pernicious" than he was that they were actually false. In a manner reminiscent of Pascal's wager, he suggested that a belief in the improvability of barbarous peoples *might* make it happen, whereas the lack of such a belief ruled out the possibility.

Tocqueville's earlier discussion in the first volume of *Democracy in America* (published in 1835) of the whites, blacks, and Indians of the United States revealed similar assumptions. According to James Schleifer, the notebooks in which Tocqueville recorded his impressions of America in 1831 and 1832 contain a consideration and ultimately the rejection of "a biological explanation" of American national character. What convinced him that circumstances were more important than "bloodlines" in explaining the attitudes and behavior of the dominant race were the great differences he found in the habits and outlook of northern and southern whites, who seemed to him almost like two peoples. But some ambiguities remained. "In the years after," Schleifer writes,

> Tocqueville never totally discarded the idea that race played some role in the shaping of human societies. Race, for example, became an element of *l'origine*. But what precisely did he mean by race? By the end of his American journey, he thought usually in terms of tenacious but slowly evolving *mœurs*. Yet what was the exact nature of the connection between bloodlines and national character or *mœurs*? Unfortunately he failed to pinpoint the meaning of these words.

Noting that American frontiersmen did not revert to barbarism when they took to the woods, he speculated that the feelings and habits of civilized life had become too deeply ingrained to be altered by a radical change in environment. Nevertheless, Tocqueville's discussion of "The Three Races That Inhabit the United States" in Volume I of *Democracy in America,* "repeatedly emphasized the radically dissimilar social, legal, and historical circumstances of the three races. Nowhere would he defend biological determinism."[10]

A close reading of Tocqueville's long chapter on "the three races" bears out Schleifer's analysis. The differences that he found between the mental and behavioral characteristics of whites, Indians, and blacks were enormous and might have led another observer to jump to the conclusion that they belonged to separate species. The gaps were so great that no trend toward assimilation could be detected—"they have mixed without combining and each follows a separate destiny." But for Tocqueville the principal cause of this separatism and mutual hostility was the fact that the whites had established a monopoly on "enlightenment, power, and happiness" and treated the other races with arrogance and brutality. The enslaved blacks were denied "virtually all the privileges of humanity" and consequently were reduced to a state of misery and abject servility that had penetrated their very souls. Slavery, he argued, had degraded and dehumanized blacks to the point where they were unfit for freedom and would not know what to do with it if it were offered to them. Indians, on the other hand, were proud and free, but for this very reason were doomed to extinction because they would not submit to the rule or embrace the culture of the whites. "The Negro would like to mingle with the European but cannot. The Indian might to some extent succeed in that, but he scorns to attempt it. The servility of the former delivers him over into slavery, the pride of the latter leads him to death."[11]

To account for the impending doom of the American Indians, Tocqueville invoked the theory of cultural evolution previously described. As "savages," Indians were far behind the whites in the scale of human progress. They had the natural capacity to catch up, as "the success of the Cherokee" demonstrated, but the pace of white settlement and the policy of Indian removal would not allow them the time to civilize themselves. "Civilization is the result of prolonged social endeavor taking place at the same spot, an endeavor which each generation bequeaths to the next." Echoing the Jeffersonian theory of how Indians might be civilized, Tocqueville prescribed a settled agricultural existence. But their devotion to hunting and wandering, as well as the encroachment of whites on their lands whenever they tried to become rooted on the soil, made it extremely difficult, if not impossible, for them to take up farming and thereby advance to the next stage of cultural evolution.[12]

For blacks, the prospects were also dismal. Slavery for Tocqueville was an indefensible violation of natural rights and should be abolished as soon as possible, but the restriction of servitude "to one of the races of man" had created a problem for which emancipation would be no solution. In the ancient world, the freed slaves could be assimilated because they did not differ in appearance from their former masters. But in the United States, "the Negro transmits to his descendants at birth the external mark of his ignominy." For blacks to achieve equality or even a measure of acceptance, prejudice based on color would have to be eradicated. But such a transformation of white racial attitudes seemed unlikely or impossible to Tocqueville: "For my part, remembering the extreme difficulty with which aristocratic bodies, of whatever nature they may be, mingle with the mass of the people, and the excessive care they take to preserve down the centuries the artificial barriers that keep them apart, I despair of seeing an aristocracy founded on visible and indelible signs vanish." The practice of democracy among whites made the problem even more intractable than it would have been otherwise. "Some despot subjecting the Americans and their former slaves beneath the same yoke might perhaps force the races to mingle; while American democracy remains at the head of affairs no one would dare attempt any such thing, and it is possible to foresee that the freer the whites in America are, the more they will seek to isolate themselves." In these passages, Tocqueville anticipated the view of some modern historians and sociologists that the United States developed historically as a kind of "*Herrenvolk* democracy"—a society in which political and social equality was prized by white males on the understanding that equal citizenship was the prerogative of the master race. Tocqueville was less certain about the ultimate fate of African Americans than he was about the doom of the Indians, but he predicted that emancipation in the South would be followed by a race war in which blacks might conceivably hold their own, thereby gaining a southerly slice of North America for their own exclusive occupancy.[13]

What is most striking about these observations is their unrelieved pessimism about the prospects for racial equality or harmony in the United States. If genetically inherited racial traits and instincts were not what was preventing the eventual assimilation of blacks and Indians or even their peaceful coexistence with the white majority, something else was doing the job just as effectively. There is a fine line between the biological determinism that Tocqueville rejected and his fatalism about the prospects of changing the mores and social habits that distinguished the three races, separated them, and brought them into deadly conflict. Where, one wonders, was the human liberty that he generally cited in opposition to deterministic theories? More specifically, the view that white Americans could not rise above their cultural racism and overcome their color prejudices seems like a flagrant denial of Tocqueville's liberal faith in the capacity of human beings to transcend the past and improve themselves and their world.

Tocqueville's sense of the inherent obstacles that would impede and probably defeat efforts to achieve justice and equality for racially defined minorities in a liberal-democratic society may have shown the limits of his liberal faith, but they cannot be rejected on those grounds alone. Who can say with certainty that history has proved him wrong? John Stuart Mill, Tocqueville's friend and fellow giant among nineteenth-century liberal thinkers, believed that representative government worked well only among ethnically homogeneous populations. Although he never made the same point explicitly, Tocqueville's conclusion that American democracy was, and would remain, an exclusively white affair was another way of saying that governments based on the will of the people depended for their success and stability on the ethnic solidarity of the people that was expressing its will.

The success of American democracy, it might be argued from Tocquevillian premises, resulted in part from the very fact that blacks and Indians were excluded from the body politic. The only apparent alternative to exclusion and subordination was uncontrollable race conflict. Describing the presence of black slaves in one section of the United States as the greatest threat to the democratic republic, he warned presciently that the slavery issue could provoke a great cataclysm that would dissolve the Union. Some of the same American political virtues that he hoped the French could emulate, especially decentralization and local self-government, were also major obstacles to the peaceful abolition of slavery and the extension of citizenship rights to blacks. Localized white majorities would never give up their racial privileges. It would thus take some form of centralized dictatorship to accomplish such a revolutionary change. In other words, one might readily conclude that the virtues of American democracy were inseparable from its vices and that one could not have one without the other. Left to itself as an expression of the liberty and equality of the white majority, American democracy would never treat blacks and Indians fairly and decently. Only by undermining the liberty and self-government of the whites would it become possible to emancipate the blacks and protect the Indians. It was a dilemma for which Tocqueville saw no resolution.

What made the problem insoluble was Tocqueville's conception of the persistence and continuity of the "mores" of any people or ethnic group. Mores did change, but very slowly over the course of many generations. The mores of white Americans included race consciousness as a central and defining element. "The pride of origin, which is natural to the English, is most remarkably increased in the American by the personal pride derived from democratic liberty. The white man in the United States is proud of his race and proud of himself." Any effort to equalize the status of blacks would be an affront to white pride, an assault on the whites' positive sense of identity. Although not a biological determinist, Tocqueville came close to being a cultural determinist. When the mores that gave character to a nation conflicted with universalist ideals of justice and equality, he expected the ideals to give way. His denial to white Americans of a capacity to overcome their ingrained racial prejudices illustrated a general principle: "It can happen that a man will rise above the prejudices of religion, country, and race, and if that man is a king, he can bring about astonishing transformations in society, but it is not possible for a whole people to rise, as it were, above itself." From his day to ours, black nationalists and those white liberals who have despaired of overcoming the cultural racism of their fellow citizens have echoed Tocqueville's gloomy prognosis.[14]

Since France had what Tocqueville regarded as an ethnically homogeneous population, it could learn from the positive features of American democracy without being concerned about the injustice that majorities might inflict on racial minorities. This happy circumstance explains why the chapter on race was relegated to the end of the first volume of *Democracy in America* after Tocqueville had completed his "main task" of describing "the laws and mores of American democracy." He regarded the racial situation as so tragic and threatening that it could fatally undermine the American experiment, but he relegated it to a virtual appendix because he wanted the French to understand the "normal" operation of American government and society in a way that might inspire the emulation of some of its features.[15]

If France was racially homogeneous, its overseas empire was not. Tocqueville confronted the problem of the relationship between his own people and non-Europeans most directly in his writings and reports on French colonial subjects between 1837 and 1847. During the public service that he performed between his first candidacy for the

Chamber of Deputies in 1837 and his brief tenure as foreign minister after the Revolution of 1848, he was devoted to two main objects: the abolition of slavery in the French empire and the colonization of Algeria.

For Tocqueville, applied Christian ethics, which he believed lay at the root of the egalitarianism and fraternalism of the French Revolution, made the abolition of slavery a moral imperative. As he wrote in his 1843 article on *"L'émancipation,"* "It is we who have given a definite and practical meaning to the Christian idea that all men are born equal, and we have applied it to the realities of this world." It was disgraceful therefore that the French had not abolished slavery in their own colonies: "It is we who, by destroying the principle of castes and classes throughout the world, by rediscovering . . . the rights of the human race that had been lost . . . [and] by spreading throughout the universe the idea of equality of all men before the law, as Christianity had created the idea of the equality of all men before God, . . . are the true authors of the abolition of slavery."[16]

As a man of affairs who aspired to be a statesman, however, Tocqueville could not afford to be a pure idealist when the subject at hand involved French national interests. Eschewing the unconditional moralism of a William Lloyd Garrison, he took account of the practical problems created by emancipation in the specific proposals he advanced for ending slavery in the French overseas empire. In the report that he wrote for the national assembly in 1839 and in a series of articles published in 1843, he drew on what he had observed in America and on the recent experience of British emancipation in the West Indies to advance a proposal that had two main features—compensation for slaveholders and direct government responsibility for educating and controlling the former slaves. In lieu of the operations of a free-labor market, he advocated what Matthew Mancini has described as "a form of state socialism." As Tocqueville put it in the 1839 report: "The bond that now exists between [masters and slaves] should be totally dissolved. The state should become the sole guardian of the enfranchised population." He thus registered his skepticism as to whether a colonial environment could be conducive to liberty and civilization without the sustained intervention of the metropolitan authorities. Benevolent despotism, which would be destructive of liberal-democratic tendencies in France itself, would be essential for the well-being and progress of its former slave colonies, just as it would have been the only way to achieve fairness for blacks and Indians in the United States. Once again, he assumed that the habits of mind bequeathed by a history of slavery

and racial hierarchy meant that the only kind of democracy sustainable
in such an environment was the *Herrenvolk* or racially circumscribed
variety.[17]

Besides being an architect of the French abolition policy that came
to fruition in 1848, Tocqueville was a strong and influential advocate
of the colonization of Algeria. In 1830 the city of Algiers had been
taken by the French in reprisal for the insult to French honor that had
occurred when the Dey of Algiers struck the French consul with a fly
whisk during talks over a longstanding debt. During the 1830s France
occupied only a limited area around Algiers and remained uncommit-
ted to the establishment of a permanent colony. But in 1841 the government decided to embark on an expansion of the French enclave leading to the full-scale conquest and colonization of the region, a process
that was completed in 1847 after fierce indigenous resistance had been
overcome by means of a brutally repressive policy that featured mas-
sacres of noncombatants and the destruction of crops and villages.
Tocqueville took up the subject in 1837 when he was running unsuccessfully for the Chamber of Deputies. (He would succeed two years
later.) In 1841 and 1846 he traveled to Algeria to observe local conditions. After the second trip, which he made as an official representative
of the Chamber of Deputies committee on Algeria, he was the principal
author of an influential report calling for reforms of the administration
of the colony to give more freedom to the French settlers.[18]

A fervent advocate of French colonization, Tocqueville based his
case for imperialism on political rather than economic grounds.
France's place among nations required its participation in what he described to an English correspondent in 1840 as the great event of the
age: "the subjugation of four-fifths of the world by the remaining one-
fifth." In his 1837 letter on Algeria he expressed a hope that France's
"share in the partition of the Orient" would not be limited to its involvement in Algeria. Tocqueville greatly admired the British for their
domination of India, believing that the assumption of this responsibility had improved the British national character, and he wanted the
French to have the same kind of redemptive experience. The alternative, if the French failed to rise to the challenge, would not be the
preservation of Algerian independence, but rather colonization by another European power, which would thereby increase its power and
prestige at the expense of France.[19]

This strategic argument for national expansionism, which would be
echoed by many later imperialists (leading some historians to wonder if

economic motives were really at the core of the imperialist impulse), was combined with a powerful concern for French domestic politics and culture. Tocqueville despised the July Monarchy that had come to power as a result of the Revolution of 1830 for its corruption and encouragement of materialism. The best antidote that he could find for the decadence and self-seeking individualism that was threatening the French national character was the kind of patriotism that could be aroused by war and overseas adventures. The conquest of Algeria was necessary therapy for the bourgeois society of France as well as a contribution to the progress of the human race. To inspire dedication to the common good at home, it was necessary to subjugate foreign populations.[20]

Did Tocqueville's belligerent French nationalism contradict his liberalism or constitute its logical extension to the international sphere? The two leading authorities on his thought about Algeria disagree sharply on this question. Melvin Richter concludes that his position on Algeria conflicted with the principles that he applied in *Democracy in America*: "When this issue forced him to choose, he placed nationalism above liberalism; the interests of 'progressive' Christian countries above the rights of those who were not." Tzvetan Todorov, on the other hand, argues that an amoral and ruthlessly nationalistic foreign policy was the logical corollary of domestic liberalism. Personal rights, according to liberal theory, exist only within a context in which the rule of law serves to protect the individual against the *"volonté générale"* (general will). In the absence of a world government or enforceable regime of international law, there is neither a general will nor an effective limitation on the liberty of individuals (which in the international sphere are nations rather than persons). Consequently, liberty is expressed internationally by the exercise of state power on behalf of national interests. If a government were to abjure the power competition among nations, it would merely open itself to foreign conquest and domination. Hence the preservation of a nation's liberty justifies disregarding the rights of persons and communities beyond its borders.[21]

Whether the democratic rights of other peoples must be respected by those who prize them at home has in fact been a matter of dispute among liberals from Tocqueville's time to ours. Todorov's formulation has the merit of making Tocqueville comprehensible; it shows how he could imagine himself to be consistent whether he was or not. Western liberalism has, for the most part, been closely linked to nationalism and has proved to be a relatively ineffective basis for resistance to imperialism. Liberals have sometimes been anti-imperialist in principle, but more often they have called for a repudiation of colonial responsibilities on the basis of pragmatic calculations of "national interest." Yet the ethical content of liberalism would appear to conflict with the kind of nationalism that sanctions the conquest and enslavement of other peoples in the pursuit of glory and as a remedy for domestic "decadence." Tocqueville keenly felt the immorality of slavery and lamented its brutalizing effects on its victims. No considerations of national interest could assuage such feelings of guilt and remorse about how whites had treated Africans since the sixteenth century. It remains to be explained why his liberal conscience virtually ceased to function when he was confronted with an imperialist war of conquest that was conducted with ferocity and inhumanity.

Tocqueville the proponent of the civilizing mission of the Christian West came to the aid of Tocqueville the French nationalist whenever he sought a thoroughly compelling justification for the conquest of Algeria. His dual allegiance to Christianity and to the spirit of 1789 meant that he could not really be at peace with imperialism if it simply meant that the Other existed only to serve the interests of Europeans in any way they saw fit. He had in fact condemned slaveholding for the immoral and arrogant attitude that it revealed—its assumption that dark-skinned human beings, like domestic animals, could be made the instruments of those who happened to be born with lighter pigmentation. In his mind, slavery and colonial domination differed in the sense that the latter did not inevitably mean the degradation of its subjects. Conducted in the right spirit and with the right methods, it could lead to improvement in their conditions, character, and morale. The civilization of Africa and Asia by Europeans was a logical outgrowth of the abolition of slavery; it was the next great step in the progress of the human race.

But the issue in Algeria was complicated by the fact that the French had decided not merely to establish European hegemony over an indigenous society as the British had done in India, but also to introduce substantial numbers of colonists from the metropole power. Unlike India, Algeria was thought to be underpopulated and endowed with more arable land than its original inhabitants could effectively cultivate. But neither was this America; for the indigenous people were not savages who would soon die out in the face of competition from civilized white settlers. As semicivilized people and adherents of a world religion that had long held its own in the struggle with Christianity, they presented a difficult problem for the colonizers. How, Tocqueville wondered, could a just and workable relationship be created between the indigenous majority, the white colonists, and the French governing authorities? In his 1837 "Letter on Algeria," written before he had visited the country and examined the question fully, Tocqueville proposed an assimilationist policy. The only justification for placing French colonists in the midst of Arabs, he wrote, was "to establish with them a durable link and to form ultimately a single people from the two races." Practical interests, he thought, would weaken the religious zeal of the Arabs and make it possible to reconcile the two communities.[22]

After he had visited Algeria in 1841, Tocqueville changed his mind about the prospects for assimilation. He was struck by the fervor of the Muslims and concluded that the Christian and Islamic sectors of Algerian society could not be combined or amalgamated in the foreseeable future. The two communities, he found, had remained almost totally separate, and any notion that they might fuse was chimerical. As a result, it was necessary for the indefinite future to maintain segregated societies with a dual system of laws. It would be useful, he concluded, to think of the European colonists "as if they were alone, since the rules to be made for them are to be applied only to them." This meant that they should be accorded some, if not all, of the basic rights they would have enjoyed if they had remained in France, but no such rights should be extended to the indigenous inhabitants. Here and elsewhere, Tocqueville opined that Islam was a religion incompatible with human progress and enlightenment. Its fatalism and confusion of the civil and religious power meant that its adherents were incapable of citizenship in a liberal-democratic polity. Because of what he took to be the enduring cultural incompatibility of the French and the Algerians, he advocated what amounted to a system of apartheid with a European monopoly on political rights. Tocqueville did not view Algerian Arabs as racial inferiors, only as religious and cultural inferiors. Like American Indians, they had the capacity to become fully civilized but lacked the will to do so.[23]

The depth of Tocqueville's animus against Islam came out several years later in a letter to Gobineau in which he expressed a cultural intolerance that some might regard as the functional equivalent of the latter's racialist claim for Aryan superiority. His study of the Koran, he reported, had convinced him that "there have been few religions in the world as deadly to men as that of Mohammed." It was more to be feared than polytheism and was in fact "a form of decadence rather than a form of progress in relation to paganism itself." Tocqueville's willingness to support the scorched earth policies of the French army in Algeria—the destruction of crops and villages that led to mass starvation—may not have resulted simply from nationalist *Realpolitik*. In all likelihood, religious and cultural intolerance played a role in making him callous about the fate of the Algerians who were resisting French domination.[24]

In his 1847 report on Algeria, which was written after the conquest had been completed and the emotions of war had died down, Tocqueville recovered some of the high ground from which he had judged white treatment of blacks and Indians in the United States: "If we demonstrate by our behavior that we consider the native population merely as an obstacle to be circumvented or smashed, if by our rule we bring them not well-being and enlightenment but destruction then the only issue between the two races will be that of life and death. Sooner or later Algeria will become the bloody arena for a mortal combat between these two peoples with mercy neither offered nor accepted." He hoped it might be otherwise, but given what he had written in *Democracy in America* about the normal brutality of Europeans toward other races—including the kinds of policies that he himself had endorsed while the conquest of Algeria was under way—what grounds could he have had for optimism?[25]

To return to our basic question: Was Tocqueville's liberal humanism an invitation to the disparagement and domination of cultural Others or a potential deterrent to it? Postmodernist writers have concluded, for the most part, that liberalism is inherently Eurocentric and in some sense racist, and they can find support for this assessment in Tocqueville's writings. But such a verdict, in my opinion, requires a view of liberalism defined in terms of historical contingencies rather than recognizing that it is a dynamic faith subject to revision in the light of changing circumstances and further reflection on its essential meaning. What is timeless and basic in liberalism is a commitment to individual liberty and human rights. But the meaning of liberty and its recognition of the rights regarded as sacred and inalienable have expanded over time. Tocqueville apprehended some of the enduring spirit of liberalism. Most significantly, in my opinion, he demonstrated conclusively that liberal thought is not the same thing as capitalist apologetics, but in fact has a potential life of its own that can provide a basis for resisting the materialism and economic determinism of free-market ideology. But it is also obvious that his time, place, and personal circumstances put limits on how and where he could apply his liberal-humanist faith. Furthermore, his quasi-deterministic theory of the persistence of mores and national characters seriously compromised his sense of human freedom and possibility.

Liberals need to be realistic about the possibility of change, but an underlying commitment to freedom and indeterminacy should prevent them from becoming fatalists. Liberal values may indeed conflict with those of religions and cultures that deny or severely limit human freedom, but coercion or intolerance are not the answer. Tocqueville believed that the best solution for the problems of democracy was more democracy. Similarly, he might have argued, if he had followed this logic further, that peoples and nations cannot be forced to be free; they must rather be given the opportunity to become free if they so desire. Colonialism, like slavery, was a clear denial of this imperative.

If Tocqueville's thought reveals a permanent and unresolvable conflict in liberalism, it is not the one that postmodernists commonly find, the intellectual contradiction between a professed universalism and a covert racism and ethnocentrism. From a logical and philosophical perspective, a universalism that is truly universal is conceivable and would be capable of resolving this conflict. The most serious and durable split within liberalism that Tocqueville's thought exposes is the inherent conflict between the liberal philosopher and the liberal politician or statesman. The theorist may be a cosmopolitan advocate of principles that apply to humanity in general, but the locus of liberal politics is the nation-state. Conflicts will inevitably arise between the liberty and welfare of American or French citizens and those of people elsewhere in the world. When liberals debate immigration policy, for example, they generally consider only the rights and interests of the nation's current inhabitants, not those of potential immigrants from other societies. More broadly speaking, what is best for one's own society is not necessarily best for humanity in general. As long as nation-states govern the world, universalist liberalism will be unable to realize its ideals. This was Tocqueville's real dilemma—and ours.

CHAPTER SEVEN

Black-White Relations since Emancipation

The Search for a Comparative Perspective

Preeminent among historical topics that have been explored extensively from a cross-cultural perspective is the institution of slavery, especially the comparison of the Old South's "peculiar institution" with systems of unfree labor elsewhere in the world. For more than forty years, scholars have been probing the similarities and differences between African servitude in the southern United States and in other slave societies of the New World; more recently Africa itself has been brought into the comparison; and now we even have a major study of North American slavery and Russian serfdom.[1]

Some of these studies go beyond the discussion of slavery itself and argue that black-white relations in the postemancipation era were predetermined or at least strongly influenced by the character of the antecedent slave society.[2] Although it would be hard to deny that the slave regime left an enduring legacy of attitudes and habits predisposing former masters and slaves to think and behave in certain ways, it is doubtful whether one can deal effectively with the subsequent history of race relations exclusively, or even principally, from this perspective. Circumstances and events of the postemancipation era, of a kind not clearly prefigured by slavery and the attitudes associated with it, may be of more importance in understanding postemancipation race relations than the peculiarities of the slave past. This is especially true if we take the long view and consider not merely what happened to the freedmen immediately after the abolition of chattel servitude but attempt to trace the trajectory of black experience from the time of emancipation to the present. Such a longitudinal view reveals major changes as well as significant continuities, and it would seem unlikely that we could explain change and development in terms of the characteristics or effects of an institution that was abolished before these transformations took place.

The subject of race relations over the entire time span from the end of slavery to the present remains relatively undeveloped in comparative historical analysis. This paper is no more than prologue to such an undertaking, because it starts from the premise that fruitful comparison can begin only after we know what other case or cases of modern race or class relations would provide the most useful comparative perspectives on what has happened to African Americans since the Civil War. There is no substitute for in-depth bilateral or trilateral comparisons if we wish to get a purchase on particular historical experiences, but here I seek merely to point the way to appropriate comparisons without actually making them in more than a hypothetical or heuristic way.

My point of departure is a synthetic view of the course or trajectory of black-white relations in the South, and ultimately in the United States as a whole, since emancipation. From such a general understanding, it should be possible to look at some other cases or types of cases to determine what kinds of insights or perspectives a more systematic comparison might be expected to yield.

Black Americans were emancipated as the byproduct of a Civil War that was fought for the preservation of the federal union. As a result of the necessities and opportunities of war, as viewed from the Union side, emancipation was adopted as an expedient policy that also appealed to the ideals of democracy and free labor that many northerners espoused as the basis of their superiority to the "aristocratic" South with its reliance on an archaic form of unfree labor. It is often incorrectly asserted that the slaves made no significant contribution to their own liberation. In fact they voted against slavery with their feet and offered themselves *en masse* to the Union army as a source of manpower. Had they remained quietly at work on the plantations, the temptation to free them as "a war measure" would have been weaker and perhaps even resistible.[3]

By itself, emancipation did not determine the status of blacks in American society. Racial prejudice and white-supremacist ideology remained strong in the North as well as the South in the immediate postwar years, and a possible model for the role of freedmen in the new order was the status of the half-million free Negroes of the antebellum period, who had been, as much in the North as in the South, a segregated pariah class without citizenship or "rights white men were bound to respect," except the right to own their own bodies, possess such property as they might somehow be able to acquire, and choose their own employers when not apprenticed under some form of labor contract. If one could have taken a poll of white Americans immediately after the Civil War, there seems little doubt that a majority would have favored such an arrangement. It was only because the postwar agenda of the ruling Republican party required black citizenship that the constitution was amended to provide for equality under the law and nonracial suffrage. Republican motives have been much debated, and various efforts have been made to distinguish elements of principle and expediency in the formation of Radical race policy. What is important for our purposes is that some combination of practical circumstances and ideological pressures made the fundamental Law of the Land into a barrier to legalized or publicly sanctioned racial discrimination, although the question of how far it went or what precisely it covered would long remain debatable.

Constitutional reform of this kind was not sufficient to turn exslaves into citizens. Efficient enforcement and generous interpretation of the law was necessary, and these were not forthcoming except fitfully and for a relatively short period. By the late 1870s, the southern states were once again under the dominance of white supremacist majorities, and the rights accorded blacks during the Reconstruction era were largely nullified. In the period 1890–1910, the southern states, with the consent of the United States Supreme Court, segregated blacks by law in virtually all public facilities and amended their constitutions to bring about the de facto disfranchisement of most of the freedmen and their descendants. In the North, blacks retained many of their civil rights, including the right to vote and hold office, but they had no adequate defense against the private or extralegal discrimination that denied them equal access to jobs, housing, education, police protection, and public amenities. The organized and articulate black response to these developments took two forms. In the South, where opposition to black political rights was massive and unyielding, the dominant ideology was accommodationist, condoning social segregation, stressing economic self-help, and deferring aspirations for full citizenship. The accommodationist and gradualist approach of Booker T. Washington was also influential in the North, especially among a rising class of black entrepreneurs working within an increasingly segregated economy. But in the early 1900s, northern black professionals, seeking to turn back the tide of Jim Crow laws and practices, launched a protest movement, modeled on pre–Civil War abolitionism, that rejected Washington's accommodationism and called for the end of enforced segregation, disfranchisement, and all publicly sanctioned discrimination. In 1909 they joined a group of white liberals and socialists to form the organization that soon became known as the National Association for the Advancement of Colored People (NAACP).

In the meantime, economic and demographic changes were occurring that would alter the contours of black-white relations. For the first half-century of freedom, most blacks remained in the rural South as sharecroppers and farm laborers, or, in the case of a fortunate minority, as renters or owners of small farms. Except to the extent that they worked in such extractive industries as mining and lumbering, blacks were scarcely affected by industrialization; in the South most factory jobs were reserved for poor whites. Hamstrung by a credit system that kept many of them in perpetual debt, these rural blacks constituted part of a class that was not supposed to exist in America—an oppressed and impoverished peasantry, an agrarian lower stratum that had some limited access to the means of production but was denied upward mobility and full rights of citizenship.

This situation began to change in the era of the First World War when the combination of an economic boom and the restriction of European immigration provided new employment opportunities for blacks in the North, including the chance to gain a toehold in secondary industry. Except for a temporary hiatus during the Great Depression, the great migration accelerated until the 1970s.

This massive shift of black population from the South to the North and from the country to the city had profound effects on American race relations. Discrimination in the housing market, combined with the preference of American ethnic groups to cluster in their own neighborhoods, produced the great urban ghettos. As has often been noted, the North was no promised land; blacks were often frustrated in their desire to find and keep decent jobs, sometimes encountered violence in their struggle for living space, and in addition to the special disabilities imposed by racial discrimination, confronted the problems of social and cultural adjustment faced by any population of ex-peasants that finds itself thrust into an urban environment.

But great advantages also followed from the migration. Despite the racial inequities, economic and educational opportunities were nor-

mally greater than they had been in the South. Furthermore, the less repressive northern environment accorded blacks the political space to
air their grievances and mount protest movements. Blacks also regained the right to vote when they went north, and politicians began to
appeal to black interests and feelings for the first time since
Reconstruction. As early as the 1930s, it was clear that the black vote
could be crucial in municipal, state, and even national elections. With
the NAACP now functioning as a legislative lobby, blacks in the 1930s
were able to block the confirmation of a racist judge to the Supreme
Court and came close to getting a federal antilynching law through
Congress. In the same decade, blacks developed their first significant
ties to organized labor when nondiscriminatory unions recruited them
in such industries as auto manufacturing and steel. The transformation
of blacks from peasants to proletarians picked up further momentum
during World War II. Wartime labor shortages, pressures from black
organizations and movements, and federal policy encouraging nondiscriminatory hiring brought about a substantial increase in the proportion of blacks in steady, relatively skilled jobs, and the enormous gap
between the average incomes of whites and blacks began to close for
the first time.[4]

Partly on the basis of progress already made and political clout already acquired, black activists and organizations launched a successful
assault on southern segregation and disfranchisement in the post–World
War II period. But this victory was not simply a result of northern
blacks' ability to influence federal policy toward the South. The breakdown of the sharecropping economy and the accelerating urbanization
of blacks within the South in the period before, during, and after World
War II gave the growing proportion of southern African Americans living in cities greater freedom and capacity to organize for protest than
those still living under flagrantly repressive rural or small-town conditions. Urban black churches, unique in the extent to which they provided
southern blacks with an experience of autonomy and self-government,
became potential centers for community mobilization.[5] Encouraged by
favorable Supreme Court rulings and a concept of national interest that
made racism a liability in the international competition for "the hearts
and minds of men" in Asia and Africa, the nonviolent direct action
movement of the 1950s and 1960s was able to compel federal action to
eliminate "Jim Crow" segregation and a variety of obstructions to
black suffrage in the southern states. The Civil Rights Acts of 1964 and
1965 fulfilled the promise of the Reconstruction amendments to the

Constitution and at long last put equality under the law and at the ballot box on a firm foundation.

Although it did not bring full equality or total liberation, the civil
rights movement resulted in substantial and seemingly irreversible
progress toward eliminating status inequality based on race in the
United States. Its legislative and judicial successes appear to give the lie
to the common assumption that patterns of race relations, once they become firmly established, are virtually immutable. It can now be argued
on the basis of historical precedent that, however long certain people
have been assigned an inferior status and to whatever extent a dominant group may have cherished a belief in their inferiority, pariah
groups or oppressed minorities *can* gain substantive legal and political
equality with their former overlords.

One should not conclude, however, that the U.S. black-white problem has been solved; it would be more accurate to say that is has
changed character. The growing black middle class has been the main
beneficiary of the civil rights movement and the affirmative action programs that came to be viewed as an essential means for achieving its
goals. But the emergence of black judges, congressional representatives,
presidential candidates, elite professionals, executives, and entrepreneurs should not obscure the fact that the impoverished black lower
class—about a third of the black population—is in worse shape than
ever before. Trapped in inner-city ghettoes from which the black middle class has now largely fled, these blacks remain poor, unemployed or
underemployed, beset by problems of teenage pregnancy, crime, and
drug abuse, and essentially cut off from the aspirations and opportunities available to most white Americans.[6] But this is not so much a civil
rights problem in the traditional sense or even attitudinal racism as a
challenge to the political economy of late twentieth-century American
capitalism. Only reforms directed at changing the American economic
system in a fundamental way are likely to emancipate the black poor
from misery and desperation. Race-specific policies are still necessary,
but solving the problem of accumulated economic and educational disadvantage—and rehabilitating the "underclass" it produces—depends
on the growth of a broader and more inclusive movement for economic
justice and equality.

What general conclusions can be drawn from this thumbnail sketch
of the African American experience since emancipation that might inform and guide our search for a comparative perspective? It should be
clear enough, first of all, that the essential character of black-white re-

lations has not been static, but has in fact changed substantially over time—first in the direction of greater separation and segmentation between the 1870s and the First World War and thereafter in the direction of greater openness and enhanced opportunities for at least some blacks to enter the mainstream of American life. Accounting for these changes requires not only an understanding of the effect of such large-scale and long-term processes as industrialization and urbanization but also a recognition of the creative historical impact of black leaders and movements.

It is also evident, however, that one essential aspect of American race relations has not changed fundamentally—the sense of race itself as socially and politically salient. The sharp color line that was drawn during the segregation era has ceased to be the basis of invidious laws, but it lives on in the form of black-white polarization on issues such as affirmative action and the responsibility of government for the relief of poverty and its consequences. Many social questions that in other countries would be debated on their merits for the entire society—or in terms of class—tend to be viewed in the United States through a prism of calculations on how they will affect this or that racial group. Even those whites who profess a lack of prejudice or ideological racism still tend to think that there are white "interests" that clash with black "interests."

Blacks also have a strong sense of racial cohesion and group interest. It was essential to the success of the civil rights struggle that blacks develop ethnic solidarity under their own leadership. Only through the group pride that came from independent action could the masses be aroused to confront white racism in the direct and courageous way necessary to accelerate reform. Liberal whites have of course supported civil rights movements, but since the earliest years of the NAACP they have not led them or constituted a major proportion of their membership. The great paradox of the struggle for desegregation was that blacks seemingly had to separate themselves from whites in order to gain the right to come together with them. But coming together has not meant assimilation to the point of surrendering black identity. As a result of their origin and peculiar historical experience, African Americans have developed a strong sense of ethnic distinctiveness. (Even in the days when "full integration" was proclaimed as the single goal of the civil rights movement, no black leader seriously proposed eliminating separate black churches.) As long as one portion of the black population is excluded from the opportunities that American society offers to whites, and another, more successful, segment feels insecure about whether it can hold on to the gains it has recently made, race will continue to determine the political and social outlook of most African Americans. Black ethnic assertiveness risks bringing white prejudices to the surface and provoking white tribalism and violence against blacks. The color line in the mind persists long after the color line in the law has been eliminated.

The obvious way to begin a search for comparative perspectives on the experience just described is by asking to what extent the trajectory of black-white relations in the United States is the product of special American circumstances and to what extent it reflects some larger international process. As in virtually all comparative studies involving the United States, the question comes down to the issue of American "exceptionalism." But it is not very helpful to frame this question as a simple either/or proposition. It is better to begin with the assumption that the American experience will share some of the elements of situations and transformations occurring elsewhere but will also show distinctive features that may mean that different consequences will result from comparable processes. This may sound like a truism, but if so, it is often forgotten in the heat of debate over American exceptionalism.

The comparisons that most readily come to mind are with the other former colonial societies of the New World that abolished slavery during the nineteenth century and faced a similar problem of incorporating freedpeople of African descent into a new social order. For a sustained bilateral comparison, Brazil presents many analogues to events in the United States. As a large, independent continental nation with a racial composition roughly similar to the North American, it might be expected to yield valuable comparative insights. When slavery was abolished in Brazil in 1889, the freedpeople instantly became, on paper at least, citizens with equality under the law. After attempting unsuccessfully to survive as agricultural workers or subsistence farmers, substantial numbers of former plantation slaves fled the countryside and migrated to the cities where they found little demand for their labor and were often condemned to a poverty-stricken existence on the margins of a slowly developing economy. Furthermore, like North American blacks, they often faced unequal competition from white immigrants also seeking employment as wage workers in emerging industries. In some ways, the predominately black *favelas* on the periphery of Brazilian cities were analogous to the inner-city black ghettos in the United States.

Faced with pervasive, if unofficial and extralegal discrimination, black Brazilians began to organize along racial lines in the late 1920s and early 1930s, forming the *Frente Negra Brasilera* in 1931. But the Negro front was outlawed when Getulio Vargas took power in 1937 and banned all political movements. It was not until the 1970s that the political atmosphere, as well as international examples of black insurgency, permitted a renewed expression of organized black protest. That decade saw the emergence of the *Movimento Negro Unificado*.[7]

One might conclude, therefore, that Brazilian blacks have been moving in the same direction as blacks in the United States but in a slower and less continuous fashion. Industrialization and the full proletarianization of the black peasantry have been inhibited by the general slowness of economic development, and black mobilization has been impeded by a lack of democratic political conditions in the country as a whole. Yet other differences between the two racial situations make it difficult to conclude that they represent merely the same process at different speeds. Brazil has never had as clearly defined and rigid a color line as the one characteristic of the United States. The well-known fluidity of racial definition in Brazil and what Carl Degler called "the mulatto escape hatch" has meant that it was never entirely clear who was black and who was white and that upward mobility through a change in racial categorization was possible, as it has rarely been in the United States with its rigid "descent rule" for ascribing racial status.[8] Furthermore, in Brazil the segregation of even those who were both dark-skinned and poor was never mandated by law or even consistently and comprehensively enforced by custom or private action. The presence of wealthy mulattos among the "white" elite and poor whites living cheek by jowl with blacks in the *favelas* indicates an underlying pattern of race relations quite different from that of the United States.

The Brazilian comparison also suggests the extent to which an experience of segregation and overt racial discrimination may be a precondition for the development of successful black movements. Several of the black informants whom Florestan Fernandes interviewed for his classic study, *The Negro in Brazilian Society,* saw segregation as "the real cause of the Negro's progress in the United States" because it created a clear-cut set of grievances and led "Negroes to unite and fight for better things." One informant concluded that the Negro in Brazil was debilitated by a covert and "hypocritical" form of prejudice while the American Negro had "benefited" from "open" prejudice because it had "led him to look at himself and solve his own problems."[9] One need not wax lyrical over how fortunate North American blacks were to face such intense and flagrant racism to acknowledge that black mobilization and militancy came more naturally in a situation of sharp racial definition and enforced segregation than in a more fluid and ambiguous context.

Hence Brazil makes for a good comparison if one is seeking to appreciate the role of race consciousness and black-white polarization in the United States. In Brazil, it seems, nonracial determinants of class and status have been better able to bend or blur lines of demarcation based on color and ancestry. The Brazilian adage "money whitens" would be hard to apply to North American race relations, at least until very recently and in a somewhat different sense. If, however, one is seeking to learn how and why the political and social implications of a deep and polarizing sense of racial difference may change over time, Brazil is not such a useful analogue. For that purpose, it might be better to turn to another society in which official segregation and militant white supremacy emerged early in the modern industrial era and incited forms of black mobilization and protest comparable to those in the United States.

Comparing race relations in the United States and South Africa is a difficult enterprise full of traps for the unwary, particularly if one focuses on the period from the late nineteenth century to the present. In an earlier work on the development of white supremacist attitudes and policies in the two countries, I concluded that the different circumstances surrounding the practice of "segregation," as well as the actual functions performed by the legalized separation of racial groups, called into question the value of a detailed comparison of twentieth-century developments.[10] Clearly the demographic variable, the fact that blacks have been a minority in the United States (even in the South) and a substantial majority in South Africa, means that blacks have weighed differently in the social and economic calculus of whites and that the consequences of racial equality for the politics and power relations of these nations would vary enormously. Furthermore, it is difficult to make an equivalence between an ex-slave population with its fragmented or problematic culture and indigenous peoples who, in many cases, retained vital links with traditional ethnic communities.[11] In fact, I found in my earlier study of white supremacy that the South African population group most analogous to African Americans, both demographically and historically was the mixed race or Cape Colored minority rather than the African majority.[12]

Nevertheless, one does get a strong whiff of similitude from *one* kind of source—the documentary record of public discourse on the race question from both sides of the color line. Both South African segregationists and Africans who were protesting segregation drew heavily on American racial ideologies or from common sources of international thinking about black-white relations. This was especially the case between the 1880s and the 1940s. Despite the demographic and structural differences between white hegemony and black resistance in the two societies, many participants in these ethnic struggles defined the issues similarly and engaged in debates on racial policy that echoed each other, sometimes consciously. The similarities in these discourses become evident if we compare either with the rather different colloquy on race and class in Brazil.

Ideological similarity must reflect some common features in the two racial situations that would go at least part of the way toward compensating for the demographic and cultural differences that would otherwise seem to obviate comparison. In my book *White Supremacy,* I probed the origins of attitudes that promoted racial hierarchy, exclusiveness, and ultimately systematic segregation. It is a complex argument, but it involves a comparable legacy of ethnocentrism, racial slavery, reactions of the beneficiaries of racial domination to nineteenth-century humanitarianism, and the adaptation of preexisting white-supremacist habits and attitudes to an emergent industrial capitalism. In short, I found a comparable interaction between inherited premodern attitudes toward race and the exigencies of industrial modernization.[13] Brazil, on the other hand, brought to the modern era a different conception of race relations, for reasons buried deep in its history as a slave society, and has not until very recently experienced the kind of massive and rapid shift to industrial capitalism that occurred in the United States after the Civil War and in South Africa after the Anglo-Boer War. Hence there were commonalities in both the ideological traditions of whites and the economic and social transformations of the late nineteenth and early twentieth centuries that would set off the general tenor of American and South African racial doctrines and policies from those predominating in Brazil during the same period.

The United States and South Africa shared a conjuncture of inherited cultural racism and industrial capitalist development that might account for the fact that racial issues were to be framed in a similar way and even seemed at times amenable to analogous solutions. Massive movement of black peasants into the city and into industrial work was a common new development of the early-to-mid twentieth century, although, admittedly, official responses to it differed significantly. Unlike the United States, where extralegal or unofficial discrimination ghettoized the new arrivals, the South African state assumed a major role in trying to control the flow and its consequences through policies that were later centralized and extended under the name of apartheid. I refer here to the pass system, influx control, prohibition of black land ownership outside of designated reserves, and reliance on contract migratory labor.

The proposition that fruitful comparisons can be made between black-white relations in the United States since emancipation and African-white relations in South Africa in the twentieth century appears even more compelling if we view matters from the other side of the color line and examine the development of black movements and ideologies. There is first of all a rich record of black South African awareness of African American ideas and achievements and a willingness to be influenced by them. Allow me simply to enumerate some examples of the African American connection: (1) the encouragement of religious separatism, or "Ethiopianism," by missionaries and bishops from the African Methodist Church of the United States between the 1890s and the First World War; (2) the reverence for Booker T. Washington and the Tuskegee Institute among the first generation of African nationalist leaders; (3) the substantial impact in South Africa during the 1920s of Marcus Garvey and his robust version of black nationalism; (4) the great prestige of W. E. B. Du Bois and his journal *The Crisis* among educated Africans seeking to combine a Pan-African vision with a militant struggle for equal rights in a multiracial society; (5) the influence of African American music, dance, and literature on urbanized Africans seeking to fashion a syncretic culture that would transcend ethnic differences and yet remain distinctively black; (6) the way that the South African Black Consciousness Movement of the 1970s appropriated the rhetoric of the American Black Power Movement of the late 1960s. One might find an even more recent example in the civil disobedience campaign of 1989, in which black demonstrators adopted many of the techniques and even the songs of the American civil rights movement. A number of scholars are studying the role of African American influences and examples in shaping the consciousness of black South Africans, and the results to date suggest an important interchange of ideas and perspectives that only makes sense if the situation of blacks in the two societies were comparable in some significant respects.[14]

Perhaps the origins of this ideological affinity can be traced to the status situations that confronted black elites in the era of intensified white supremacy and segregationism between the turn of the century and the First World War. During the late-nineteenth century, a new class of educated blacks, the product of mission education or its equivalent, emerged in both countries and sought the opportunities for social mobility and incorporation in the larger society that seemed to be promised by the theoretically color-blind liberalism of the mid-Victorian era. Bitterly disappointed by the resurgence of ideological racism and discriminatory policies around the turn of the century—culminating by 1913 in such symbolically similar actions as the segregation of federal employees in the United States and the denial to Africans of the right to purchase or rent land in the "white" areas of South Africa—the black intelligentsia moved from optimistic accommodation to moderate protest. The founding of the NAACP in 1909 and the South African Native National Congress (later the African National Congress) in 1912 were parallel expressions of black elite dissatisfaction with new color bars and diminishing opportunities for educated, Christianized, or "civilized" blacks. Although black elites organized increasingly along racial lines, they resisted an exclusionary nationalism and based their plea for equal treatment on a liberal and interracial vision of a just society. The Americans, who had been promised more, demanded more—the universal black suffrage and full public equality that had been affirmed during the Reconstruction era. The early South African nationalists claimed only the equal rights for a "civilized" minority that was the essence of the "Cape liberal tradition"; under its aegis blacks who could meet a general property and literacy qualification had been voting in the Cape Colony since 1852. The struggles of both movements for inclusion in a white-dominated political and economic system were based on an assumption that peaceful agitation, the petitioning of those in authority, legislative lobbying, and legal action based on constitutional guarantees or English common-law traditions would eventually induce the whites to live up to their own professed principles of equal opportunity and democratic citizenship.[15]

Because the NAACP had only a modest initial success and the ANC virtually none at all, and because both organizations failed to address the most pressing problems of black peasants and workers, they were challenged during the 1920s by popular movements drawing on a heightened racial or ethnic consciousness. These movements sanctioned overtly antiwhite sentiments and put forth utopian visions of a separate black nation. It is in this context that the appeal in both countries of Marcus Garvey and his Universal Negro Improvement Association can best be understood.

As the extravagant expectations of the ultranationalist and millennialist movements of the 1920s shattered against the obdurate reality of white power, a different and seemingly more efficacious conception of revolutionary change gained·a following among middle-class black intellectuals, as well as among the politically conscious members of an emerging industrial working class. Marxian socialism did not gain a mass following among blacks in either the United States or South Africa through the Great Depression and through the Second World War, but it had significant impact on leaders and political activists. Serious efforts emanating from the Comintern to combine an orthodox Marxian class analysis with recognition of the primacy in some societies of a race or national question engendered similar debates among black and white leftists in both countries.

Enough has perhaps been said to give at least a crude sense of how it is possible to see a similar trajectory for black ideologies and movements in the United States and South Africa through the Second World War, and one could go on to suggest parallels between the coming of nonviolent mass protest to South Africa in the early 1950s and to the southern United States in the late fifties and early sixties. But in the postwar period the outcomes of comparable protest initiatives diverged widely and the American example became increasingly less relevant to the calculations of the South African resistance. The massive nonviolent American campaigns of the 1960s did not come until after the African National Congress had already tried such tactics and been forced to abandon them by a repressive regime.

The turning point for both societies was possibly the election of 1948. In that year the Nationalist party came to power in South Africa and began to implement an even more rigid and systematic policy of racial separation and discrimination. The same year saw the surprising victory of Harry S. Truman and the Democratic party in the United States, despite the fact that the Democrats had a civil rights plank in their platform and faced a third-party challenge from southern white supremacists. In effect the black vote in the North more than counterbalanced the white defections in the South. Up to 1948 it might have been possible to argue that South Africa's prospects for racial reform were comparable to those in the United States. Hopes for a peaceful evolution toward equal rights became patently unrealistic in one context at the same time that they were becoming quite credible in the other.

The shift from parallelism to divergence might be explained in many ways. Some were suggested by our earlier discussion of the factors involved in the victories of the American civil rights movement, none of which were present, or present to the same degree, in the South African case. Demography, legal-constitutional traditions, and geopolitical circumstances were clearly more conducive to reform in one case than the other. An international development with significant implications for the status of blacks in white-dominated societies—decolonization and the emergence of independent nations in black Africa—had quite contrary effects on short-term black prospects. In the United States, it gave added weight to the cause of reform, while in South Africa it provoked a beleaguered white minority to greater repression. But the elections of 1948 brought one crucial factor into sharp relief. In one election the black vote was a decisive factor, in the other it did not figure at all, for the electorate was all white except for a small number of "Coloreds" who would soon be disfranchised by the Nationalist government.

If any general truth emerges from this admittedly very tentative exploration of comparative possibilities, it is that politics and power are crucial to understanding evolving patterns of race relations. In Brazil blacks have not been able to challenge a system that makes them de facto, if not de jure, inferiors because a confused and ambiguous ideological situation, a lack of group resources, and an unstable, often undemocratic, political system have made it impossible for them to exert political power as a distinctive element of the population. In South Africa blacks gained a clear understanding of their situation and what would be required to change it, but, until 1990, when Nelson Mandela was released from prison and the ANC was unbanned, ruthless repression denied them the capability to influence the government by peaceful means or through nonrevolutionary, reformist politics. In the United States blacks have been able to acquire some power and leverage within a functioning democratic political system—not enough to address the problems of an impoverished lower class but enough to keep hopes of progressive reform alive. In short, the history of race relations should be viewed, not as illustrating some iron law of social and cultural determinism, but rather as the record of a dynamic process that can be made to change course as a result of political action and initiative. Black people, like people in general, make their own history even if they cannot make it exactly as they choose.

PART THREE

Twentieth-Century Freedom Struggles

CHAPTER EIGHT

Reform and Revolution in American and South African Freedom Struggles

Different though they may be in other ways, the histories of the United States and South Africa have been similar in one notable respect. To an extent unique in the modern world, these societies generated patterns of racial domination that culminated by the twentieth century in national or regional policies requiring the forced segregation of people designated as black or African. Consequently, historians and social scientists have compared these two racial orders with useful results.[1] But the work published in the 1980s on white supremacy in the two societies had one significant limitation: it focused almost exclusively on the thought and action of the oppressors. Left out of the comparison or treated in cursory fashion was the resistance of Africans and African Americans to white hegemony. In the introduction to my own book, *White Supremacy,* I acknowledged this limitation and called for work that would look at black-white relations in the two societies from the subaltern side of the color line.[2] Eventually I decided to take up my own challenge, and the full results have recently appeared in a book that offers a detailed treatment of a series of comparable phases of black ideological development over a period of about 150 years.[3] The research for that book obviously informs this essay, but here I explore a set of recurring themes that are embedded but not concisely articulated in the larger study.

Like the book, this essay is based on the assumption that the organized and programmatic black opposition to white supremacy in the

United States and in South Africa can be compared in ways that will contribute to our understanding of both "freedom struggles." Despite the important differences in the background and circumstances of black people in the United States and South Africa, leaders of the resistance against racial oppression have embraced similar ideologies and engaged in comparable debates over ultimate objectives and strategies for achieving them. This discursive affinity derives for the most part from the analogous forms of racial oppression in both societies and has been nurtured to a significant extent by mutual awareness and cross-fertilization.

Similar ideological debates and divisions have arisen on two crucial issues. The first concerns future relations with whites. Is liberation to come through equal citizenship in a multiracial polity, or is the proper aim of the struggle the achievement of some form of independent nationhood? One answer draws on universalist standards of justice and human rights to reject a racially circumscribed political destiny; the other emphasizes racial or ethnic particularism and asserts that blacks cannot achieve self-realization by joining with whites in a unitary state. For convenience, I will label the two perspectives *cosmopolitan* and *ethnocentric*. The second dichotomy, which is not automatically resolved by adopting a cosmopolitan or an ethnocentric orientation, concerns the nature of the struggle: will it be carried on by reformist or revolutionary methods?

Cosmopolitans might believe that all people can be incorporated as equals into a common society through gradual elimination of the racist aspects of an otherwise acceptable political and social order. Or they might believe that racism is an integral part of the social and economic system and that the only way to eliminate it is to overthrow the system itself. Ethnic nationalists can also be reformist or revolutionary: they can either hope to gain their autonomy through peaceful negotiation or conclude that they must seize it by force of arms.

Using these dichotomies to analyze American and South African freedom struggles reveals some striking similarities. The most obvious is the predominance of cosmopolitan perspectives in the programs and ideologies of the most durable and historically influential black movements and associations. The principal American civil rights organization, the National Association for the Advancement of Colored People, has rarely wavered from the commitment to a racially integrated republic that it proclaimed at its founding in 1909. The more militant organizations that assaulted southern segregation in the late 1950s and early 1960s—The Southern Christian Leadership Conference (SCLC), the Committee on Racial Equality (CORE), and the Student Nonviolent Coordinating Committee (SNCC)—all aimed, during this period at least, at removing the barriers to equal participation in a common society. Similarly, the African National Congress (ANC), founded in 1912, has consistently advocated a multiracial or nonracial South Africa, in which opportunity and citizenship would no longer depend on skin color and ancestry. Like the American civil rights organizations, it has normally welcomed white support and participation in the struggle against segregation. It has also avoided the strong temptation, obviously absent in the American case, to conceive of the future postapartheid nation as an exclusive expression of black or African ethnicity. As the Freedom Charter of 1955 proclaimed, "South Africa belongs to all who live in it, black and white."[4]

These cosmopolitan or nonracial attitudes did not go unchallenged in either country. The most obvious characteristic of the oppressors was their pigmentation. Fraternity with conquerors or former slaveowners was hard for many black people to imagine, and it was often psychologically easier to hate whites and to wish to be rid of them than to distinguish between the sinners and their sins. The fact that black-white relations did not become the kind of zero-sum struggle-to-the-death between competing racial or ethnic groups that has developed in other parts of the world may seem miraculous given the flagrantly unjust treatment of blacks in the United States and South Africa. This achievement of mainstream black leaders was, and continues to be, a fragile one that has been under constant challenge from a variety of nationalist or separatist movements.

In the United States, a persistent undercurrent of separatist nationalism has ebbed and flowed since the early-to-mid nineteenth century, mainly in the form of African emigration movements. At times, this impulse has also taken the form of demands for territorial separation to establish the basis for a black nation within the existing boundaries of the United States. Major twentieth-century manifestations of the search for ethnic self-determination have included such notable mass movements as Marcus Garvey's Africa-oriented Universal Negro Improvement Association of the 1920s and the Nation of Islam—the so-called Black Muslims, who came to prominence in the 1950s and have retained substantial support up to the present day. For Garvey, the only way black Americans could liberate themselves from racism was to participate in the creation of an independent Africa. He saw no long-term future for blacks in the United States because he viewed white racism as ineradicable. In the 1960s and 1970s, the Black Muslims, the Republic of New Africa, and other separatist groups called for the creation of a sovereign black nation within the current borders of the United States.[5] At the present time black nationalist sentiment appears to be reviving within an African American community that is suffering from an intensification of white hostility and discrimination. But, up to now, this feeling has expressed itself mainly in the form of cultural separation within the American educational system and has not produced a definite plan or program for political independence from a white-dominated America.

In South Africa the ANC's multiracial or nonracial ideology has been continually challenged from within the organization as well as from outside by groups or movements usually designated as "Africanist." The Africanist perspective derives ultimately from the natural desire of conquered peoples to regain their land and was first articulated in the slogan "Africa for the Africans," which was associated with the rise of an independent black Christianity around the turn of the century. It was later expressed in a variety of messianic movements of the 1920s, some of them influenced by Garveyism, which heralded a racial apocalypse in which some supernatural power, or, alternatively, black American aviators flying bombing planes, would exterminate all of the whites or drive them into the sea.[6]

A more secular and sophisticated version of Africanism emerged within the ANC during the period after World War II, partially in response to the Pan-Africanist ideology of independence movements elsewhere on the continent. The ANC Youth League of the mid-to-late 1940s, in which Nelson Mandela, Oliver Tambo, and Walter Sisulu began their political careers, had a pronounced Africanist orientation in its early years. But in 1948 it explicitly repudiated the Garveyite slogan of "Africa for the Africans," indicating that African ascendancy would not mean exclusion or expulsion of whites from a liberated South Africa.[7] After the ANC reaffirmed its multiracial vision of South Africa's future in the Freedom Charter of 1955, the minority that favored a nationalism based on consciousness of racial character and destiny seceded to form the Pan-Africanist Congress (PAC) in 1959. The Black Consciousness Movement of the 1970s retained some elements of the Pan-Africanist perspective, and in the 1990s the Africanist or ethnic nationalist strain of black liberationist thought survives in modified form (synthesized to some extent with Marxian class perspectives) in the PAC, the Azanian People's Organization, and allied groups.[8]

Given their appeal to deep-seated popular emotions, it may seem remarkable that racially defined nationalisms have thus far failed to predominate in the politics of black protest and resistance in either country. This failure is especially remarkable in the case of South Africa. In the United States, the legacy of slavery, emancipation achieved with white allies, and the egalitarian amendments to the constitution passed during the Reconstruction era served to distance many black Americans from their African roots and raise enduring hopes for equality within a democratized republic. But some black South African nations lost their independence a little more than a century ago under conditions that permitted them to retain a sense of national or tribal identity. The continued if diminishing vitality of traditional African cultures and the intensification of white oppression and discrimination after 1910 might have been expected to undermine hopes for a common society based on racial equality and cooperation. One reason this did not happen is that universalist, cosmopolitan ideologies—especially Christian humanitarianism and Marxism—have exerted such a powerful influence on African elites.

During the early stages of twentieth-century black protest politics in both countries, the predominant ideology was a color-blind, cosmopolitan liberalism inherited from the nineteenth century. In the American context this was the tradition of Frederick Douglass and the interracial abolitionist and Radical Republican movements. In South Africa it was the legacy of "Cape liberalism"—the notion of "equal rights for every civilized man regardless of race or color" that had been proclaimed, often somewhat hypocritically, by white English-speaking "friends of the natives" in the Cape Colony in the decades just before the unification of South Africa in 1910. In the minds of many twentieth-century black leaders, most of whom were educated by white missionaries, this universalist liberalism was linked with Christianity and its ideal of human brotherhood. Normally, however, Christian liberalism is not a revolutionary creed. For the most part the ideologies that dominated black protest movements in South Africa until the 1950s and in the United States until the mid-1960s advocated incremental racial reformism rather than sudden and fundamental changes in the social and economic system.

The first serious efforts to redefine the black struggle in terms of a *revolutionary* cosmopolitanism came after the Russian Revolution when Communists in both societies confronted the race issue and sought to mobilize blacks in the cause of proletarian revolution. The Communist campaign to overthrow capitalism in the United States and South Africa went through three similar stages. Initially the emphasis was on enrolling class-conscious white workers, even if this meant tactical concessions to their feelings of racial superiority and fears of economic competition with blacks willing to work for lower wages. (In 1922, the South African party, to support a strike against the displacement of white miners by lower-paid Africans, actually endorsed the slogan "Workers of the world unite for a white South Africa.") When a class appeal directed at whites failed to achieve mass support, Communists shifted some of their attention to blacks, basing their appeal on antiracism and calls for the solidarity of black and white workers. Finally, in 1928 the Comintern examined closely "the Negro question" in both the United States and South Africa and determined that a program based strictly on class would not be effective in attracting mass black support. Impressed by the popularity of the Garvey movement, the Comintern embraced the cause of black nationalism, calling for "a native republic" in South Africa and national self-determination for the Black Belt of the southern United States.[9]

This controversial redefinition did not involve accepting an essentialist view of race and cannot be attributed entirely to tactical cynicism. The new policy was rooted in the Leninist doctrine of attacking capitalism by encouraging national struggles against imperial domination, which required mobilization of the peasantry as a revolutionary force. In the late 1920s the majority of Africans and African Americans were still trapped in rural poverty and could plausibly be described as peasants whose subjugation and exploitation followed a color line and were rationalized in terms or race or ethnicity. Communists believed that these pre-proletarian victims of capitalism could most readily be aroused to insurrectionary action if the party promulgated a conception of liberation that appealed to their repressed desires for national or ethnic self-determination.

As a device for winning support among American blacks, the slogan had a very limited success. Robin Kelley has shown that a practical application of the slogan to the condition of southern sharecroppers, in the form of a demand that blacks be given ownership of the land they worked, had great resonance among a people who believed that they had once been promised some of the land that they had cultivated as slaves. The substantial if ephemeral success of the Communist-dominated

Alabama Sharecroppers Union was based in part on an interpretation of "Negro self-determination" that was congruent with the folk traditions of those being organized.[10] But the slogan was applicable only to the rural South and thus could not serve as an effective means to coopt the ghetto nationalism expressed in the Garvey movement. In northern urban areas Communists persisted in their efforts to encourage interracial solidarity among industrial and commercial workers and in the early thirties withheld their support from the "don't buy where you can't work" campaigns of black activists because they considered them incompatible with a continued emphasis on interracial class solidarity. While occasionally giving lip service to the aim of "self-determination for the Black Belt," most American Communists in the 1930s concentrated on the economic or class issues brought to the fore by the Great Depression. The slogan virtually disappeared from Communist propaganda directed at African Americans after 1934 when a change in the international party line deemphasized anti-imperialist revolutions. Between 1934 and 1939 the highest priority of the Soviet Union was to encourage within Western democratic nations a united front of antifascist elements, which came to include not only white social democrats but also bourgeois "progressives."

Communist appeals to nationalism in South Africa during the late twenties and thirties were also intermittent and of limited impact, despite their apparent compatibility with the situation of Africans as a colonized people. In the late 1920s, after having been expelled from the Industrial and Commercial Worker's Union (ICU)—an important independent association of black workers and peasants—Communists made their first serious effort to gain influence within the African National Congress. They succeeded in winning the cooperation of ANC president J. T. Gumede, who became sympathetic to Communism after a visit to the Soviet Union. But Gumede was ousted from the ANC leadership in 1930 by a conservative faction and the organization entered a nonmilitant accommodationist phase that lasted until the end of the decade. Torn by purges, factional conflict, and confusion about how to apply the "black republic" slogan, the South African Communist party also went into eclipse and did not revive until the Second World War. Free from significant left-wing influence, the mainstream black organizations—the ANC and the All-African Convention of the mid thirties—limited themselves to protesting against new legislative assaults on African rights, hoping in vain to reverse the tide of racial segregation and discrimination through peaceful and legal forms of protest.

The perspective of the American Communist party and of others who took a Marxist or socialist view of the racial question reached its high point of influence among African Americans in the mid-to-late 1930s. Helped by the economic desperation of blacks and whites alike during the Great Depression, hopes of cooperation between black and white workers revived among leftists and also influenced a broad spectrum of black leaders and intellectuals. But the party's favorable image in the black community stemmed primarily from its endorsement of traditional civil rights objectives and its essentially reformist stance during the Popular Front era. Instead of trying to convert large numbers of blacks to a revolutionary ideology, Communists curried favor by accommodating themselves in the short run to the dominant tradition of cosmopolitan reformism.

World War II and the Cold War brought a striking reversal of the situation of the radical left in both countries. In the United States, Marxists lost influence among blacks, and Communists were relegated to the periphery of an intensifying black civil rights struggle. In South Africa, Communists became major participants in the struggle for black liberation, forging a working alliance with the African National Congress that has proved remarkably durable. In the period between 1940 and 1960 reformism became more dominant than ever in the American movement; simultaneously an overtly revolutionary ideology was becoming increasingly influential in the South African struggle.

The decline of radical, potentially revolutionary, influences on American racial movements stemmed in part from Communist blunders and miscalculations during the war years, which made the party seem less militant and committed to black equality than thoroughly reformist groups like the NAACP and the March on Washington movement (at least until 1944 when the Soviet Union was no longer in danger, and it again became acceptable in party circles to agitate militantly against Jim Crow). After the war, the McCarthyite hysteria affected mainstream black movements and induced them to keep Communists at arm's length. At the same time, reformism was beginning to pay off in favorable court decisions against the segregation and disfranchisement of southern blacks and in growing black influence on the national Democratic party. Once the repressive McCarthyite phase of the late 1940s and early 1950s had run its course, the Cold War actually encouraged gains in civil rights because policymaking elites became aware that America's practice of racial discrimination impeded the propaganda struggle for the "hearts and minds" of people of color in Africa and Asia.

In South Africa the triumph of the Nationalist party in 1948 led to the extension and intensification of racial segregation under the banner of apartheid; consequently the futility of reformism became increasingly evident. In 1949 a younger generation, influenced by Africanism as well as Marxism, came to power in the ANC and launched a campaign of militant nonviolent resistance against the apartheid regime. The example of independence movements elsewhere in Africa encouraged aspirations for a nationalist revolution in South Africa. In the 1950s the ethnocentric or Africanist impulse was marginalized, partly as a result of Communist influence. The basis for cooperation between the ANC and the CP was set forth by Moses Kotane, a black Communist who was also an ANC leader. According to this doctrine, the South African revolution would be a two-stage affair, first a struggle for national self-determination to achieve democratic majority rule, and then a freely chosen transformation to socialism. Even if the majority of the ANC did not endorse the second revolution or was uncertain about it, there was no justification for refusing Communist assistance in achieving the primary objective, especially since the ANC's great tradition was cooperation with sympathetic whites, and most of the whites who fully endorsed racial equality and "one person, one vote" in South Africa during the immediate postwar period were Communists or fellow-traveling radicals. Making common cause with Communists made sense to staunch opponents of the South African regime at a time when the Soviet Union, unlike the United States, was strongly supportive of the struggle against apartheid. When nonviolent acts of civil disobedience were shown to be suicidal at Sharpeville in 1960 and both the ANC and PAC were forced underground, the National Congress's reluctant acceptance of violent resistance took the form of establishing, jointly with the Communist party, a military organization committed to sabotage and ultimately to guerrilla warfare. The turn to revolutionary cosmopolitanism seemed irrevocable. The ANC's slogan of the 1980s— "Apartheid cannot be reformed"—was taken to mean that it must be overthrown.[11]

As American and South African freedom struggles diverged, it began to seem more and more obvious that the situations in the two countries were radically different. A black majority can hope to make a revolution by itself, but a black minority can scarcely expect to do so. Furthermore the United States Constitution encouraged hopes for equal citizenship, whereas South Africa's constitutional and legal framework was unequivocally white supremacist and would have to be completely reconstituted if blacks were to have any semblance of equal rights. But what has occurred in black thinking and consciousness since the 1960s shows that revolutionary attitudes could reemerge in the American context and that reformist tactics could again seem relevant or necessary in the South African.

The more militant and confrontational American civil rights movement of the early 1960s was often described at the time as a "nonviolent revolution" or as "the Negro revolution." In a special sense, the term is entirely appropriate. The movement used disruptive and coercive methods—sit-ins, boycotts, mass marches, and demonstrations—that violated state and local laws and went beyond normal American limits on peaceful dissent and reformist agitation. If these methods were nonviolent, they were likely to provoke violence and were to some extent intended to do so; although, as Adam Fairclough has shown, careful planning helped to minimize the bloodshed.[12] Furthermore, civil rights activists rejected gradualism, insisting on "Freedom, Now." Within the context of a southern social order based on legalized racism, the movement was indeed revolutionary in its intentions and achievements.

Within a national context, however, its *reformist* characteristics were apparent. Supreme Court decisions reinterpreting constitutional provisions for equal rights gave the movement legitimacy and put the onus of law-breaking on the southern segregationists. In 1964 and 1965 the U. S. Congress enacted most of the program of southern protesters, reflecting a decision of national elites to remove the embarrassing anomaly of legalized segregation and denial of voting rights in one section of the country. In bringing southern racial practices into harmony with the rest of the country, national legislators and policymakers were promoting the health and safety of the American social and economic system as a whole. The civil rights legislation can therefore be viewed as the culmination of a successful reform movement, one that strengthened and legitimized fundamental social and economic arrangements rather than calling them into question and inciting radical resistance to the status quo.

Nevertheless, the legislative success of the civil rights movement failed to pacify African Americans; indeed its aftermath was the most devastating and bloody wave of urban disorders in American history— the ghetto insurrections of 1965–1968. The failure of civil rights reform to address the economic disadvantages under which most blacks labored and its inability to meet the rising expectations of a better life that the movement's rhetoric had called forth, encouraged a bitter and rebellious mood in the black urban communities of the North and West. The result was the upsurge of revolutionary rhetoric associated with the slogan "Black Power." But the rhetoric did not easily crystallize into effective political ideology, because it was hard to imagine how a black revolution could actually take place within a nation that was mostly white. The most plausible formulation was probably that of the Black Panther party, which eventually went beyond a strictly black nationalist viewpoint and envisioned an American dispossessed class, composed mainly but not exclusively of dark-skinned victims of racism, acting in support of the struggle of third-world peoples against Western imperialism.[13]

By itself the Black Power slogan had limited revolutionary potential, despite its capacity to stimulate localized disorders, because it so readily lent itself to essentially reformist purposes. It normally meant rejection of nonviolent tactics but only to the extent that self-defense was sanctioned. Its call for racial mobilization could, and often did, mean merely the organization of black voters into an ethnic bloc and the encouragement of black capitalist enterprise. As Stokely Carmichael and others explicitly proclaimed, Black Power was in the American tradition of ethnic mobilization for political and economic advantage, as pioneered by the Irish, the Jews, and other white ethnic minorities.[14] From this perspective Black Power was not so much a radical and revolutionary separatism as a tough-minded and somewhat cynical program for group incorporation into a society that was conceived as culturally pluralist rather than homogeneous and as more responsive to physical power than to assertions of democratic values. In its most common applications Black Power turned out to be an ethnocentric reformism, which departed from the cosmopolitan reformism of the civil rights movement in its stress on racial identity and integrity rather than in its social and economic radicalism. In fact Martin Luther King, Jr., during the last years of his life, was more consistently radical on social and economic questions than many Black Power advocates.[15]

The South African Black Consciousness Movement of the 1970s borrowed some of its rhetoric from the American Black Power movement. There was a similar emphasis on psychological and organizational independence from liberal or even radical whites. But, as Steve Biko made clear in an explicit comparison of the two movements, there

was a great difference between a minority movement aimed at incorporation on its own terms and a majority movement seeking to gain
control of its own country.[16] Although repression prevented the Black
Consciousness Movement from openly avowing its revolutionary aims
(at times it explicitly denied them), it was clear to everyone who
thought much about it, including the South African government, that
BC could not achieve its aims except by a nationalist revolution. By
broadening the conception of "black" to include Indians and
"Coloreds," it transcended the Africanist tradition, but its rejection of
whites put it in obvious conflict with the ANC's nonracial cosmopolitanism.[17]

After the Soweto uprising of 1976, which was inspired in part by the
Black Consciousness Movement, some commentators predicted that
the ANC's nonracialism would soon cease to dominate the antiapartheid movement and that a racially defined nationalism would come
to the fore in the black struggle. But during the 1980s the mainstream
domestic movement, represented principally by the United Democratic
Front (UDF), proclaimed its allegiance to the cosmopolitan Freedom
Charter and opened its ranks to white supporters, thus relegating
groups with an exclusivist Black Consciousness orientation, like the
Azanian People's Organization, to the periphery of the struggle. Now
linked to a vigorous internal movement, the ANC gained in international prestige and recognition, utterly eclipsing the PAC, the other
exile organization. In the mid-eighties the increasing level of violent and
nonviolent resistance to the regime and the government's desperate and
draconian efforts to repress the antiapartheid movement made it seem
more likely than ever that South Africa was in a classic revolutionary
situation. However long it might take, it seemed inevitable that white
tyranny would be overthrown; it also seemed clear that it would have
to be overthrown by revolutionary action, because the government
gave no signs of a willingness to negotiate a peaceful transfer of power
to the black majority.[18]

The surprising turn of events in 1989–1990—the emergence of nonviolent mass resistance against segregation laws for the first time since
1960; the unprecedented success of this movement in gaining the right
to protest and in pressuring the government to phase out petty
apartheid; the dramatic release of Nelson Mandela; the beginning of
discussions between the government and the ANC; and the subsequent
negotiations that have led to a new constitution, democratic elections,
and the presidency of Nelson Mandela—have called into question the

conventional wisdom on the inevitability of a South African revolution. Many observers of the late 1980s had described the situation as a stalemate or impasse—the African resistance lacked the power to overthrow the regime, but the government lacked the ability to suppress the level of black opposition to a point where it could feel secure. Furthermore, the economy, seriously damaged by international sanctions that were intensified by the domestic upheaval and repression of the 1980s, was in such bad shape that it threatened to undermine white expectations of prosperity under apartheid.[19]

What these observers had for the most part failed to anticipate was that this impasse would prove so unsatisfactory for both sides that they would jointly seek a negotiated settlement rather than risk a long, uncertain, and debilitating struggle for the unconditional surrender of their opponents. In opting for negotiations, the ANC realized that it could not achieve all its objectives in the near future. The white minority did not surrender unconditionally, because it had no necessity or incentive to do so. Hence it is not surprising that the ANC accepted some compromises, agreeing to an interim arrangement that fell short of achieving its professed goal of untrammeled black majority rule in a unitary state. Mandela and the leadership of the ANC concluded that a compromise constitutional settlement, involving some checks and balances to protect the white minority's economic and social privileges, would open the way to the eventual achievement of a substantive form of black majority rule. But the entrenchment of market capitalism and the recognition of most existing white property rights was the price that had to be paid to open up the political system to Africans by some means short of actually driving the whites from power after a prolonged and bloody revolutionary struggle.

Major reform, with revolutionary implications for the racial status order but not for the character of other social and economic relationships, is one way to describe what has taken place in South Africa during the last seven years. As in the American South, however, that reform was forced from below by militant confrontational tactics rather than imposed from above in an effort to head off trouble that had not yet reached crisis proportions. In such cases the maintenance of a sharp dichotomy between reform and revolution becomes problematic. Clearly the analogy with what happened in the United States during the 1960s is not so far-fetched as many, including myself, thought it would be in the 1980s. In both countries, it now appears, the cause of black liberation has entered a new phase. The current challenge is

how to go beyond an effective mobilization against legalized segregation and denial of voting rights to mount a successful political challenge
to the de facto inequality of white and black circumstances in the two
societies—a gap that in the United States, by some measures, is actually
increasing. A new synthesis of reformist and revolutionary methods or
perspectives will be required to move the two freedom struggles to a
higher stage.

CHAPTER NINE

Prophets of
Black Liberation

Close comparisons of the "freedom struggles" of African Americans and black South Africans are difficult to make because of the great differences in the situation and the prospects of people of color in the two societies. One fundamental difference was brought home to me in the spring of 1989 when I visited the Reverend Allan Boesak, then a leading figure in the domestic resistance to apartheid, in his office in a "Colored" suburb of Cape Town. In both his inner and his outer offices, Boesak had hung large portraits of Martin Luther King, Jr. I knew also that he had written a dissertation in theology at the University of Leiden on the ethics of Dr. King and Malcolm X.[1] But when I asked him to reflect on the relationship between the black American movements of the 1960s and his own antiapartheid campaign, he argued that there was a big difference between a minority's battle for equality in a predominantly white society and a black majority's effort to overthrow the rule of a white minority. The distinction that he made between an essentially reformist civil rights movement and a revolutionary effort to empower a disenfranchised majority seemed totally persuasive.

But the unexpected events of the past several years have blurred this distinction. By deciding to give up the armed struggle and negotiate with the de Klerk government, the African National Congress did not abandon its goal of winning power for the black majority, but the methods it had to use to achieve this end may bear comparison with those used by African Americans to dismantle legalized segregation in the 1960s. In the period immediately after its legalization, the ANC did not have much success in mobilizing the masses for nonviolent action to put pressure on the government for a new constitution based on one-person, one-vote; it was preoccupied with violent challenges to its claim to speak for blacks, especially from the Zulu-based Inkatha movement. But in its later efforts to build an effective and disciplined popular movement—one that could give muscle to the negotiating position of its leaders by calling for consumer boycotts, general strikes, and mass demonstrations—it may have found that the southern civil rights movement offered some useful tactical lessons.

Despite the obvious differences in racial demography (and the subtler differences between a population descended from slaves who were transported by force from one continent to another, and one deriving mainly from conquered peoples, who were dominated and oppressed but left with some shreds of autonomy and dignity), black South African leaders and intellectuals have often in the past looked to African American movements and ideologies for inspiration and guidance. Odd as it may seem now, some of the men who founded the African National Congress (originally called the South African Native National Congress) in 1912 were under the spell of Booker T. Washington and his doctrine of black self-help and accommodation to white authority. In his acceptance speech, the first president of the Congress called Washington his "guiding star," because he was "the most famous and the best living example of our Africa's sons."[2] Marcus Garvey, the Jamaican black nationalist who based his "Africa for the Africans" movement in Harlem and attracted widespread African American support just after World War I, also had a vogue in South Africa. Besides gaining the admiration of some members of the African elite, he inspired messianic popular movements fed by a prophecy that he would appear at the head of a black American army to overthrow white rule.[3]

In the 1940s, the ANC was led by an American-educated physician who drew inspiration from the civil rights activities of the NAACP. Dr. A. B. Xuma, president of the ANC from 1940 to 1949, had studied in the United States for thirteen years. (At the University of Minnesota he met Roy Wilkins, the future head of the NAACP, who was to be a lifelong friend.) At the time he headed the ANC, Xuma had an African American wife and remained in close touch with American developments.[4] During the late 1960s and early 1970s, the

Black Power movement in the United States provided most of the rhetoric and some of the ideas for the Black Consciousness movement in South Africa.[5] Julie Frederikse's documentary history of ideological currents in the antiapartheid struggle, *The Unbreakable Thread*, provides new evidence of how the thinking of young Africans in the early 1970s could be revolutionized from reading Malcolm X, Stokely Carmichael, and Eldridge Cleaver.[6]

But there is a conspicuous and revealing gap in the history of African American influence and example in South Africa. Martin Luther King, Jr., and the nonviolent direct action for equal rights that he represented had relatively little meaning for the antiapartheid resistance in South Africa. There is nothing mysterious about this. In 1952, three years before the Montgomery Bus Boycott, the African National Congress, under a new leadership, including Nelson Mandela, that was more militant and confrontational than the elite that previously ran it, had embarked on a campaign of nonviolent resistance. Ruthless repression, culminating in the massacre at Sharpeville in 1960, convinced the African nationalist leadership that nonviolence would not work in the face of an implacable and unscrupulous racist regime, and that force, initially limited to sabotage but later including guerrilla warfare, would have to be employed.

Thus, at about the time that King was achieving international recognition as an advocate and practitioner of nonviolent direct action, the South African struggle had taken a turn that tended to make his philosophy outdated and irrelevant. In James H. Cone's comparative biography of Martin Luther King and Malcolm X, *Martin & Malcolm & America*, we discover that in a 1964 radio talk in Britain Malcolm X used Nelson Mandela's conversion to violence as a reason for describing King's nonviolent philosophy as "bankrupt." Cone also notes that King was always more popular in Europe than in the third world: "His philosophy of nonviolence was ignored in many Third World countries as their Colored inhabitants took up arms against European colonizers."[7]

What happened in the African National Congress between the 1940s and the 1960s—or between the age of Xuma and that of Mandela— was that the struggle was redefined. An earlier, more moderate ANC leadership had viewed their cause as one of gradual reform to achieve equal rights, a clear counterpart to the NAACP's program for the United States; a new and more militant leadership, emerging from the

ANC Youth League of the 1940s, moved from nonviolent confrontation to armed struggle, with an increasing conviction that their model was anticolonialist revolution rather than an American-style civil rights movement. Only when revolutionary, anti-imperialist rhetoric began to come from black Americans in the late 1960s did African American thought again strike a chord with a substantial number of black South African activists.

If one looks for the recurring themes in the history of dialogue and cross-fertilization between African Americans and black South African thought about equality or liberation, it becomes evident that blacks in the two societies have shared a common problem that did not have to be faced by most anticolonial revolutionaries. In simplest terms, it was the question of what to do about the whites. Although only a minority in South Africa (currently about 15 percent of the total population), Europeans have been there for almost as long as those in the United States and seem likely to stay. Occasionally there has been talk of pushing the white man into the sea, but prominent black leaders of all ideological persuasions have tended to accept the white presence as an unalterable fact of life.

In the United States, an extreme version of black nationalism has emerged from time to time to call for a total separation of the races through black emigration or by ceding blacks a part of the Untied States, but most black thinkers and political leaders have assumed that African Americans would continue to live with whites in a common society and under a single government. The difficult question, applicable to both situations, is whether blacks should go it alone in their struggle against white supremacy or whether they should cooperate with those whites who profess a commitment to racial justice. The nationalist position is that blacks have to fight their own battles. White allies will be unreliable because few will be able to overcome completely their culture's assumption of white superiority, and undesirable because their presence in a black liberation movement will endanger the racial solidarity and spirit of self-determination deemed essential to group pride and mobilization. (Malcolm X's verdict on the white liberal was that "when the chips are down, you'll find that as fixed in him as his bone structure is his sometimes unconscious conviction that he's better than anybody black.")[8]

Interracialists, or (to use the South African terminology) "nonracialists," welcome the involvement of some antiracist whites because the cause is defined as a crusade to transcend race in the name of color-

blind conception of democracy. The actual history of a debate over relations with whites is not, however, as neat and simple as this abstract
dichotomy would suggest. In practice, the lines between interracialism
and separatist nationalism could blur in response to the opportunities
or exigencies of the moment. For example, it was sometimes argued
that blacks needed to go it alone in the short term in order to develop
the strength and self-confidence to interact and make common cause
with sympathetic whites at some time in the future—when they could
do so on the basis of feeling equal. Because of similarities in the ways
such issues were formulated and resolved, there are some instructive
analogies between the "separate or together" debate of the 1960s in the
United States and the South African debate that began in the 1950s and
continues today between "nonracialists" and advocates of "Africanism" or "Black Consciousness."

James H. Cone's *Martin & Malcolm & America* is an illuminating
discussion of how the issue of integration vs. separatism was played
out in the thought of the two most influential black leaders of the
1960s. Although unknown to most whites, Cone himself is a major figure in recent black intellectual history. A professor for many years at
Union Theological Seminary, he is usually regarded as the father of
"black theology"—the synthesis of Christian belief and Black Power
ideology that emerged out of the ferment of the late 1960s.[9] Because he
went beyond narrow ethnocentrism and made the plight of blacks in
the United States a symbol of the oppression of the poor throughout
the world, arguing that Christ's message for the modern age was social
revolution, he influenced the founders of Latin American liberation
theology (which may explain why *Martin & Malcolm* was published
by the Maryknoll fathers). He also helped to inspire the development
of a Black Theology in South Africa and has engaged in a serious, ongoing dialogue with black South African churchmen opposed to
apartheid.[10]

Much of Cone's original inspiration came from Malcolm X, and his
early work might be seen as an effort to give a Christian justification to
Malcolm's black nationalism. One might therefore expect that his book
comparing "Martin and Malcolm" would be a brief for the latter and
a rejection of the former. But in fact he tries to show that both were au-
thentic representatives of black America and that their views were not
as irreconcilable as is generally supposed. He begins by putting each
leader in a particular sociological setting. King embodied the potential
for liberation of the southern black middle class. Steeped in the

Christian universalism of the southern black church; the self-help, character-building philosophy of Booker T. Washington; and the progressive civil rights activism of the NAACP; King was in a good position to lead a nonviolent campaign against legalized segregation. But in giving voice to the aspirations of southern and middle-class blacks, he failed to address the problems and concerns of lower- or working-class blacks, especially in the northern urban ghettos.

As King himself came to recognize, the desperate and deteriorating economic and social conditions of the ghetto poor could not be remedied by civil rights laws aimed at the southern Jim Crow system. Furthermore, the values to which he appealed on behalf of nonviolence and integration had little meaning to those trapped in the ghetto by structural or institutional forms of racism that made integration seem like a pipe dream. For many blacks whose principal contacts with whites came in the form of police harassment and brutality, a doctrine of integration through nonviolent protest seemed more like a device to pacify blacks and salve the consciences of white liberals than a program for black liberation.

According to Cone, Malcolm X gave voice to the genuine feelings and aspirations of the mass of northern urban blacks. By calling on them to value their blackness and separate themselves voluntarily from whites, he provided the only basis for pride and positive identity that was in fact available to them. By sanctioning violence, at least for the purposes of self-defense, he endorsed attitudes toward whites that were more natural and appropriate to the circumstances of most blacks than King's seemingly impossible demand that blacks turn the other cheek and love their oppressors. When Malcolm rejected America and told blacks that they had no stake in what he considered an irremediably white-supremacist society, he reflected the reality of ghetto life as many blacks felt and perceived it.

It is hard to accept Cone's view that Malcolm's "vituperative language against whites did not mean that he hated whites or that he was trying to make blacks hate them."[11] During his period as a minister for the Nation of Islam, and before he broke with Elijah Muhammed, was he not in effect arguing that whites deserved to be hated? But he had tapped a deep vein of justifiable anger and resentment within the black community. To say that racism breeds counterracism does not deny the importance of Malcolm X. In exposing whites to the real feelings of many blacks, he revealed the dimensions of the American racial problem to an extent that the King of the early 1960s was unable to do.

Cone's contrast of King's position before 1965 and Malcolm's before he broke with the Black Muslims in 1964 contains few surprises for anyone who has a keen memory of the events of the period—although it is useful to have such a vivid reminder of the fierce debates of the time. More original and potentially more controversial is Cone's contention that both men changed their views late in their tragically abbreviated lives in ways that substantially narrowed the gap between them and removed the necessity to choose between their philosophies. After breaking with Elijah Muhammed and becoming an orthodox Muslim, Malcolm X emphatically repudiated his cosmic racialism and admitted into his thinking a conception of human brotherhood. He even conceded that not all white Americans were "devils" and that some whites might contribute positively to the cause of African American liberation—not however by joining black organizations, such as Malcolm's own Organization for Afro-American Unity, but rather by working to combat racism within their own communities.

Malcolm remained a separatist and black nationalist, and his new nonsectarian version of black self-determination was perhaps the main intellectual source for the Black Power movement that arose after his death in 1965. But his categorical antipathy to whites—which has to be considered racist—was abandoned, along with his assumption that blacks had no conceivable place in America. He now seemed to entertain the hope, if not the expectation, that a unified black community might be able to transform America itself into some kind of democratic plural society in which blacks could feel at home without having to reject their identity as people with African roots and a distinctive culture.

Malcolm's movement toward a qualified, pluralistic form of interracialism is well known to hundreds of thousands of readers of his autobiography. Less well recognized is King's acknowledgment toward the end of his life that not all forms of black separatism and self-segregation were bad. The disillusionment with America that set in after the Watts riot of 1965, the failure of his Chicago open housing campaign, and the nation's deepening commitment to what he came to regard as an imperialist war in Vietnam did not make King repudiate his dream of an integrated America, but it did force a reassessment of how hard it would be to get there.

The plight of black America, he began to realize, was inseparable from the inequities of a capitalist society; true equality would require more than the abolition of legalized segregation and the protection of black voting rights. Along with his well-documented turn toward democratic socialism went a certain disenchantment with the mainstream white liberals who had backed the Civil Rights Act but had no stomach for the elimination of poverty through the redistribution of wealth.[12]

Cone shows that King also softened his opposition to black separatism. In 1967 and 1968 he acknowledged the need for "temporary segregation" in cases where desegregation was not, for the time being, a practical possibility (as in the inner cities), or where integration meant a loss of group power. "There may be periods," he told a Miami audience in February 1968, "where segregation may be a temporary way-station to an integrated society," and expressed the fear that in cases of desegregation in which the dissolution of black-run institutions or associations was involved, blacks might be "integrated *out* of power."[13]

In the last analysis, despite Cone's efforts, King does not make a very convincing black nationalist and it is hard to believe that he and Malcolm would ever have fully agreed on the separate-or-together issue even if both had lived to a ripe old age. On one question, as Cone readily concedes, they remained in deep disagreement—the choice of violence or nonviolence as the path to black liberation in the United States. And here, somewhat surprisingly, in view of his endorsement of black violence in his early expositions of black theology, Cone comes down on the side of King. He also proclaims that King's vision of a "beloved community" united across racial lines by Christian love remains "the ultimate goal" of the black freedom movement:

> As important as black nationalism is for the African-American struggle, it cannot be the ultimate goal. The beloved community must remain the primary objective for which we are striving. On this point Martin was right: "for better or worse we are all on this particular land together at the same time, and we have to work it out together."[14]

Cone concludes by invoking the contemporary image of America as a multicultural "rainbow" composed of diverse "members of one human family," in which no group claims genetic or cultural superiority over the others. From his perspective of the 1990s, Cone argues that the achievement of King's beloved community requires not only elimination of the racism that he and Malcolm understood and fought so courageously, but also the "classism" that they more dimly perceived, and the "sexism" that they completely failed to recognize and struggle against.

Cone's attempt to synthesize the ideas of King and Malcolm and update their insights to conform with more recent trends in "liberationist" thought is a major contribution to the discussion of race and ethnicity in modern America. But one unresolved tension in his thinking exposes the philosophical problem at the root of current debates about cultural pluralism. At one point, Cone seems to be criticizing King for his "universalism" and praising Malcolm for his ethnic particularism:

> Martin's faith was universal; that is, it was meant to embrace *everybody*, which meant, in the modern world of Euro-America, that it was ultimately defined by *white people* and those who shared their values. Martin had to reinterpret a white religion, designed to enslave blacks, into a religion of black liberation. Malcolm, however, contended that black people "need a religious expression that is not dictated and controlled by their enemies," but rather by themselves.[15]

Cone praises Malcolm X for rejecting Black Muslim ideas and turning to orthodox Islam, because this allowed him to "move toward a universal perspective on humanity that was centered on his commitment to the black liberation struggle in America."[16] Cone seems to assume that a universalism derived from the European tradition is fatally contaminated by racism, whereas one that is based on a non-Western source such as Islam is justified because of its putative link to the struggle against white or Western domination.

Beyond the obvious question of how Cone justifies his own adherence to Christianity, there is the more serious issue of the complex relationship of "Western values" to the liberation struggles of people of non-Western origins. Although racism, broadly defined, may not be uniquely Western, the rationalized, pseudoscientific form of racism that served to justify a worldwide system of domination and exploitation undoubtedly is. But antiracism and the ideal of universal human rights are at least in their characteristic modern formulations also products of Western civilization. Those non-Western struggles for freedom or self-determination that have proclaimed some form of democracy as their objective have appealed to conceptions of human rights first abstractly set forth by eighteenth-century European or American thinkers and revolutionaries; and they were given new social and economic content by nineteenth-century European socialists. It is no more accurate to say that Western thought is inherently racist than to say that is inherently antiracist. It can be either, depending on how it is interpreted and on what is regarded as essential and what is seen as the betrayal of its essence.

King's creative appropriation of Christian altruism and the Social Gospel was a powerful and persuasive argument for black liberation from Jim Crow, just as Fredrick Douglass's appropriation of Enlightenment conceptions of natural rights furthered the cause of abolitionism in the nineteenth century. Wholesale rejection of Western values, as opposed to the appropriation of those that seem truly universal in their capacity to liberate and humanize "everybody," seems to me self-denying and possibly self-defeating. It is difficult to see what else can serve as the basis for the egalitarian rainbow society that Cone proclaims as his ultimate goal.

Julie Frederikse's *The Unbreakable Thread: Non-Racialism in South Africa* demonstrates that the South African antiapartheid movement has rejected racial separatism, even as a temporary phase of the struggle, and has embraced a color-blind universalism without worrying about its cultural antecedents. Frederikse, who has been a correspondent for National Public Radio in South Africa, uses oral history interviews and documents to demonstrate that the black nationalist or Afrocentric conceptions of the cause have had a hearing but have remained a minority viewpoint and that the main currents of the movement have remained resolutely "nonracialist" in outlook. If King's nonviolence and specifically Christian form of universalism put limits on his capacity to inspire antiapartheid freedom fighters in South Africa, a secular ideology of human liberation that is mainly Western in derivation has resolved the "separate or together" issue by choosing a form of "integration" that seems, on the surface at least, akin to what King was fighting for. Malcolm X and his Black Power disciples appear in this account in the role of pied pipers who led some young South African blacks away from the straight-and-narrow path of nonracialism in the 1970s by promulgating "Black Consciousness"; fortunately, in Frederikse's view, most of these young militants later found their way back to the true cause of color-blind liberation.

Americans, especially liberal whites, who look back with nostalgia on the "black and white together" spirit of the civil rights movement of the early 1960s might be tempted to contrast South African nonracial-ism with the tendency toward race consciousness and separatism that has persisted in African American politics and ideology since the late 1960s (a black nationalist strain that is evident not only in Cone's book but also in the popular films of Spike Lee and in the social relations that are visible on every college campus) and to wonder how we might em-ulate the South African spirit of togetherness.

It would be a serious mistake, however, to make Frederikse's "non-racialism" a synonym for what was usually meant by "integration" in the 1960s. Integration meant primarily the assimilation of African Americans with middle-class credentials into the white middle class. Frederikse firmly repudiates such a program for incorporating a black bourgeoisie into the existing social and economic system. She identifies such a doctrine with a South African liberal tradition that sought to maintain white supremacy and avoid the liberation of the black masses by creating and coopting a black capitalist elite. Frederikse's version of nonracialism is unlikely to travel well to the United States, because its fundamental assumptions are Marxist rather than liberal-capitalist.

The Unbreakable Thread presents a kind of conversion narrative in which an advocate of Black Consciousness comes to realize that the basis of apartheid is "class" not "race" and that racism is caused by capitalism. It follows that racism can only be eliminated by the over-throw of capitalism and the establishment of a socialist order. The kind of whites who can hope to become brothers-or-sisters-in-arms with blacks in the antiapartheid struggle are described succinctly and clearly in the ANC policy document of 1969 admitting whites for the first time to full membership in the organization:

> Whatever instruments are created to give expression to the unity of the lib-eration drive, they must accommodate two fundamental propositions. Firstly, they must not be ambiguous on the primary role of the most op-pressed African mass, and secondly, those belonging to other oppressed groups and *those few white revolutionaries* [my italics] who show them-selves ready to make common cause with our aspirations must be fully inte-grated on the basis of individual equality.[17]

In practice "white revolutionaries" usually meant white members of the South African Communist party. One of them, Joe Slovo, rose to a top leadership position. When it was an underground revolutionary or-ganization, the ANC's version of an "integrated" movement meant the incorporation of the only whites the leadership found trustworthy, those who were committed to a Marxist conception of the struggle.

White liberals and social democrats, even those who joined the integrated and resolutely nonracial Liberal party in the 1950s and 1960s,
were not, for the most part, considered potential allies mainly because
their anticommunism was viewed as divisive.

If Frederikse's documentary history were the whole story of nonracialism, one might have legitimate reason to view her ideas as merely
an extrapolation from Marxist doctrine and also conclude that the
ANC was a thoroughly Communist-dominated organization during the
period from its banning in 1960 to 1989 (where her coverage ends). But
she somewhat slights the other main source of the nonracialist tradition—the South African variant of the social Christianity that influenced Martin Luther King, Jr., in the United States. Entirely absent
from the documents demonstrating the meaning of nonracialism are ex-
tracts from the speeches of Albert Lutuli, the non-Marxist Christian
who was president-general of the ANC from 1952 to 1967, or testimony from notable Christian supporters of the ANC who could have
been interviewed, such as Archbishop Desmond Tutu, the Rev. Allan
Boesak, and the Reverend Beyers Naudé.

It is useful to hear the views of the white leftists who are featured in
the volume, but their secular and materialist perspective does not exhaust the meaning of nonracialism. The decision of the ANC leadership
to include Naudé, an Afrikaner ordained in the Dutch Reformed
Church, as one of two whites on its negotiating team showed the leadership was more sensitive than Frederikse is to the contribution of
Christians who were led by their faith into antiapartheid activism.
Conflict between the Christians and the Marxists in the organization
has been minimal. For the most part the Christian element in the ANC
was committed to a liberation theology, similar to that of Latin
American clerical revolutionaries, and therefore viewed a struggle
against capitalism on behalf of God's poor as a fulfillment of the
Gospel.[18]

In sharp contrast to Cone's effort to synthesize aspects of the nationalist and integrationist traditions in African American thought,
Frederikse treats the black nationalist strain in the struggle against
apartheid as an unfortunate deviation from the nonracialism triumphant in the ANC. She provides documents reflecting the views of
the Pan-Africanist Congress (PAC), founded in 1959 by a group of former ANC activists who objected to the kind of cooperation between
Africans and radical whites and Indians that the ANC was then pre-

scribing. She includes an account of the Black Consciousness movement of the late 1960s and 1970s that broadened the definition of "black" to include Indians and "Coloreds," but rejected association with white opponents of apartheid. But the testimony presented from recent interviews with people who were involved with such movements in the past stresses the extent to which they outgrew such a limiting philosophy. Some of them see Black Consciousness as a stage that had to be gone through on the path to nonracialism, while others have come to the conclusion that such notions were misguided from the beginning. A good example of the ANC view of Black Consciousness comes from Steve Tshwete, who was imprisoned on Robben Island from 1964 to 1979 and who had much to do with changing the views of the Black Consciousness advocates who were added to the community of political prisoners in the late 1970s:

> We knew that it was the responsibility of the revolutionary movement to direct the Black Consciousness Movement into more progressive positions. I mean, we certainly knew that BC could give problems in the long run, by reason of it being colour politics. Colour politics are dangerous. They are just as bad as tribal politics, you know. That's why we know that the imperialist countries were very much interested in boosting Black Consciousness, knowing that politics of the skin are going to blunt the revolutionary drive of the working class, and in particular, the anti-imperialist nature of the struggle.[19]

Advocacy of nonracialism has served the antiapartheid cause well. It has given the movement an ethical legitimacy in the eyes of most of the world that a particularistic, black nationalist emphasis could not have provided. In its specifically Marxist formulation, well reflected in Tshwete's comments, it identified the movement with an international struggle against capitalism and imperialism and consequently evoked substantial aid from the "socialist nations" and became a favorite cause of the far left in Western societies. But since it could also be interpreted as an embodiment of Christian ethics or liberal humanism, it attracted support well beyond the anticapitalist left and became the great international cause célèbre that in the 1980s led Western capitalist democracies to impose sanctions against South Africa, thereby helping to force the white supremacist regime to begin dismantling apartheid.

Frederikse's book, coming as it did at a time when the left throughout the world was having to reevaluate some of its traditional positions, invited a harder look at the ANC conception of nonracialism than one might have been inclined to take a few years earlier. Viewed simply as a judgment that racism is a great evil and that a just society has no place for racial and ethnic discrimination, it is unexceptionable. But the way the concept is used by Frederikse—which is also how it was used by an influential element in the ANC—poses a number of problems. At a time when orthodox Marxism was in retreat throughout the world, could it have been expected to provide a workable philosophy for a postapartheid South Africa? If not, what could take its place, given the fact that the most dedicated and effective opponents of apartheid based their opposition to white racism and black chauvinism on essentially Marxist assumptions?

I was struck in 1988 when I participated in a seminar on South African history and politics at Oxford that the students, most of whom were South Africans representing the full spectrum of racial groups, tended to embrace a Marxist fundamentalism that seemed totally impervious to what was then occurring in Eastern Europe. This was especially true of the whites among them. In visiting South African campuses at about the same time, I found more adherence to orthodox Marxism among white students and faculty than one would be likely to find in any American university.

What this phenomenon reflected, I think, was a long tradition of viewing the struggle as an either/or choice of socialist revolutionism or racist capitalism. As a practical matter, given the characteristic weakness and indecisiveness of liberals in South Africa and the exacting ideological standards that the ANC applied to white adherents, virtually the only way that antiracist whites were able to attach themselves directly to the black-led struggle against apartheid was to affiliate with or support the South African Communist party. Frederikse's book clearly reflects this circumstance, since most of the examples of white nonracialism that she presents are from Communists or their sympathizers. But, it seems necessary to ask, can a genuinely nonracial South Africa be built on such an apparently outmoded sectarianism? As the ANC itself later conceded, its socialist inclinations have to be restrained if blacks are to share in the fruits of a growing South African economy. (Which is not to say that it must or can accept the opposite extreme of unfettered free-market capitalism.)

Another problem with the conception of nonracialism emerges from *The Unbreakable Thread*. It carries the concept to the point that denies all significance to race and ethnicity. It is one thing to say that race is a social and cultural construction rather than a natural phenomenon that predetermines the relations among people. It is another to maintain, as some of the activists in this book do, that one can forget about it entirely in planning the future of what historically has been an ethnically and racially divided society. Consciousness of race or ethnicity reflects the historical experiences of whites and blacks, Afrikaners and English, Zulus and Xhosa. To some extent ethnic loyalties or identities have broken down under the homogenizing effects of industrialization and urbanization, but they remain psychologically powerful and will continue to be influential long after the legal basis of group differentiation has been removed. Simply denying their importance—as Frederikse's nonracialists tend to do—would seem to be a prescription for disappointment and disillusionment. A nonutopian approach to nonracialism would acknowledge the validity of ethnic loyalties and identities that do not actually involve racism—i.e., the impulse to maintain or establish domination over other groups. *The Unbreakable Thread* nowhere seems to acknowledge that an egalitarian cultural pluralism could have a part in the struggle against racism. The notion that class consciousness will totally supplant race consciousness in a democratic South Africa seems naive, and is contradicted by much historical experience.

Perhaps proponents of black liberation in South Africa have something to learn from African American thinkers with roots in the black nationalist tradition, like James Cone. If Frederikse's nonracialism were to be advanced as a solution for the American race problem, it is likely that Cone and many other African American intellectuals would reject it out of hand as a threat to black identity and pride. Of course a black minority is in a very different situation from a black majority. South African blacks have little reason to be worried about being swallowed up or assimilated out of existence. But a democratic and majoritarian South Africa contains large white, Indian, and Colored minorities. One-person, one-vote will not automatically protect their right to cultural freedom. One limitation of the dominant form of nonracialism is that it gives little or no thought to such matters. Before the end of apartheid, it could be argued, it was tactically unwise to pay attention to divisions among the oppressed, and unnecessary, or beside the point, to worry about how white communities would fare in a black-dominated South Africa. But in the 1990s, such issues have to be confronted. It is doubtful that an orthodox Marxist version of nonracialism provides an adequate basis to deal with them justly and effectively.

Benjamin Pogrund's *Sobukwe and Apartheid* gives us the opportunity to evaluate other visions of the struggle against apartheid.
The author is a white liberal journalist, and the subject, Robert
Sobukwe, was the leading proponent of an "Africanist" alternative
to the ANC's brand of nonracialism in the late 1950s. Somewhat in
the vein of Donald Wood's book about Steve Biko, it is the history
of a friendship across racial and ideological lines as well as a biography.[20]

Robert Sobukwe was an intellectual and politician of mixed tribal
background—his mother was a Xhosa, his father a Sotho—who joined
the militant ANC Youth League while a student at South African
Native College at Fort Hare in the Eastern Cape Province during the
late 1940s. In the 1950s, first as a teacher in African high schools and
then as a lecturer in African languages at the white University of the
Witwatersrand, he took an increasingly dim view of the decision by the
new ANC leaders, mainly former Youth Leaguers like himself, to compromise the original Youth League aim of turning the ANC into an orthodox nationalist movement for liberation from colonial domination,
similar to those emerging elsewhere in Africa.

What Sobukwe and his supporters found intolerable was the tendency to downgrade black African nationalism and the right of
Africans to self-determination that resulted from ANC collaboration
with radical members of other racial groups. He objected most strongly
to the conspicuous role that white Communists seemed to be playing in
the "multiracial" Congress Alliance of the mid-to-late 1950s. Like
Malcolm X and his black nationalist successors in the United States,
Sobukwe distrusted whites who embraced the black cause and sought
to keep them at arm's length. He feared they would blunt the edge of
black solidarity and self-reliance by influencing the movement to pursue goals that blacks had not established for themselves. He did not,
however, make the kind of vituperative attacks on whites as a race that
earned Malcolm X his early reputation as a black supremacist, and he
proclaimed that the ultimate goal of his racially based struggle was a
truly nonracial society in which each person would be accorded equal
rights regardless of color or ethnicity. Indeed, he criticized the leadership of the ANC in the 1950s for its tactic of multiracial federalism in
which Africans, Coloreds, Indians, and whites organized themselves
separately and were viewed as having rights as groups.[21] Although sympathetic to some form of socialism that would reflect African commu-

nal traditions, he regarded Marxism as an alien, European ideology that would distort the meaning of African liberation from racial oppression. In other words, he dissented vigorously from the orthodox nonracialism canonized by Frederikse. In a letter to Pogrund, sent from Robben Island, where Sobukwe was imprisoned in the 1960s, he summed up his lifelong conviction that race, not class, was the central element in the South African struggle:

> The point is, Benjie, when we talk of European experiences, we talk in terms of class. . . . But in Africa particularly, though I believe this goes for Asia too, to a large extent, class interests are either nonexistent or irrelevant or muted. The oppression and the struggles are group oppressions and group struggles. In Europe when a member of the middle class wrote about the lower classes, he was writing about a different people. In this country the dichotomy is a colour one. Class distinctions within the group are muted and perhaps even discouraged and emphasis is placed on the solidarity and unity of the group.[22]

In 1958 Sobukwe called for the secession of the Africanist faction from the ANC, and in 1959 he was elected the first president of the rival Pan-Africanist Congress. In 1960 he mounted the extensive campaign of civil disobedience to apartheid that led to the Sharpeville massacre and the banning of both the PAC and the ANC. Arrested for his part in the protest, Sobukwe was sentenced to prison for three years. When his term had been served, his imprisonment was extended indefinitely as the result of a special act of parliament. He was finally released from prison in 1969 but was kept under house arrest at his home in Kimberley until he died of cancer in 1978.

Pogrund first met Sobukwe in Johannesburg in 1957, and a friendship developed that would last until Sobukwe's death. At the time of their meeting, Pogrund was active in the Liberal party, a racially integrated organization founded by antiapartheid whites who had come to disapprove of the ANC's officially sanctioned white auxiliary, the Congress of Democrats, because of a well-founded belief that the latter was Communist-dominated. Pogrund and Sobukwe agreed that communism was an inherently undemocratic doctrine that would substitute one form of oppression for another, but they obviously could not agree on whether the struggle against apartheid should be an interracial or an all-African affair.

Contrary to his popular image, Pogrund assures us, Sobukwe was not a black racist who hated all white people. His commitment to the idea that Africans should go it alone was based on the tactical consideration that only a racially exclusive nationalist orientation would address the realities of racial oppression in South Africa and bring the masses of black people into the struggle. Pogrund argued in vain that racial consciousness and hostility to whites were not attitudes that could be easily changed after white domination was ended; like other liberals, he worried about the danger of white supremacy turning into black supremacy and was not reassured by Sobukwe's personal commitment to the "ultimate" achievement of a nonracial, egalitarian society.

Although Pogrund does not make a point of it, Sobukwe can also be criticized for his disastrous miscalculation of the possibilities for sudden black liberation in 1960. Unlike the ANC, which had learned from earlier campaigns that the apartheid regime should not be confronted by widespread direct action until the people at the grass roots had been effectively organized and educated, the PAC leadership believed that promulgating the correct liberationist doctrine (essentially that Africans should rise up to reclaim their birthright as masters of their ancestral homeland), and the exemplary action of PAC supporters going to jail rather than obeying racist laws, would evoke a spontaneous uprising of the masses that would quickly bring the apartheid regime to its knees.

When the PAC led crowds of Africans to turn in their passes and accept imprisonment, hoping that the movement would grow when they did so, they failed to take account of the readiness to shoot down unarmed blacks that the police would demonstrate at Sharpeville and the capacity of the government to respond in a repressive fashion to the violence and disorder that its propaganda subsequently blamed on the African protesters. They also overestimated the readiness of the masses to risk everything in a bid for liberation. Their romantic, populist conception of black revolution led to the banning and virtual decimation of their own organization and also forced the rival ANC underground and into exile.[23]

Whatever limitations might be found in its ideology, the ANC was, and has remained, a more realistic and tactically supple organization than the PAC. (The characteristic idealism and rigidity of the PAC was manifested in the early 1990s in its opposition to all negotiations with the white government.) Communist influence in the ANC has probably contributed to this pragmatism and flexibility, just as it has helped to sustain the ideal of nonracialism. Communist doctrine has no place for "premature revolutionaries" or for "propaganda of the deed." It also favors "popular fronts" with non-Communist "progressive" forces at times when revolutionary conditions do not exist. Paradoxically, therefore, the Communists have been, on the whole, a moderating and steadying element in the ANC; however objectionable their underlying ideology and ultimate objectives may be, they have contributed to the discipline and cohesiveness of the ANC as a liberation movement.

It is not surprising, therefore, that those non-Communist African nationalists who have rejected the romantic, all-or-nothing revolutionism of the PAC and have objected on Christian or humanistic grounds to its racial chauvinism found Communists to be congenial and useful allies. Thus Sobukwe and Pogrund deserve credit for their recognition of the antidemocratic implications of Communist ideology, but it also needs to be said that their polemics had the practical consequence of dividing and weakening the antiapartheid forces. Whether the longstanding alliance of the ANC and the South African Communist party is still functional and mutually advantageous under current conditions in South Africa is another question. But there is no doubt in my mind that the longstanding marriage of convenience between Communists and democratic nationalists will be difficult to dissolve.

Pogrund exonerates the imprisoned Sobukwe from any responsibility for the often disastrous career of the PAC after 1960. He maintains that Sobukwe neither authorized nor approved of the random terrorism carried out by *Poqo,* the PAC's underground offshoot in the early 1960s, and it is self-evident that he cannot be held accountable for the blunders, including the terrorist policy itself that virtually destroyed the movement within a few years of its banning. More surprising is Pogrund's claim that Sobukwe recanted his separatist Africanism and professed a new willingness to admit whites into the liberation movement.

What apparently persuaded him that a go-it-alone strategy should be abandoned was what he learned from Pogrund about the courageous actions of some white liberals during the Sharpeville crisis. In Cape Town, where huge PAC-led demonstrations protesting the massacre penetrated the center of the city and made the apartheid regime seem temporarily fragile and in retreat, a close working relationship developed between members of the left wing of the Liberal party and young, inexperienced PAC leaders. Liberals smuggled food to townships that were cordoned off and blockaded by government forces, made all their offices and facilities available to the PAC, and, in defiance of the State of Emergency, used their own journal to disseminate information about the protests. Their leader, Patrick Duncan (who later became the first white member of the PAC), also helped avert bloodshed by acting as an intermediary between demonstrators and the police. Other accounts of these events do not present the role of the Liberals in so favorable a light.[24] But whatever the facts may have been, Sobukwe reportedly concluded from the accounts he received in prison that

> A number of whites had given clear proof of their willingness to work as equals with blacks in a completely disinterested spirit. . . .
> If the PAC were to be re-formed now, it would in his view be on a wholly non-racial basis.[25]

One can only speculate what might have happened had Sobukwe gotten out of detention, lived longer, and been allowed to work politically either in South Africa or in exile. Perhaps he would have been able to create an anti-Communist, antiapartheid alliance of white social democrats and black nationalists. (Frederikse's cursory attention to the Liberal party shows at least that its position on economic reform in the 1960s was clearly social-democratic rather than liberal-capitalist.)[26] Such a grouping does not exist in contemporary South Africa, and there seems to be little basis for its emergence. There may be reason to regard this gap in the political spectrum as a misfortune.

Sobukwe's funeral in 1978, as described by Pogrund, was the scene of events that foreshadowed later developments with greater accuracy. A small riot occurred when Sobukwe's young admirers forcibly ejected Chief Mangosuthu Buthelezi and some other attending black dignitaries who were adjudged to be collaborators with the apartheid regime. (Pogrund himself remained throughout the services but was prevented from delivering the eulogy that he had prepared.) This incident helped to shed light on the violent animosities currently surrounding Buthelezi and his Inkatha movement. Before he accepted office in KwaZulu homeland created by apartheid legislation, Buthelezi had been a supporter of Nelson Mandela and the ANC. For several years Pogrund and Sobukwe had a running argument on whether Buthelezi's decision to work within the apartheid system was justified. Sobukwe, even earlier than the African National Congress, concluded that Buthelezi was a traitor to the cause of African liberation because of his willingness to accept office under the regime and because of the way he based his influence on divisive Zulu ethnic claims. Pogrund, unlike most South African liberals, eventually became converted to the negative view of Buthelezi that Sobukwe shared with the ANC, the Black Consciousness movement, and virtually all other Africans with strong claims to being part of the liberation struggle.

The subsequent violence between Inkatha and supporters of the ANC in townships had complex origins. Government backing for Inkatha, as demonstrated conclusively by revelations in the *Rand Weekly Mail,* encouraged Inkatha attacks on ANC supporters, often with the active support of the police. But an essential part of the background was the widespread view outside Inkatha (even before the scandal over government financing of Inkatha broke) that Buthelezi had betrayed the cause and collaborated with the enemy. However reasonable he may have sounded to many Americans, Buthelezi was absolutely anathema to a substantial part of the politically conscious African population, including many Zulus. Asking that he be seated on their side of the table during the negotiations over a new constitution invited a reaction roughly similar to what would have happened if Americans had been asked to accept Benedict Arnold as one of their negotiators at the peace conference to establish American independence from Great Britain. Revelations that the de Klerk government subsidized Inkatha activities in 1989 and 1990 gave new substance to the old charge that Buthelezi was a government stooge.

During his imprisonment Sobukwe developed a keen interest in American affairs, which he followed in the newspapers and magazine to which he was allowed access. Most remarkably, he became a devoted admirer of President Lyndon B. Johnson, to whom he gave much of the credit for the civil rights breakthrough in the United States. In a letter to Pogrund, apparently written in 1965, he characterized U.S. and South African race policies as polar opposites. Johnson, he opined, "is implementing his policy of complete equality determinedly and successfully," much to the chagrin of the South African government, which believed that racial integration could never work. Hendrick Verwoerd, the South African prime minister at the time, stood at the head of white supremacist forces throughout the world, while Johnson was "the hope of all those who stand for nonracialism."[27] Even Johnson's deepening and debilitating involvement in Vietnam did not completely dampen Sobukwe's enthusiasm for the much-maligned Texan. In 1968 he expressed regret that Robert Kennedy was reportedly on the verge of challenging LBJ for the Democratic nomination and argued that if Johnson had followed his own instincts rather than the advice he had been receiving, he would have readily negotiated his way out of Vietnam.

> He has one outstanding virtue for which I like him. He feels. Some say he is sentimental. And that is the man for me any day: A man who can be moved; a man who can feel anger; who can feel deep compassion. But above all a man who can weep in the presence of great sorrow and suffering.[28]

This tribute from a South African revolutionary in solitary confinement to a reformist American president who was being repudiated by the left in his own country is unexpected and idiosyncratic, but it is nevertheless worth attention. It recalls that amazing moment in 1965 when Johnson appeared on television to give strong support to the Voting Rights Act. When the President, his voice quivering with emotion, appropriated the slogan of the Civil Rights movement, "We Shall Overcome," Martin Luther King, Jr., watching at a friend's house, reportedly burst into tears. According to King's most authoritative biographer, "His colleagues and friends had never seen him cry before."[29] From the perspective of subsequent events that dimmed Johnson's luster and made him seem a tragic figure to his former admirers and merely pathetic to more cynical observers, it is difficult to recapture what may have been the finest single moment in the history of the American presidency. Somehow, Robert Sobukwe sensed the authenticity of LBJ's flash of greatness and identified with it.

The contrast that Sobukwe found between a United States heading resolutely toward racial equality and a South Africa dominated by a bigoted, racist government was a reasonable interpretation of the state of affairs in the two countries in 1965. The Civil Rights Acts of 1964 and 1965, mostly the achievement of the civil rights movement but requiring the endorsement and political skills of Lyndon Johnson to turn the chants of protesters into the law of the land, had indeed "overcome" the American equivalent of South Africa's apartheid legislation. And for a time, it seemed that the struggle for equality might be broadened and carried to fruition by becoming a war on poverty and, more specifically, on the economic disadvantage entailed on African Americans by three or more centuries of slavery and racial discrimination. This at least was what Johnson forcefully advocated in his notable address to the graduates of Howard University in June 1965:

> You do not take a person who for years has been hobbled by chains, liberate him, bring him up to the starting line of a race and then say, "You are free to compete with all the others," and still justly believe you have been completely fair.[30]

But, as James H. Cone shows in his account of Martin Luther King's disillusionment between the triumph of 1965 and his assassination in 1968, national leadership faltered as the war in Vietnam made racial justice of less national concern and white opinion turned against measures to deal with the misery of northern urban blacks that was so dramatically exposed in the ghetto riots of those years. King's dream of integration and the beloved community faded; a quarter century later it has not been recaptured. The current ideal of "multiculturalism" that Cone endorses is not really an equivalent because it emphasizes what differentiates Americans rather than what might unite them.

Those Americans who still yearn for a unifying vision, a conception of integration that avoids the biases of class and culture that made the 1960s version vulnerable to the attacks of Malcolm X and the black nationalists, might learn something from South Africa. For reasons already set forth, the conception of "nonracialism," stressed in Julie Frederikse's *Unbreakable Thread* carries ideological freight that makes it questionable for South Africa and clearly inapplicable to American circumstances. But Robert Sobukwe's non-Marxist version of the concept—whatever one thinks of his belief that Lyndon Johnson was its exemplar—might serve as a passable ideal for both societies. Sobukwe's goal (which would be shared today by the dominant element in the ANC) was a society committed to the rights of the individual, in which race or ethnicity will in no way be a disadvantage. What must unite such a society is a commitment to the essentially liberal ideal of personal freedom and equality. By protecting the rights of the individual, it gives to voluntary associations of individuals the ability to maintain distinctive religious or cultural traditions but it gives no formal, constitutional recognition to cultural pluralism. Equal rights as a fair distribution of opportunities may require the curtailment of economic laissez faire; but freedom of thought and association makes cultural laissez faire a necessity.

It might be objected that such a system of beliefs is merely a restatement of conventional Western liberalism and is what theoretically already exits in the United States. But the fact remains that we have failed to apply such values successfully to hierarchies of race, as well as to other persistent inequalities that can be defined as denial of equal rights. The problem facing both the United States and South Africa is how to make rights a reality and not merely pro forma. Existing concentrations of power and privilege, even when they are no longer sanctioned by law, make this exceedingly difficult—some would say impossible. But if we survey the historical and contemporary examples of societies based on different principles—ranging from dictatorship of the proletariat to the various modes of constitutional privilege and empowerment based on race, ethnicity, or religion—no better model is likely to be found.

CHAPTER TEN

Nonviolent Resistance to White Supremacy

The American Civil Rights Movement and the South African Defiance Campaigns

During the 1950s and early 1960s nonviolent protesters challenged legalized racial segregation and discrimination in the only two places where such blatant manifestations of white supremacy could then be found—the southern United States and the Union of South Africa. Comparing these roughly contemporaneous movements and looking for connections between them may give historians a better perspective on the recent history of black liberation struggles in the two societies, while at the same time providing social scientists with material that should be helpful to them in their search for a theoretical understanding of social and political movements aimed at overthrowing established racial or ethnic hierarchies.

The ANC's "Campaign of Defiance against Unjust Laws" in 1952 resulted in the arrest of approximately eight thousand blacks (including Indians and Coloreds as well as Africans) and a handful of whites for planned acts of civil disobedience against recently enacted apartheid legislation. The campaign did not make the government alter its course, and it was called off early in 1953 after riots broke out in the wake of nonviolent actions in the Eastern Cape. Repressive legislation, making deliberate transgression of the law for political purposes a serious crime in its own right, made the ANC wary of again attempting a nationwide campaign of civil disobedience, but it could not prevent the Congress and other black or interracial organizations from protesting nonviolently in other ways and refusing generally to cooperate with the regime in its efforts to erect barriers between blacks and whites in all aspects of life. School boycotts, bus boycotts, noncooperation with the program of removing blacks to new townships, and mass marches to protest efforts to force African women to carry passes were among the actions of the mid-to-late fifties which the ANC led or supported. In 1960 the Pan-Africanist Congress—a militant faction that had recently seceded from the ANC because of its objections to the parent organization's policy of cooperating with the congresses established by other racial groups as well as to its relatively cautious approach to mass action—launched a campaign of civil disobedience against the pass laws that ended with the massacre of sixty-nine unarmed protesters at Sharpeville. Chief Albert Lutuli, president-general of the ANC, showed his sympathy for the Sharpeville victims by publicly burning his own pass, and the one-day stay-at-home that the Congress called to register its solidarity with the PAC was well supported. But the government quickly suppressed all public protest, and both the ANC and the PAC were banned and driven underground. After Sharpeville, nonviolent direct action no longer seemed a viable option for the liberation movement, and in 1961 some ANC leaders, in cooperation with the South African Communist party, inaugurated the era of armed struggle by establishing a separate organization to carry on acts of sabotage against hard targets.[1]

The nonviolent phase of the American civil rights movement began with the Montgomery bus boycott of 1955–1956 and culminated in the great Birmingham, Mississippi, and Selma campaigns of 1963–1965. Viewed narrowly as an attack on legalized segregation and disfranchisement in the southern states, the movement was remarkably successful. It led to the Civil Rights Acts of 1964 and 1965, which effectively outlawed Jim Crow and assured southern blacks access to the ballot box. It becomes immediately apparent therefore that a fundamental difference between the two movements is that one can be regarded as successful in achieving its immediate objectives while the other was a conspicuous failure.[2]

Fully explaining success or failure obviously requires an assessment of the context—what each movement was up against and what outside help it could expect in its struggle. But before looking at such limiting or favoring circumstances, we must describe and analyze the movements themselves in an effort to compare the resources and capabilities that each brought to the confrontation with white power. Furthermore, it would be mechanistic and ahistorical to ignore the possibility that movements emerging at about the same time and involving people who in both instances defined themselves as black victims of white oppression may have influenced each other in some direct and important way. We need to know what they had in common and how they differed in ideology, organization, and leadership. What do similarities and differences in political thought and behavior as well as in social and cultural characteristics tell us about the situation of black people in these racist societies during the 1950s and 1960s? What role, if any, did internal differences play in determining the success or failure of nonviolence?

Somewhat surprisingly, there is little evidence to indicate that the two nonviolent movements influenced each other in a significant way. Before World War II, African American influence on black South African ideologies and movements had been substantial, but the use of black America as inspiration and example appears to have tapered off during the postwar years. Before the triumph of the Nationalists in 1948, black American interest in South Africa had been limited and intermittent; the African Methodist Episcopal Church had provided the most important and durable connection when it established itself in South Africa at the turn of the century. For most African Americans, Africa meant West Africa, but awareness of the white-dominated nation at the tip of the continent increased rapidly after the rise of apartheid showed that South Africa was out of step with a world that seemed at last to be moving toward an acceptance of the principle of racial equality.[3]

Nevertheless, the Defiance Campaign does not seem to have made a great impression on African Americans. The Council on African Affairs, a group of black radicals who sought to influence American opinion on behalf of decolonization, circulated a petition supporting the Campaign that garnered 3,800 signatures—many of which came from white radicals—and $835 in donations; but this appears to be the most significant expression of African American concern. The campaign was also mentioned in passing in a November 1952 petition to the United Nations on African issues sponsored by twenty-five organizations, including the NAACP, but the Association's organ *The Crisis,* which commented frequently in 1952 and 1953 on the rise of apartheid, did not cover the campaign against it. By 1952 black Americans were beginning to notice African developments, especially the first stirring of independence movements in West Africa, but interest was far less intense than would be the case a few years later.[4]

Black Americans might have been more aroused by the Defiance Campaign if it had not occurred at a time when interest in direct action as a possible form of protest in the United States was at a low ebb. Nonviolence had been placed on the agenda of civil rights activity during and immediately after World War II with A. Philip Randolph's March on Washington Movement of 1941–1945 and the founding and first sit-ins of CORE; but by 1952 McCarthyism and the generally conservative mood in the country had made established black leaders reluctant to endorse actions that opponents of civil rights could describe as radical or subversive; they feared a backlash that would weaken popular support for a legalistic and gradualist reform strategy that was beginning to bear fruit, especially in court decisions affirming the basic constitutional rights of African Americans. When interest in nonviolence revived after the onset of the Montgomery bus boycott in 1955–1956, scarcely anyone seems to have thought of invoking the South African precedent.[5]

Montgomery, in turn, does not appear to have inspired in any significant way the dramatic bus boycott that took place in the Johannesburg township of Alexandria in 1957. Martin Luther King reacted to the Alexandria boycott by expressing his admiration for protesters who had to walk ten or fifteen miles, noting that those in Montgomery had often been driven to work, but he did not claim any connection between the two movements. The Alexandria boycott was a desperate act of resistance to a fare increase, not a protest against segregation or denial of civil rights, and replicated a similar action in the same township during World War II. At the time when Martin Luther King and the American nonviolent movement was first attracting the attention of the world, the faith of black South Africans in passive resistance was wearing thin. When direct action on a broad front commenced in the United States in 1960 and 1961, the ANC was in the process of rejecting nonviolence in favor of armed struggle.[6]

The movements were connected historically in one sense, however. Both were inspired to some extent by the same prototype—Mahatma Gandhi's use of militant nonviolence in the struggle for Indian independence. King of course made much of the Gandhian example and tried to apply the spirit and discipline of *satyagraha* to nonviolent protests in the American South. The official statements of purpose or philosophy issued by SCLC and SNCC in the early 1960s were permeated with Gandhian rhetoric and philosophy. Gandhi was less often invoked explicitly by the Defiance Campaigners, but their methods, especially their public announcements of where, when, and by whom laws would be disobeyed and their refusal to make bail in an effort to "fill the jails," could have been learned from a Gandhian textbook.[7]

If both movements drew inspiration from the great Indian apostle of nonviolence, they received the message by different routes. Gandhism came to King and the American movement by way of a radical pacifism that derived mostly from the left wing of the Protestant Social Gospel tradition. King's nonviolent antecedents and mentors were from the Christian pacifist Fellowship of Reconciliation and its antisegregation-ist offshoot, CORE. Mainly the creation of white Christian radicals like the Rev. A. J. Muste, this intellectual and spiritual tradition lacked deep roots in the black community, although it did have some notable black adherents like Bayard Rustin and James Farmer. Nevertheless, as a recent study has shown, there was a long history of African American admiration for Gandhi as a brown man who was fighting for the freedom of his people from white or European oppression. Black newspapers sometimes expressed the hope that a Negro Gandhi might someday appear to lead a nonviolent movement against racial oppression in the United States.[8]

Gandhi cast an even longer shadow in South Africa, because he had first experimented with *satyagraha* as the leader of the South African Indian community's struggle for rights as British subjects in the period between 1906 and 1914. The South African Native National Congress had been so impressed with Gandhi's mobilization of Indians for non-violent resistance that they included "passive action" as one of the methods they proposed to use in their struggle for African citizenship rights. In 1919 the Congress actually engaged in "passive action" on the Witwatersrand in an unsuccessful attempt to render the pass laws unenforceable through a mass refusal to obey them, but for the next thirty years this potential weapon lay rusting in the ANC's arsenal as the politics of passing resolutions and petitioning the government prevailed. A politically aroused segment of the Indian minority revived the Gandhian mode of protest in 1946 and 1947 when, with the encouragement of Gandhi and the newly independent Indian government, it engaged in "passive resistance" against new legislation restricting Indian residential and trading rights. With the triumph of the Nationalists in 1948 and the coming of apartheid, the Indian passive resisters gave up their separate struggle and allied themselves with the ANC. The Defiance Campaign itself was in fact jointly sponsored by the ANC and the South African Indian Congress, and several veterans of earlier Indian passive resistance struggles played conspicuous roles teaching and demonstrating Gandhian nonviolent techniques, as well as helping to plan the campaign and participating in its actions.[9]

In neither case, however, does a tracing of the Gandhian legacy provide a full picture of the ideological origins of mass nonviolent action. Mass pressure tactics do not require a specifically Gandhian rationale; they may derive simply from a sense that less militant and confrontational tactics have proved fruitless and that it is now time to challenge the oppressor in a more direct and disruptive way. The decision of a group to engage in nonviolent direct action usually constitutes a major escalation of resistance, a shift from legally authorized protest by an elite to initiatives that are more threatening and potentially violence-provoking because they involve bringing masses of aggrieved people into the streets. A philosophical or religious commitment to nonviolence is not necessary to a choice of boycotts and civil disobedience as vehicles of resistance. In fact groups committed ultimately to a revolutionary overthrow of the existing order often embrace nonviolent action as a means of raising consciousness and encouraging the kind of polarization that will make a revolutionary upheaval more likely. In the United States, the Communist party and its allies had engaged in a variety of nonviolent protests against racial discrimination during the 1930s, including the first mass march on Washington.[10]

Communists were excluded from A. Philip Randolph's March on Washington Movement of 1941, but Randolph was clearly influenced by their example in his effort to create an all-black movement for equal rights that would go beyond the customary legalistic methods of the NAACP and use mass action to pressure the government. As a trade unionist he was also aware of the sit-down strike and other examples of labor militancy that owed nothing to Christianity or pacifism. Neither religious nor a pacifist, he found Gandhi's campaigns attractive because they showed what could be achieved by "nonviolent goodwill direct action." He represented a way of thinking that could endorse everything Martin Luther King, Jr., was doing without accepting his nonviolent theology. For Randolph and those in the movement who shared his views, it was sufficient that nonviolent direct action was a practical means for African Americans to improve their position in society—while violent resistance, however defensible it might be in the abstract, was not in their view a viable option for a racial minority. King himself not only tolerated this viewpoint in his associates but at times came close to embracing it himself, at least to the extent that he came to realize that the effectiveness of nonviolence resulted more from its ability to coerce or intimidate the oppressor than from any appeal it made to his conscience or better nature.[11]

In South Africa non-Gandhian pressures for nonviolent mass action came during the 1940s from the young rebels in the ANC Youth League who had grown impatient with the older generation's willingness to work within the system of black "representation" established by the preapartheid white supremacist governments of Prime Ministers J. B. M. Hertzog and Jan Smuts. The Youth Leaguers, among whom were Nelson Mandela, Walter Sisulu, and Oliver Tambo, favored a boycott of segregated political institutions and experimentation with more militant and confrontational methods of protest than the organization had hitherto employed. In 1949 the Youth Leaguers won control of the ANC, and the Programme of Action that was subsequently enacted called for "immediate and active boycott, strike, civil disobedience, non-cooperation. . . ." The spirit of the Youth League and of the Defiance Campaign that was the fruit of its action program was not based to any significant degree on a belief in the power of love to convert enemies into friends or in the higher morality of nonviolence. Indeed the very use of the term "defiance" suggests that anger more than *agape* was the emotion being called forth. The campaign, as its chief planner Walter Sisulu and its tactical leader, volunteer-in-chief Nelson Mandela, conceived it, was designed to enable an unarmed and impoverished majority to carry on its struggle against the tyrannical rule of an armed and wealthy minority in a more forceful and effective manner. If nonviolent methods failed, there was no firm ideological barrier to prevent the young turks of the ANC from embracing other means of struggle.[12]

But there were still influential older figures in the Congress who were nonviolent in principle and not purely out of expediency. Among them was Chief Albert Lutuli whose fervent Methodist Christianity strongly predisposed him against taking up arms and sustained his hopes that oppressors could be redeemed by the sufferings of the oppressed. "The road to freedom is via the cross" was the memorable last line of the statement he made after the government had dismissed him from his chieftainship because he would not resign from the ANC. The fact that the idealistic Lutuli was elected president-general of the ANC in 1952 showed that the ANC of the 1950s, like the southern civil rights movement of the 1960s, brought together those who regarded nonviolence simply as a tactic and those who viewed it as an ethic.[13]

Besides sharing the ideological ambiguity that seems to be inescapable when nonviolence becomes coercive mass action, the two movements tended to view the relationship of nonviolence to "normal" democratic politics in similar ways. Some forms of nonviolence are difficult to reconcile with democratic theory because they frankly seek to override or nullify decisions made by a properly constituted majority. But in both of these instances the protesters were denied the right to vote and were therefore able to argue that their employment of extraordinary means of exerting pressures were justified by their lack of access to other forms of political expression. One-person, one-vote was a major goal of both movements, and the attainment of it would presumably reduce, if not eliminate entirely, the need for nonviolent mass action, especially in South Africa where blacks would then constitute a majority of the electorate. As Chief Lutuli put it in 1952, "Nonviolent Passive Resistance" is "a most legitimate and human political pressure technique for a people denied all effective forms of constitutional striving."[14] Speaking at the Prayer Pilgrimage to Washington in 1957, King made a litany of the phrase "Give us the ballot," and promised that if it were done "we will no longer have to worry the federal government about our basic rights. . . . We will no longer plead—we will write the proper laws on the books."[15]

In addition to such similarities of ideology and ethos, the leadership of the two movements came from a similarly situated social group—what might be described as the educated elite of a subordinate color caste. Studies of the social composition of the ANC through the 1950s have shown conclusively that the organization was dominated by members of "an African bourgeoisie" or "petty bourgeoisie" that was characterized mainly by educational and professional achievements.[16] Examinations of the origins of the southern Civil Rights movement have found the spur for militant action in the rise in southern cities and towns of what one historian calls "a relatively independent black professional class."[17]

It was a special product of legalized racial segregation that such elites were not—as is often the case under less stringent forms of ethnic or colonial domination—subject to detachment and alienation from their communities by a system of rewards and opportunities that allows a favored few to move into the lower ranks of the governing institutions established by the dominant group. It might be taken as axiomatic that where race per se is the main line of division in a society, as it obviously was in South Africa and the American South, that resistance will take the form of a cross-class movement led by members of the educated middle class. This does not mean, however, that less educated and working-class blacks made little contribution to whatever success these movements achieved. It was of course the plain folk who sustained the boycotts, often at great personal sacrifice. The point is that these freedom struggles were, and had to be, movements of peoples or communities rather than of social classes.

These similarities in the ideological and social character of the two movements did not preclude significant structural and cultural differences, to say nothing as yet of the obvious contrast of situations. The most significant structural difference between the Defiance Campaign and the nonviolent civil rights movement was that the latter grew out of a number of local struggles and was sustained by strong organizations and institutions at the community level, whereas the former was for the most part a centrally planned, top-down operation. The one area where the Defiance Campaign achieved something like mass involvement was in the cities of the Eastern Cape, where, as historian Tom Lodge has shown, it was able to build on the firm base provided by a recent history of local mobilization and protest activity. But nothing like the network of "movement centers" that was the source of the American movement existed to buttress nonviolent campaigns in South Africa. Where such centers existed in South Africa they were usually tied to labor organization and trade unions; in the United States it was the black churches and black colleges that did most to sustain local activism. Since every southern city had relatively prosperous black churches and many had some kind of higher educational facility for blacks, such an institutional matrix for community protest was widely available, whereas black unions were well-established in only a few places in the South Africa of the 1950s. Furthermore, South African black townships of the 1950s were quite different from southern black urban communities. Their populations, which included a large number of transients and illegal residents, were less socially stable and significantly poorer; there were fewer well-established cultural or religious institutions; there was a proportionately much smaller middle class and relatively little black entrepreneurship or business activity. Efforts were indeed made to establish community associations, but they had much less success than comparable efforts in Montgomery or Birmingham.[18]

Even if the forces opposing each movement had been identical in strength and determination—which of course they were not—there seems little doubt that a centralized movement like the South African one would have been easier to repress than the more decentralized and diffuse American movement. Even before the ANC was outlawed, the government was able to hobble it severely simply by banning or arresting its top leaders. In the American South in the 1950s the NAACP was rendered ineffectual by state legal harassment that in some states amounted to an outright ban. It was partly to fill the vacuum created by persecution of the NAACP that independent local movements developed. These grassroots movements were more difficult to suppress by state action, and they flourished in places where the NAACP could no longer show itself. If such strong local communities and institutions had existed in South Africa, the government might have faced a variety of local actions that would have been much more difficult to counter than the centrally directed campaign of the ANC in 1952. (This in fact is what happened in the 1980s with the rise of the United Democratic Front, which was a federation of the community organizations that had sprung up in the 1970s and early 1980s.) When, during the mid-1950s, the Congress attempted to assume the leadership of local struggles over housing or transportation, it fell short of effectively adjusting its methods and organizational style to accommodate grassroots initiatives. The ANC supported the Alexandria bus boycott of 1957 and helped it roll back a fare increase, but it failed to turn this spontaneous expression of community grievances into a durable township organization committed to broader objectives. In the later stages of the civil rights movement, SCLC was sometimes accused of coopting local campaigns and undercutting local initiatives. But its great successes in Birmingham and Selma were the product of a skillful coordination of local, regional, and national perspectives. SCLS's genius was that it could channel and harness community energies and initiatives to make them serve the cause of national civil rights reform.[19]

Besides differing structurally, the two campaigns also diverged in the less tangible realm of movement culture and ethos. As the special prominence of ministers and churches in the American movement strongly suggests, religious belief and emotion directly inspired and animated the African American protesters to an extent that could not be paralleled in South Africa. The charisma of King as prophet/saint of the movement was instrumental in making it a moral and religious crusade rather than merely the self-interested action of a social group. The opposition of large numbers of black churches and churchmen to nonviolent direct action belies any notion that African American Christianity necessarily or automatically sanctions militant protest, but

King's creative interpretation and application of the Gospel showed that it had the capacity to do so. The South African struggle, unlike the American, did not produce a Gandhi-like figure who could inspire the masses by persuading them that nonviolent protest was God's will. There was a reservoir of religious belief and practice that might have been tapped—it surfaced at times in local actions that featured prayer and hymn-singing. But the ANC leadership was composed of highly educated men who had gone to mission schools and whose religious beliefs had little connection with those of the masses of Africans, especially those who were members of the independent "Zionist" churches that served a large proportion of urbanized Africans. The rival PAC formed in 1959 made a greater effort to draw the independent churches into the struggle, but it did not have time to accomplish much before it was banned in 1960. What King did that no South African leader was able to do was to weave together the black folk Christianity that was his own cultural heritage with the Gandhian conception of nonviolent resistance to empower a cause that both inspired its followers and disarmed the opposition of many whites. Hence the nonviolence of the American movement had a soul-stirring quality, both for its practitioners and for many white observers, that the more obviously conditional and pragmatic civil disobedience characterizing the Defiance Campaign normally failed to project. Of course this resonance was in part the result of the extensive and usually sympathetic way that the national press covered the American movement and, by the 1960s, of its exposure on national television. The Defiance Campaign by contrast received relatively little attention from the white South African press and was not widely noticed abroad (which is one reason it did not serve as a model for African American passive resisters).[20]

The possibly decisive effects of contrasting press or media treatment suggest that the differences in the nature of the movements may tell us less about why they ultimately succeeded or failed than we are likely to learn from examining their external circumstances—what they were up against. The American protesters faced a divided, fragmented, and uncertain governmental opposition. The most important division among whites that the movement was able to exploit was between northerners who lacked a regional commitment to legalized segregation and southerners who believed that Jim Crow was central to their way of life. The success of the movement stemmed ultimately from its ability to get the federal government on its side and to utilize the U.S. Constitution

against the outmoded states' rights philosophy of the southern segregationists. When King proclaimed that "civil disobedience to local laws is
civil obedience to national laws," he exploited a tactical advantage the
South African resisters did not possess; for they had no alternative to a
direct confrontation with centralized state power. South African black
protest leaders had long tried to drive a wedge between British imperial and South African settler regimes, but the withdrawal of British
power and influence beginning as early as 1906 and virtually complete
by the 1930s had rendered such hopes illusory. For all practical purposes South African whites in the 1950s were monolithic in their defense of perpetual white domination. In the United States it was of
course federal intervention to overrule state practices of segregation
and disfranchisement in the southern states that brought an end to Jim
Crow. In South Africa there was no such power to which protesters
could appeal against apartheid.[21]

The geopolitical context of the Cold War and decolonization of
Africa and Asia also cut in opposite ways, ultimately helping the
American movement and hindering the South African. In the United
States the competition with the Soviet Union for the "hearts and
minds" of Africans and Asians, especially by the early 1960s when several African nations achieved independence, made legalized segregation
a serious international liability for the Eisenhower, Kennedy, and
Johnson administrations. As reasons of state were added to other factors working against Jim Crow, the federal government became more
susceptible to pressures from the civil rights movement. In South
Africa, on the other hand, fears of Communist subversion within the
country and of Soviet influence in the newly independent African states
of southern and central Africa panicked the white political leadership
into pressing ahead with more radical schemes for the "separate development" and political repression of the black majority. Underlying
these contrary assessments of the dangers of black insurgency was the
basic difference between a white majority facing a demand for the inclusion of a minority and a white minority conscious that the extension
of democratic rights would empower a black majority.

It would be cynical, however, to see nothing in the positive responses
of many white Americans to the civil rights movement except self-
interested calculations. White America has not been of one mind historically on the place of blacks in the republic. In the North, at least,
there was an alternative or oppositional tradition in white racial
thought, originating in the antislavery movement, that advocated the

public equality of the races and offered a standing challenge—although one that was only intermittently influential—to the deeply rooted white supremacist tradition that was a legacy of African American slavery. At times, as during Reconstruction and in the mid-1960s, racial liberals became ideologically dominant and were in a position to respond to black demands for civil and political equality with major reforms. (But, being liberals, they had great difficulty in addressing the problem of economic inequality.) In South Africa, by contrast, there was no white liberal tradition that went beyond a benevolent paternalism and no deep reservoir of theoretically color-blind attitudes toward democratic reform that could be appealed to. Nelson Mandela caught this difference when asked by an American journalist in one of his rare prison interviews during the 1980s why he had not followed the example of Martin Luther King and remained nonviolent:

> Mr. Mandela said that conditions in South Africa are "totally different" from conditions in the United States in the 1960s. In the United States, he said, democracy was deeply entrenched, and people struggling then had access to institutions that protected human rights. The white community in the United States was more liberal than whites in South Africa, and public authorities were restrained by law.[22]

Was it therefore inevitable that a nonviolent movement for basic civil rights would succeed in the United States and fail in South Africa? As probable as these outcomes might seem to be, one can imagine things turning out differently. It is arguable that without the astute and inspirational leadership provided by King and others that the struggle for black civil and political equality would have taken much longer. Any claim that the Civil Rights Acts of 1964 and 1965 were inevitable obscures the creative achievements of the liberation movement. For South Africa the argument has been made that the 1961 decision of the ANC to sanction some forms of violence was a mistake; the full potential of nonviolent resistance had not been exhausted, and the sabotage campaign that resulted from the decision was itself a disastrous failure that devastated the organization. To support this viewpoint, one could point, as historian Tom Lodge has done, to the relative success of the last mass nonviolent action of the 1960s—the three-day stay-at-home of 1961. Lodge has also noted that the one ANC-related organization that was not banned shortly after Sharpeville—the South African Congress of Trade Unions—had a capability for politically motivated strikes that was never fully exploited. Clearly the sabotage campaign that became the center of resistance activity in the 1960s posed little threat to white domination and turned out very badly for the ANC because it exposed its top leadership to arrest and imprisonment. If nonviolence had its inherent limitations as a resistance strategy under the kinds of conditions that prevailed in South Africa, it would be hard to establish from its record of achievement in the 1960s and 1970s that the resort to violence, however justifiable in the abstract, represented a more effective method of struggle. Of course the key historical actors, like Nelson Mandela, Walter Sisulu, and Oliver Tambo, did not have the benefit of historical hindsight and can scarcely be condemned for trying something different when nonviolent resistance had obviously failed to move the regime and had become more and more difficult to undertake.[23]

Although Martin Luther King, Jr., had shown some awareness of the South African campaigns of the mid-1950s—in 1957 he discussed them with the Rev. Michael Scott when both were in Ghana for the independence celebration—he first indicated a deep and abiding interest in South African developments in 1959 when he wrote to Chief Lutuli to express his admiration for the latter's courage and dignity and to forward a copy of *Stride Toward Freedom*. The Sharpeville massacre in 1960 and the awarding of the Nobel Peace Prize to Lutuli in 1961 for his espousal of nonviolent resistance heightened King's interest and prompted him to speak out vigorously against apartheid. In a 1962 address to the NAACP national convention, King exemplified his doctrine of nonviolence by referring to Lutuli: "If I lived in South Africa today, I would join Chief Lithuli [*sic*] as he says to his people, 'Break this law. Don't take the unjust pass system where you must have passes. Take them and tear them up and throw them away.'"[24]

King made his fullest statement about South Africa in a speech given in London on 7 December 1964, as he was en route to receiving his own Nobel Peace Prize in Oslo.

> In our struggle for freedom and justice in the U.S., which has also been so long and arduous, we feel a powerful sense of identification with those in the far more deadly struggle for freedom in South Africa. We know how Africans there, and their friends of other races, strove for half a century to win their freedom by nonviolent methods, and we know how this nonviolence was met by increasing violence from the state, increasing repression, culminating in the shootings of Sharpeville and all that has happened since . . . even in Mississippi we can organize people in nonviolent action. But in South Africa, even the mildest form of nonviolent resistance meets with years of punishment, and leaders over many years have been silenced and imprisoned. We can understand how in that situation people felt so desperate that they turned to other methods, such as sabotage.[25]

Like Mandela two decades later, King was sensitive to differences between the two contexts that would make nonviolence more feasible and effective in the American case. But in the same speech he indicated a way that nonviolence could be brought to bear against apartheid. "Our responsibility presents us with a unique opportunity," he told his British audience. "We can join in the one form of nonviolent *action* that could bring freedom and justice to South Africa; the action which African leaders have appealed for in a massive movement for economic sanctions." Almost exactly one year after his London speech, King made another strong appeal for sanctions in an address on behalf of the American Committee on Africa. "The international potential of nonviolence has never been employed," he said. "Nonviolence has been practiced within national borders in India, the U.S., and in regions of Africa with spectacular success. The time has come fully to utilize nonviolence through a massive international boycott."[26]

King, who gave vigorous support to the sanctions movement for the remaining three years of his life, did not of course live to see the anti-apartheid movement succeed without unleashing the violent revolution that so many observers had believed would be necessary for the overthrow of white supremacy. It is now possible to argue that the breakthrough that came with the release of Nelson Mandela and the unbanning of the ANC was as much, if not more, the result of international nonviolence as the fruit of a strategy of violent resistance inaugurated by the Congress in the 1960s. The apartheid regime was not in fact decisively defeated on the battlefield or driven from power by a domestic insurrection. The armed struggle of the ANC served to remind the world that blacks were determined to be liberated from white oppression, but it was the ethical disapproval of much of humanity that destroyed the morale and self-confidence of South Africa's ruling whites, and the increasingly effective economic sanctions that persuaded its business community and those in the government whom they influenced that apartheid had no future. Of course those sanctions would undoubtedly have been lighter and the disapprobation less sharp if the domestic resistance of the late 1980s had not provoked the government into a final desperate effort to suppress dissent by force. But that domestic resistance was primarily a matter of withdrawing cooperation from the regime. Not entirely nonviolent, it was predominantly so—a great domestic boycott to parallel the international one. The spirit of Gandhi, long since repudiated by the ANC in exile, was alive and well in the United Democratic Front, the domestic movement that rallied behind the ANC's goal of a nonracial democratic South Africa. In 1989, with the emergence of the Mass Democratic Movement, South Africa once again saw massive nonviolent actions against segregation, led this time by clergymen like Allan Boesak and Desmond Tutu—both of whom had been greatly influenced by King and the church-based American Freedom Struggle—and featuring the singing of African American freedom songs. Nonviolence may not have been sufficient to liberate South Africa, but it played a major role in bringing that nation to democracy. It would not be beyond the power of historical analogy to describe the successful antiapartheid movement as Birmingham and Selma on a world scale.[27]

CHAPTER ELEVEN

From Black Power to Black Consciousness

In the early 1980s the pioneer comparative historians of South Africa and the United States focused most of their attention on the structures and ideologies of white domination. More recently, however, the spotlight has shifted to the experiences of those oppressed by racism and their resistance to it. "Top-down" comparisons have been superseded by "bottom-up" studies of the commonalities and interaction of black struggles against white political and cultural hegemony. These studies reveal the salience of black America as an example or inspiration for South African blacks in the period between the 1880s and the 1940s and suggest that there was more of a sense of identity or similarity than might have been anticipated from the comparisons of patterns of domination.[1] But the study of connections and comparisons of black ideologies and movements in the two societies has not often been extended into the post–World War II era. The radicalization of the South African struggle during the postwar period made the relatively moderate American civil rights movement seem less and less relevant.[2]

Nevertheless, African American rhetoric and ideas reentered the South African struggle with the rise of the Black Consciousness movement in the late 1960s and early 1970s. In a pioneering work published in 1978, the American political scientist Gail M. Gerhart briefly explored the connection between the Black Power movement in the United States and its analogue in South Africa. Her work was highly suggestive; but it was not based on a deep and precise knowledge of Black Power, and it lacked the perspective that awareness of the subsequent history of the two movements can now provide. It is worthwhile, therefore, to reexamine the relationship between Black Power and Black Consciousness in light of the enhanced understanding of the two movements made possible by the passage of time and the appearance of new scholarship.[3]

The Black Power movement in the United States was in some respects a revival of the black nationalism promulgated in the 1920s by Marcus Garvey. But its immediate precursor and patron saint was Malcolm X, the renegade minister of the Nation of Islam. Between 1963 and his assassination in 1965, Malcolm asserted a black separatist perspective in opposition to the racial integrationism advocated by the Reverend Martin Luther King, Jr. According to Julius Lester, an intellectual exponent of Black Power writing in 1968: "More than any other person, Malcolm X was responsible for the growing consciousness and new militancy of black people."[4]

The actual emergence of Black Power as the rallying cry for a movement took place in the context of the southern civil rights struggle of the mid 1960s. By 1965 young black activists in the Student Nonviolent Coordinating Committee (SNCC) had become disillusioned with the two cardinal principles that had previously guided the Civil Rights movement as defined by the Reverend Martin Luther King, Jr.—interracialism and nonviolence. The failure of the Democratic party in its 1964 national convention to seat the insurgent black delegation from Mississippi had helped to discredit the white liberalism to which King had appealed. In both SNCC and CORE the spirit of "black and white together" that had characterized both organizations before 1963 had given way by 1965 to a growing feeling that the presence of whites in the movement was inhibiting the growth of black pride and initiative. By 1966 racial exclusiveness was the basic policy of both SNCC and CORE. Even stronger emotions surrounded the issue of nonviolence vs. self-defense. The brutal beatings and killings of civil rights workers who had followed King's rules for nonviolent engagement and whose pleas for federal protection had gone unanswered had created a deep reservoir of frustration and anger.[5]

Preparations for a civil rights march in Mississippi in June 1966 brought into the open the long-simmering conflicts between King and SCLC, and SNCC, now led by the young firebrand Stokely Carmichael. The immediate issues in Mississippi were whether whites should be allowed to participate in the march and whether a black self-defense organization, the Deacons for Defense, should provide armed protection. The compromise hammered out authorized the inclusion of both the

Deacons and white sympathizers, although relatively few whites actually showed up. On the march itself a rhetorical struggle developed between King's gospel of racial reconciliation and Carmichael's stress on polarization and conflict. Finally in Greenwood on June 16, Carmichael, fresh from being been held by the police, announced that he was fed up with going to jail and tired of asking whites for freedom. "What we gonna start saying we want now is 'black power.'" He then shouted "black power" several times and the audience shouted it back. The context reveals that the original implications of Black Power were self-defense against racist violence and an unwillingness to continue petitioning whites for equality. From now on, Carmichael urged, blacks should confront power with power rather than offer love in return for hate.[6]

The panic over the Black Power slogan in the white press in 1966 was due primarily to its association with violence, which made it seem part of the same spirit that was manifested in the civil disorders then taking place in northern urban ghettos. But, initially at least, the only violence that was being sanctioned was self-defense against racist assaults. The secondary association with racial exclusiveness was particularly shocking to white liberals who had identified strongly with the ideal of integration. Charges of black racism compelled African Americans to make the argument, originally put forth by Malcolm X, that blacks could not be racist because they lacked the power and inclination to dominate whites the way that whites continued to dominate blacks. Here differing definitions of racism—for liberal whites it was a prejudiced attitude and for Black Power advocates it was a hierarchical social order—made communication difficult. But the essence of Black Power was neither violence nor the exclusion of whites; it was rather self-determination for black people. According to Julius Lester, it meant simply that "black people would control their own lives, destinies, communities. They would no longer allow white people to call them ugly." Blacks were tired of having whites define who they were and what they might become, especially since white "friends of the Negro" often failed to deliver on their promises of racial justice and at times used their egalitarian rhetoric to cover up substantive inequalities.[7]

During the racial polarization that took place in the years between 1966 and 1968, liberal whites tended to withdraw their active support from the struggle for racial equality, either because they believed that the goal had already been achieved or because they saw no place for themselves in the reconstituted freedom struggle. At the same time blacks from a variety of ideological backgrounds were endorsing Black Power in the basic sense of community control and self-determination. Shortly after the events in Mississippi, a prominent group of black clergymen took out an ad in the *New York Times* endorsing the idea that blacks must develop "group power," because they had been oppressed as a group and not as individuals and had as much right as other American racial or ethnic groups to unify and exercise power on behalf of their own community. In 1967 a national Black Power conference was held at which a range of black organizations, including the traditionally integrationist NAACP and the National Urban League, were represented. Its principal convener, the Reverend Nathan Wright, Jr., described the purpose of Black Power as going beyond civil rights and getting black people to address themselves to "the far more basic business of the development by black people for the growth in self-sufficiency and self-respect of black people."[8]

These early formulations of the Black Power program did not directly challenge the status quo of American society. They did not in fact sanction either a total and permanent separation of the races or revolutionary action to liberate blacks from oppression. They merely substituted the idea of corporate or group integration for the individualist version that had previously prevailed. According to Nathan Wright, "The thrust of Black Power is toward freeing the latent power of Negroes to enrich the life of the whole nation." What blacks were doing, he argued, was following the example of other ethnic groups: "The basic American tradition is for each rising ethnic group to devise and execute its own plan for economic, political, and civic freedom and development. So it must be with the Black people of our land." Individualist integration, according to Wright, had not been a goal of other groups, and it need not be for blacks.[9]

To be sure, Wright was one of the least militant of the major Black Power advocates of 1966 and 1967; he was essentially a conservative whose thinking recalled at times the accommodationist "self-help" tradition of Booker T. Washington. But those who used a more confrontational rhetoric often ended up advocating a reformist ethnic pluralism similar to Wright's. According to the book that in 1967 was taken as the definitive statement of the new racial philosophy, *Black Power* by Stokely Carmichael and Charles V. Hamilton, "The concept of Black Power rests on a fundamental premise: *Before a group can enter the open society, it must first close ranks.*" The aim was "bargaining strength in a pluralistic society," and the model to be followed was the way that white American immigrant groups like the Jews, Irish, and Italians had been able to exert political power by voting as a bloc.[10]

But another argument in the book had more radical implications— the analogy made in the first chapter between the situation of African Americans and that of colonized peoples of Africa and Asia. Here the authors likened the internal form of colonialism that characterized black-white relations in the United States to the oppressive system of white domination that prevailed in South Africa and Rhodesia. If, in fact, "black people in this country form a colony, and it is not in the interest of the colonial power to liberate them," what reason was there to expect that the mobilization of blacks as a pressure group within the American political and economic system would result in their incorporation on a basis of equality? In his speeches and writings of 1966 and 1967, Carmichael gradually shifted his allegiance from the reformist model of ethnic mobilization in a pluralist society to a revolutionary model of national liberation from colonialism. "Traditionally for each new ethnic group," he had told the readers of the *Massachusetts Review* in September 1966, "the route to social and political integration in America's pluralistic society has been through the organization of their own institutions with which to represent their communal needs within the larger society. This is simply what the advocates of Black Power are saying." But in a speech in London in July 1967, he sounded a different note:

> Black Power to us means that black people see themselves as part of a new force, sometimes called the Third World: that we see our struggle as closely related to liberation struggles around the world. We must hook up with these struggles. We must, for example, ask ourselves: when black people in Africa begin to storm Johannesburg, what will be the reaction of the United States?. . . . Black people in the United States have the responsibility to oppose, certainly to neutralize, white America's efforts.[11]

In London Carmichael stopped short of calling for an African American insurrection in support of the international antiimperialist struggle. By 1968, however, he was openly advocating revolution and paying homage to Frantz Fanon as the prophet of decolonization through violence. But dissension quickly developed within the radical wing of the Black Power movement between those like Carmichael who believed that blacks were victimized primarily as a race and must therefore endeavor to separate themselves from whites and deepen their connections to the African motherland and those who believed that they also were oppressed as a class and might therefore establish alliances with other potentially revolutionary segments of American society.[12]

The most conspicuous exponents of the latter position were the supporters of the Black Panther party, initially established in 1966 in Oakland, California, and by 1968, according to historian Manning Marable, "the most revolutionary national organization in the United States." When Stokely Carmichael and other militants from SNCC attempted to combine forces with the Black Panthers, the differences of opinion on the nature of black oppression came into the open. Carmichael resigned as prime minister of the Panthers in 1969 because of the ties the party had established with white leftists. Those who had begun as Black Power radicals increasingly divided into two warring factions—those who stressed racial separatism and cultural nationalism and those who, following the Black Panthers, moved toward the Marxist conception of an anticapitalist revolution—but with the provisos that the revolution in the United States would be led by blacks from the ghettos rather than by the predominantly white industrial working class and that in the international struggle people of color rather than the most advanced segments of the proletariat would be in the vanguard. Huey Newton, the leader of the Panthers, derided those who looked to African culture as the basis of a separatist identity as "pork chop nationalists," and in Los Angeles the Panthers engaged in violent skirmishes with members of an extreme separatist and cultural nationalist group (called simply US) led by Ron Karenga. Well into the 1970s there were bitter quarrels among black radicals between separatist nationalists, who tended to become more inward looking and less confrontational as time went on, and revolutionary nationalists, influenced by Marxism-Leninism, who bore the brunt of official repression.[13]

But many of those who invoked the Black Power slogan in the late 1960s and early 1970s never embraced a radical black nationalism of either variety and continued to stress the reformist ethnic pluralism that had been the original meaning of the slogan. Besides the radical versions, there were conservative and liberal interpretations of what proved to be an extremely elastic conception. These formulations eventually forced many of the radicals to disown the slogan or to see it as merely representing a stage on the way to a fully developed national consciousness. Economically conservative black leaders emphasized black self-help and entrepreneurship, virtually replicating the procapitalist "bootstrap" philosophy of Booker T. Washington. Black politicians in the Democratic party generally defined the concept as a mobilization of black voters behind stronger civil rights legislation and liberal reform.[14]

As the radical sixties gave way to the relatively conservative seventies, it became clear that the Black Power movement had made a significant difference in the attitudes of black America. Especially evident was a significant increase in racial pride and self-esteem. The slogan "black is beautiful" summed up the positive affirmation of black identity that had replaced the widespread sense of ugliness and inferiority that psychologists in the 1950s had found to be widespread among blacks. There was also an increasing willingness to identify with African culture; African Americans in the late 1960s and early 1970s wore African clothes, adopted African hairstyles, and began to celebrate African holidays. A coherent African American cultural ethnicity was in the process of being constructed out of a combination of African and specifically African American traditions. But in political and social terms what had triumphed was a validation of black ethnic solidarity and action within the context of a liberal pluralist society and not the radical alienation from the American political and social system that had characterized the black nationalism of a Stokely Carmichael, a Huey Newton, a James Foreman, or an Imamu Baraka.[15]

The South African Black Consciousness Movement of the 1970s appears at first glance to have been the most obvious case of imitating an American movement in the entire history of black protest in South Africa. But close examination of the circumstances of its growth and the content of its ideology shows that the African American influences were less important than local conditions and indigenous currents of thought. The reading of Stokely Carmichael, Eldridge Cleaver, Malcolm X, James Cone, and other American Black Power advocates was clearly a stimulus, but the adaptation of African American concepts and slogans was selective rather than wholesale, and the ideas appropriated were often reinterpreted to fit South African conditions.

Black Consciousness rose to fill the vacuum created by the banning of the African National Congress and the more militant Pan-Africanist Congress in 1960, but only after a hiatus of nearly a decade that saw little organized and visible political activity among Africans. The repression that succeeded in making the Congresses virtually invisible within South Africa in the mid-to-late 1960s meant that they existed thereafter mainly as émigré organizations seeking to organize guerrilla forces in neighboring African states and to rally international support against the apartheid regime. Inside South Africa the voices raised in public against the government's racist policies during the mid-to-late 1960s tended to be those of white dissidents.[16]

The antiapartheid liberalism of the white dissenters had little influence on the white electorate, but it did find a home on the campuses of the English-speaking white universities and came to predominate in the principal political organization on these campuses, the National Union of South African Students (NUSAS). NUSAS was opposed to racial segregation and sought to involve blacks in its own activities. Although the organization was not permitted to organize on the campuses of the "tribal colleges" established under apartheid, it recruited among the small and diminishing number of Africans allowed to attend the predominantly white universities through loopholes in the separate education laws and also solicited representatives from the African colleges to attend its conventions as guests or observers.[17]

At the 1967 annual NUSAS conference at Rhodes University in Grahamstown, the black delegates were forced by the host institution to eat separately from whites and to occupy separate living quarters far from the conference venue. Among those subjected to this treatment was Steve Biko, a student at a medical school for nonwhites established under the auspices of the University of Natal in Durban. At the July 1968 conference Biko provoked a searching discussion of whether there was any point in Africans continuing their affiliation with NUSAS in the light of their minority status and second-class treatment. He pressed the issue again at a meeting of the University Christian Movement (UCM), another interracial organization that also met during the winter vacation period of 1968. UCM, which was allowed to organize formally on black campuses because of its seemingly nonpolitical religious character, had more black members than white, making it a better springboard for independent black political action than NUSAS. At its meetings Biko proposed the establishment of an all-black student movement to supplement NUSAS. A year later the South African Students' Organization (SASO), with Biko as its first president, was formally established. At first SASO operated under the umbrella of NUSAS, which it continued to recognize as the "national organization" of students. But in 1970 it severed all ties with the parent body and endeavored to extend the influence of its separatist philosophy—summed up in the slogan "Black man, you are on your own"—beyond black students and into the larger African community. In 1972 the Black People's Convention (BPC) was founded as a coalition of African organizations committed to the ideology that was now being called "Black Consciousness." Another wing of the movement and perhaps its most active and creative component in the early 1970s was Black Community Programmes (BCP), the coordinating body for a variety of local self-help initiatives, such as community medical clinics and home industries for the unemployed poor. These were run by blacks for blacks, but were financed mainly by antiapartheid church groups both within the country and abroad.[18]

The government hoped for a time that the racial separatism of the movement would make it tolerant of the autonomy and eventual "independence" of black "homelands." But in 1972 the leadership of Black Consciousness rejected all governmental schemes for separate development. It did not thereby endorse violence or revolution, but its repudiation of territorial separation meant, in principle, that all of South Africa, rather than the small portions assigned to Africans by the government, was the birthright of blacks. In Biko's own words, "We black people should all the time keep in mind that South Africa is our country and that all of it belongs to us."[19]

This assertion of exclusive black ownership was an intentional repudiation of the African National Congress's policy of multiracialism. It took direct issue with the famous opening line of the Freedom Charter of 1955: "South Africa belongs to all who live in it, black and white." In some respects Black Consciousness was a revival of the black separatist ideas of the Pan-Africanist Congress, which had seceded from the ANC in 1959 on the issue of whether Africans should cooperate with other racial groups. In 1972 Biko's paper at a Cape Town conference on "Student Perspectives on South Africa" explicitly traced the BC ideology back to a "group of young men [in the 1950s] who were beginning to 'grasp the notion of their peculiar uniqueness' and who were eager to define who they were and what." These forerunners of BC opposed "the ease with which the leadership [of the ANC] accepted coalitions with organizations other than those run by blacks. The 'People's Charter' adopted in Kliptown in 1955 was evidence of this." In Biko's view, therefore, the Africanists of the 1950s—those who opposed the Freedom Charter and eventually broke away to form the PAC—produced "the first real signs that the blacks in South Africa were beginning to realize the need to go it alone and to evolve a philosophy based on, and directed by, blacks. In other words, Black Consciousness was slowly manifesting itself." A reluctance to cooperate with white liberals and radicals on the grounds that all whites were beneficiaries of the system of oppression and could not be trusted to act on behalf of the black community was an attitude common to Pan-Africanism, Black Consciousness, and Black Power.[20]

But Black Consciousness departed in some significant respects from Pan-Africanism, most obviously in its definition of "black." For Biko and his colleagues, all those previously described in negative terms as "nonwhites"—Indians and "Coloreds" as well as indigenous Africans—were to be considered "black" so long as they identified with the struggle against racial oppression. Blackness then became a matter less of ancestry than of a raised consciousness. On the other hand, not all people of African ancestry and pigmentation were automatically black; those who accepted white domination and cooperated with their oppressors continued to deserve the appellation "nonwhite."[21]

This repudiation of a strictly genetic view of blackness paralleled a subtle and little noticed difference between the African American nationalism of the 1960s and the earlier varieties associated with Edward Blyden, Alexander Crummell, and Marcus Garvey. These forerunners were men of dark complexions who distrusted mulattos and at times openly disparaged them. But in the 1960s the foremost champion of blackness could be the light-skinned and red-haired Malcolm X. Obviously no strict genetic test was being applied, and discussion of the historical significance of skin-color variations among African Americans became virtually taboo. The implicit message was that one was as black as one felt, and that people of African ancestry who retained the integrationist view that white culture was superior to black culture continued to be "Negroes" rather than "blacks," however dark-complexioned they happened to be. Even people who were of mostly white ancestry and appearance could be as black as any other African American provided that they were part of the group that had been historically classified and treated as such (in accordance with the extraordinary American custom of considering anyone of known black ancestry to be black) and provided also that they currently identified themselves with the struggle for black liberation and self-determination. Whether or not the new American affirmation of a nongenetic blackness influenced the racial thinking of Black Consciousness, there can be no doubt that both movements made a significant innovation in identifying a race consciousness that was a matter more of existential choice and political awareness than of biological determination.[22]

Another way that Black Consciousness departed from the Pan-Africanist precedent and drew closer to American black nationalism of the 1960s was in its emphasis on psychological rehabilitation as a precondition for political resistance. The Pan-Africanists of the 1950s had believed that the masses were fully conscious of the injustices perpetrated upon them because of their race and that the anger they naturally felt made them ready at any time for a massive uprising against white domination. Leaders needed only to provide the spark in the form of some dramatic act of confrontation and provocation. But the fact that the massacre of PAC demonstrators at Sharpeville in 1960 had led to massive repression and political quiescence rather than to a general uprising of Africans had cast doubt on their belief in revolutionary spontaneity. For the advocates of Black Consciousness, the state of affairs in post-Sharpeville South Africa revealed that blacks were held in subjugation not merely by force but by their own sense of impotence and inferiority. Consequently, the primary task of their movement was to "conscientize" black people, which meant giving them a sense of pride or a belief in their own strength and worthiness. Only in this way could the psychologically debilitating effects of white domination be overcome. BC's rejection of alliances with white liberals and radicals was based on a conviction that the whites in such relationships tended to assume authority and behave paternalistically, thus preventing blacks from overcoming their inferiority feelings. Malcolm X's distinction between forced segregation and voluntary "separation" was central to the South African Black Consciousness Movement, and the slogan "Black is beautiful" had as much resonance for its adherents as it did for American Black Power advocates.[23]

But the idealist view that consciousness precedes praxis was more clearly and insistently affirmed in South Africa than in the United States—at least in the early and classic formulations of the Black Consciousness philosophy. The very difference in the names generally assigned to the two movements suggests a muted philosophical difference. In the United States the growth of black pride and a positive sense of identity was not divorced conceptually in most formulations from the actual exercise of black power. Awareness of a positive black identity was indeed a precondition for community organization and the application of political pressure, but consciousness was expected to be translated quickly into forceful action, and the exercise of power in turn was supposed to be essential for the full development of consciousness.

The most obvious reason that consciousness was divorced more sharply from power in early Black Consciousness thinking was the significant difference in the political rights and economic conditions of blacks in the United States and South Africa. Only people who could vote could plan to exercise power at the polls, and it was futile to think about a separate black economy if blacks had few resources they could mobilize. Furthermore, the South African government was willing to tolerate the public expression of BC ideology only as long as it remained convinced that the movement was a purely intellectual and cultural one that was not actually proposing any kind of political resistance. After the Black People's Convention was established in December 1971 as a broad-based "political" expression of Black Consciousness, the government concluded that the rhetoric of "conscientization" was a cover for seditious action and that BC ideology could act as a stimulus to acts of defiance and insurrection. Eight BC leaders, including Biko himself, were banned in early 1973. The following year the leading BC activists in Durban were arrested for treason after they defied a government ban on holding a rally to celebrate the victory of FRELIMO over the Portuguese in Mozambique.[24]

But the idea that consciousness was itself a kind of power had an intellectual basis as well as a tactical one. One of the features of Black Consciousness that distinguishes it from the mainstream of the African American movement, was the extent to which religious beliefs and associations shaped its ideology and mode of operation. Virtually all its leaders were practicing Christians with affiliations to one or another of the mainstream interracial churches, and the movement's institutional origins were as much in churches and religious associations as in student organizations. It will be recalled that the United Christian Movement was the cradle of SASO and that the principal white patronage and financial support that the movement received was from church groups both in South Africa and abroad. Of particular importance in aiding and abetting the movement was the resolutely anti-apartheid Christian Institute, led by radical white clergy. Antiracist white ministers like the Methodist Basil Moore, the renegade Dutch Reform *predikant* Beyers Naudé, and Anglican priest Aelred Stubbs were strong supporters and major facilitators of the Black Consciousness Movement. The ban on cooperation with white liberals did not extend to radical clergymen who saw BC as a religious movement designed to purge the church of the sin of white supremacy. A large number of black ministers, mostly within the "historic" churches originally established by European missionaries, became prominent advocates of Black Consciousness; they predominated in the leadership of the "adult" wing of the movement—the Black People's Convention. To some extent, to be sure, association with religion was a matter of convenience for the student activists who remained in the forefront of the movement. The one place in the late 1960s and early 1970s where blacks could express themselves with some freedom was within the churches or in associations that enjoyed religious sponsorship. But it would be cynical to leave it at that and ignore genuine religious convictions of a Steve Biko and a Barney Pityana, to say nothing of the religious basis reflected in the philosophy itself. The belief that a new consciousness could transform physical reality, or that spiritual truth could overcome vast differences in power, was a profoundly religious one. It assumed that God was on the side of the most downtrodden and despised portions of humanity, and that once the sufferers realized that they were the chosen of God, the end of their agonies would be in sight.[25]

The aspect of the American Black Power movement that had the most direct and significant impact in South Africa was an intellectual tendency that is usually viewed as peripheral to the mainstream development of black nationalism—the effort of clergy and religious thinkers to formulate a Black Theology. Beginning with the 1966 defense of Black Power by a distinguished group of African American ministers and emerging full-blown with the publication of James Cone's seminal *Black Theology* in 1969, this doctrine caused much controversy within religious circles but attracted relatively little attention outside of them. That the black nationalist revival of the 1960s began with Malcolm X's categorical condemnation of Christianity as a white man's religion and was stimulated by a negative reaction to Martin Luther King's Christian nonviolence made Christian theology seem like an unpromising source of Black Power sentiments. Furthermore, none of the more radical exponents of Black Power who attracted the attention of the press in the late sixties—Stokely Carmichael, Rap Brown, James Foreman, T. Huey Newton, or Eldridge Cleaver—manifested a positive view of Christianity. But a small number of black ministers and theologians went to work in the late 1960s and early 1970s reformulating Christian doctrine in light of the Black Power revolt and the resurgence of nationalist and separatist ideas in the black community. When South Africans sought inspiration for a black theology of their own, they found it primarily in the writings of James Cone, a prolific author of serious theological works who was appointed a professor at Union Theological Seminary in New York after the publication of his first book in 1969. Cone was not merely a distant intellectual stimulus; he established direct connections with black theologians in South Africa, contributing papers to their symposia and commenting on their work.[26]

Cone and the theologians of Black Consciousness in South Africa agreed that white missionaries had preached a form of Christianity that helped to sustain racist and colonialist oppression. It had not only helped to justify slavery and imperialism but also taught black converts that their cultural traditions were worthless and that resistance to white domination was sinful. But this was not the fault of the Gospel itself; it had resulted rather from an interpretation of it that served the selfish interests and sinful appetites of Europeans. Blacks had the right and the need to interpret the Christian religion in light of their own situation as an oppressed people. Passages in the New Testament that presented Jesus as the champion of the poor and oppressed were the basis for a theology of liberation. Christ himself was black, if not literally at least in the sense that blackness had come to symbolize the state of being oppressed that He had been sent to overcome. In Cone's formulation of 1970, "Blackness is an ontological symbol and a visible reality which best describes what oppression means in America." For the South African black theologians, it stood for oppression in their country in an even more obvious sense. To affirm blackness as a positive identity in either society was to be freed in spirit and committed to a struggle for liberation from physical oppression. As the South African theologian Manas Buthelezi put it: "As long as somebody says to you, 'You are black, you are black', blackness as a concept remains a symbol of oppression and something that conjures up feelings of inferiority. But when the black man himself says, 'I am black, I am black', blackness assumes a different meaning altogether. It then becomes a symbol of liberation and self-articulation."[27]

It would be wrong to suppose, however, that those in South Africa who were stimulated by Cone to pursue the project of creating a distinctive black theology ended in total agreement with his forthright apology for Black Power. In the end Cone was too extreme in his separatist rejection of whites to meet the needs of African clergy who served denominations that had both white and black communicants. Despite a recognition of the need to adapt Christian principles to particular situations, they retained a strong underlying commitment to Christian universalism.[28]

When Cone denied the universality of Christ's offer of salvation, arguing that "Jesus is not for all, but for the oppressed, the poor and unwanted of society, and against oppressors," he was coming too close for the comfort of the South Africans to saying that whites were beyond re-demption. According to Lutheran bishop Manas Buthelezi, the Gospel dictated a very different attitude: "It is now time to evangelize and hu-manize the white man," he wrote in 1973, thus reversing the original mission relationship without sacrificing the basic Christian idea of a universal salvation. In his early writings, Cone often expressed a cate-gorical hostility to whites that seemed to make reconciliation with them impossible. He also flirted with what more orthodox Christians could only view as heresy when he affirmed that "Black Power is not only consistent with the gospel of Jesus Christ, but . . . it is the gospel of Jesus Christ." For Black Consciousness theologians like Buthelezi and the Colored Dutch Reformed minister Allan Boesak, reconciliation of the races could not be achieved without black liberation but it re-mained the ultimate goal of genuine Christians; for them the Gospel transcended human ideologies and could never be reduced to a finite political meaning. Boesak, in an important book of 1977 endorsed Black Power as "the power to be," but rejected the tendency in American Black Theology toward "a complete identification [of the Gospel] with Black Power's political program (in all its expressions.)" As critics of Afrikaner nationalism with its idolatry of the *Volk*, South African black theologians were on guard against making national feel-ing and religious faith synonymous.[29]

The differences between the versions of Black Theology promul-gated in the two countries support the more general conclusion that the Black Consciousness Movement was influenced by the American Black Power philosophy but did not slavishly imitate it. The most ob-vious borrowings can be found in early SASO documents. The Policy Manifesto of 1970 featured the free appropriation of current African American ideas and slogans, suggesting strongly that there were sig-nificant similarities in the situation of black people in the two societies and comparable solutions to their problems. Repeating almost verba-tim a famous phrase from Carmichael and Hamilton's *Black Power*, the Manifesto accepted "the premise that before the black people should join the open society, they should first close their ranks, to form themselves into a solid group to oppose the definite racism that is meted out by the white society, to work out their direction clearly and bargain from a position of strength." The Manifesto repudiated "integration" if it meant "the assimilation of blacks into an already established set of norms drawn up and motivated by white society," but went on to en-dorse an integration based on "the proportionate contribution to the

joint culture of the society by all constituent groups." In this formulation Black Consciousness was not yet a revolutionary black nationalism but rather a reformist pluralism similar to the moderate or mainstream version of Black Power. It is difficult to determine whether this
seemingly unrealistic conception of what was possible in South Africa
without violent confrontation reflected the honest beliefs of Biko and
the founders of SASO or was, on the contrary, an expedient cover for
the political organization of blacks under the eyes of a government intensely fearful of the revolutionary potential of the African majority.[30]

Gail M. Gerhart has uncovered an internal SASO document describing a 1970 seminar discussion on the applicability of the Carmichael and
Hamilton injunction that "before entering the open society we must
close ranks," which shows an appreciation of the differing contexts of
Black Power and Black Consciousness. "This group," the document reports, "made the observation that an open society in this country can
only be created by blacks, and that for as long as whites are in power,
they shall seek to make it closed in one way or the other. We then defined what we meant by an open society. . . . The group ended up by
stating that the original statement should read 'before *creating* the open
society we should first close our ranks.'"[31]

In his 1971 paper at the conference on Student Perspectives on South
Africa, Biko discussed at some length the relationship of Black
Consciousness to Black Power and argued that the influence of the latter on the former had been exaggerated. A more important impetus, he
claimed, was "the attainment of independence by so many African
states in so short a time. . . . The fact that American terminology has
often been used to express our thoughts is merely because all new ideas
seem to get extensive publicity in the United States." Five years later,
when the government brought some Black Consciousness leaders to
trial for celebrating the victory of FRELIMO in Mozambique, Biko was
called to the stand and questioned closely about the origins of the
movement. In answer to a question on the relationship to Black Power,
he made a fundamental distinction between the two manifestations of
black self-determination:

> I think the end result of Black Power is fundamentally different from the
> goal of Black Consciousness in this country, that is, Black Power . . . is the
> preparation of a group for participation in an already established society, a
> society which is essentially a majority society, and Black Power therefore in
> the States operates as a minority philosophy. Like you have Jewish power,
> Italian power, Irish power and so on in the United States. The Black people

are merely saying that it is high time that they are not used as pawns by the other pressure groups operating in American society.[32]

Biko's understanding of Black Power, which was probably derived mainly from Carmichael and Hamilton's book, was actually a fairly accurate perception of the concept that had survived the suppression and decline of the more radical black movements. But in distinguishing between the operation of Black Power within the context of a potentially benign American ethnic pluralism and the implied claims of Black Consciousness as a "majority philosophy" in an undemocratic South Africa, he shied away from drawing the conclusion to which his logic pointed —that reform, persuasion, and peaceful pressure, which might work in the United States, had little chance in South Africa. Elsewhere in his testimony he explicitly denied that Black Consciousness would lead to a black revolution. In a somewhat tortuous interpretation of the practical meaning of a statement of the Black People's Convention that blacks needed to form a "power bloc" for the purpose of bargaining on the basis of strength with the white community, he conceded that blacks were not yet strong enough to make radical demands and that it might take "over twenty years of dialogue between blacks and whites" to achieve real success. Eschewing "armed struggle" or even "confrontational methods" leading to civil disobedience, he affirmed that "our operation is basically that of bargaining and there is no alternative to it. It is based mainly on the fact that we believe we have interpreted history correctly that the white man anyway is going to have to accept the inevitable." Biko seemed to be saying that the methods that would work for a minority in the context of democratic pluralism in the United States would also work for a disfranchised majority in South Africa. But a more realistic assessment of the situation might have suggested that a racist minority could not be persuaded to cede power to a black majority without a fight and that it would do everything in its power to prevent the majority from gaining the kind of leverage that Biko predicted it would gradually and peacefully acquire. Biko may well have been masking his real views in an effort to keep his movement alive and within the law. But if we take him at his word, there is a considerable gap between his analysis of the situation and how it differed from the American and the kind of action that he was publicly prepared to contemplate.[33]

Biko's advocacy of organization, self-help, and "conscientization"— with no clearly specified program for political resistance—resembled the stance of cultural nationalists in the United States. Like them he seemed to be saying that for the time being black people should devote themselves mainly to building their self-esteem. Just as the African American cultural nationalists were criticized by the Black Panthers and other revolutionary nationalists for their lack of political militancy and failure to address the class basis of racial oppression, so Biko was criticized by the ANC, the South African Communist party, and assorted freelance Marxists for his idealist conception of the power of consciousness and his failure to link up effectively with the struggle of black workers for economic justice.[34]

But the Black Consciousness movement was not without political consequences. The circulation of its ideas beyond the colleges and universities to the high school students of Soweto helped to set off the revolt of June 1976. The brutal suppression of student protests against government efforts to require African students to have instruction in the hated oppressor language of Afrikaans touched off student strikes and riots throughout the country and plunged South Africa into its most serious domestic crisis since Sharpeville. The organization that called the demonstration of June 16—upon which the police fired with bloody proficiency—was the Soweto Students' Representative Council, which had been founded by the local members of the South African Students' Movement, a national organizational of black high school students inspired by SASO and under BC influence. The government had no doubt about who was ultimately responsible, and it proceeded to ban all of the Black Consciousness groups. The arrest, torture, and murder of Steve Biko in 1977 climaxed the massive effort to stamp out the movement with which he was identified.[35]

Unlike what happened after Sharpeville, the repression that followed Soweto did not lead to a long period of political inactivity and apparent black resignation in the face of overwhelming white power. Soweto in fact is now recognized as a turning point in recent South African history; as a result of the impression it conveyed to the world of the utter viciousness of the white regime, it energized and empowered the international antiapartheid movement. Less easy to calculate but nevertheless undeniable was the effect on black South Africans of the fact that their children had been willing to risk their lives by defying the regime on an issue that involved black pride and cultural identity. The adult Black Consciousness organizations did not plan or direct the uprising, but they could take some credit for instilling the mood of black self-assertion that produced it.

Nevertheless, the historical fate of the Black Consciousness ideology after 1977 defied predictions made at the time that its way of thinking would soon predominate in the black resistance movement, eclipsing the nonracial nationalism of the ANC. An estimated 60 percent of the student rebels who fled the country after the uprising were recruited into the guerrilla army that the ANC was organizing in friendly African states. The Pan-Africanist Congress, which as we have seen was ideologically closer to Black Consciousness, was in no position to receive them in large numbers. Disabled by factionalism and incompetent leadership—and without the reliable supply of arms that the ANC received from the Soviet Union and the nonmilitary help it obtained from Western supporters—the PAC was virtually defunct by the late 1970s. While young recruits in the guerrilla army camps were being indoctrinated in the ANC view of the world by veteran émigrés, the Black Consciousness activists who were arrested and sent to Robben Island were being reeducated by Nelson Mandela, Walter Sisulu, Gavin Mbeki, and other ANC leaders who had been incarcerated there since the early 1960s. Hence it was the ANC and not organizations that tried to carry on in the Black Consciousness tradition that derived the most benefit from the "conscientization" of blacks that was occurring in the late 1970s.[36]

The main source of domestic resistance to the apartheid regime beginning in the 1980s was the interracial United Democratic Front (UDF), a coalition of organizations—African, Colored, Indian, *and* white—that was originally established in 1983 to protest against the constitutional changes that the government was proposing in order to give a limited form of political representation to Indians and Coloreds, but not to Africans. Indicative of the new interracialism was the fact that NUSAS, the predominantly white student organization from which SASO had seceded in 1970, was among the affiliating groups that founded the UDF, and one of its former presidents became a member of the UDF's National Executive Committee.[37]

The new federation quickly identified itself with the Freedom Charter and, becoming bolder, with the ANC itself. One impetus for making this connection was the fact that the ANC had grown in strength and visibility since the time before Soweto when it seemed to be merely an exile group with virtually no visible presence within the country. Its forces augmented by refugees from the Soweto uprising, the ANC was able to carry out a number of spectacular acts of sabotage within South Africa in the late 1970s and early 1980s. Since the rival

PAC remained considerably smaller and less active, the conviction grew within the black communities of South Africa that the main source of resistance against apartheid was the ANC and that its camp was the place to be if one wanted results. Embracing the Freedom Charter meant welcoming all racial groups, including whites, into the movement and setting as the goal of the struggle a racially inclusive democratic South Africa rather than a state that gave official priority to African interests and cultural values. The opposition to the Charterists, as they were now called, came from The Azanian Peoples Organization (AZAPO) and the Black Consciousness alternative to the UDF as a confederation of community groups, the National Forum. But it was clearly the UDF that won the support of most blacks and that took the lead in the wave of boycotts, strikes, and demonstrations that characterized the mid-1980s and created the last great crisis of apartheid. The rise of the Congress of South African Trade Unions (COSATU), a labor federation closely allied to the UDF and the ANC, made possible a coordination of political and industrial action against the regime that went far beyond any earlier black challenge to apartheid and could be held in check only by an unprecedented (and internationally unacceptable) level of repression.[38]

Did the Black Consciousness movement and the closely related tradition of Pan-Africanism therefore simply shrivel up and die except in the thinking of a minority that was relegated to the periphery of the struggle? Some former advocates of BC who now joined the Charterist movement maintained that their previous persuasion had served its historical function by increasing black self-confidence and willingness to challenge white supremacy but that its racial exclusionism had outlived its usefulness. Since blacks were clearly in charge of the movement and white supporters were deferring to their leadership, the old problem of white paternalism and black deference no longer seemed to exist. Long-standing fears of "alien" Communist domination of the liberation struggle receded in the 1980s as the Soviet Union withdrew from involvement in African conflicts and as the Cold War itself began to wind down. At the same time, the Communists and Marxists of all races who continued to be influential in the organization could be counted upon to fight for a nonracialism compatible with their basic belief that consciousness of class and not of race was the key to revolutionary change.[39]

Black Power and Black Consciousness had a great deal in common, beyond the sharing of slogans like "Black is beautiful" and "Before a group can enter [or create] the open society, it must first close ranks." Perhaps the most durable contribution of both was to instill in many black people a new sense of self-worth and competence that made traditional patterns of racial deference impossible to maintain. The rejection of white leadership and significant participation in the freedom struggle that the two movements shared had more lasting effects in the United States, but the contrast must be qualified by the acknowledgement that a minority has reason to feel more anxious about its ability to determine its own destiny than a majority; it can much more easily find itself the instrument of some other interest than its own. Clearly the ideal of total assimilation into a middle-class society and culture that reflected only European or Euro-American values and historical experiences was now recognized as a confession of cultural inferiority and was no longer an acceptable ambition for blacks in either society. Those in the United States who had been lured by the image of a melting pot of races and nationalities and those in South Africa who had been persuaded by missionaries that Africans could be reborn as white Christians with dark skins had learned that proposing to whiten black people—literally or figuratively—was a genteel way of advocating genocide. On a more practical level the emphasis on community organization and self-help that was common to both movements had empowering consequences. In South Africa the communal resistance of the 1980s built to some extent on the community organizing of the 1970s, much of which was associated with the Black Consciousness movement. In the United States the election of African Americans in substantial and increasing numbers to federal, state, and local offices was the result not simply of voting rights legislation but also of Black Power's call for mobilizing the vote behind black candidates and causes. In 1986 American Black Power asserted itself on behalf of South African liberation when the political clout of African Americans was instrumental in getting Congress to pass, over a presidential veto, strong sanctions against South Africa. On balance, therefore, both movements had healthy and liberating consequences.[40]

But the movements were far from identical, which is scarcely surprising given the fact that the contexts in which they operated were in some ways radically different. The American movement was more diverse and variegated. In a strict sense it was not a single movement at all but several related tendencies of thought and action, ranging from accommodationist "Black Capitalism" to a few attempts at antiwhite terrorism by tiny urban guerrilla groups. Between the fringes the movement divided into ethnic pluralists, separatist nationalists, and revolutionary nationalists. The pluralists were likely to believe that mobilizing blacks as a pressure group could reform America's liberal capitalist system; the separatists wanted to secede from it culturally and, if possible, physically; and the revolutionists envisioned blacks leading an uprising of oppressed peoples and classes to overthrow it. The most militant debated among themselves the importance of a distinctive black culture in group mobilization. For some, cultural autonomy was crucial, almost an end in itself; for others it was a diversion from the politics of making a revolution against American capitalism and imperialism (which would include making appropriate alliances with other oppressed peoples). The Black Consciousness Movement, by contrast, was relatively unified in policy and leadership. It was not entirely monolithic; differences were developing even before the Soweto crisis between those who considered the oppression of blacks purely a matter of race and those who were beginning to perceive that apartheid also had a profound class dimension. But there were no dramatic schisms or major public disagreements within the movement before its suppression in 1977.[41]

This difference reflected the contrast between protest in a liberal democracy with constitutional protection of civil liberties and in a state that permitted some freedom of speech to its white citizens but tried to maintain totalitarian control over black expression. The contrast was not absolute; SNCC, the Black Panthers, and other militant groups were victims of FBI and police harassment, "dirty tricks," and even murderous attacks. But these assaults did not occur until after the groups had worked out and promulgated their basic ideas and programs in relative freedom. The chance to write and speak freely invited a diversity of views about how best to respond to the post–civil rights predicament of blacks and provided ample opportunity for ideological and tactical disagreements. In South Africa, Black Consciousness adherents knew from the beginning that advocacy of violence or even militant nonviolence would lead to immediate proscription. The movement had to walk a tightrope between accommodation to the regime and revolutionary assertion; this balancing act limited the scope of discourse and action. Part of the explanation for the fact that Black Consciousness relied so heavily on churches and church-sponsored organizations as a vehicle for its message was that religious expression was less closely monitored than other forms. In the United States the more charismatic or notorious Black Power advocates had many forums; they were interviewed on television and radio, wrote articles for prominent liberal journals, had their utterances reported (sometimes accurately) in daily newspapers, and published their books with major commercial publishers.

Steve Biko put his finger on the basic difference between the situations faced by the two movements. One embodied—in its most characteristic and durable expressions—the desire of a minority to be included, *but on its own terms*, within a society that it could never dominate. The other reflected the ambition of a majority to rule in its native land. This difference seems so fundamental that the degree of similarity our inquiry has revealed may seem surprising. But numbers are not the whole story. Blacks in South Africa were even more of a minority from the standpoint of the power they were officially allowed to exercise than African Americans. But their potential power was of course much greater. The sense of that potential power, however long it might take to be realized, may be part of the reason why representative expressions of black protest in South Africa since the 1960s have generally seemed to be delivered in a more confident and less angry tone of voice than the equivalent expressions of African American grievance.

From a pragmatic point of view, Black Power was a greater success than Black Consciousness. The pluralist version, especially in its political manifestation, clearly increased the ability of blacks to advance their own interests and defend themselves against racism. Black Consciousness, by contrast, failed to exert sufficient pressure to make apartheid unworkable and was superseded by a movement that played down BC's message of black pride and solidarity. Black Consciousness failed in practical terms because the white minority government of the 1970s was unwilling to allow blacks to acquire the kind of bargaining power that might bring genuine reform and had the strength and ruthlessness to prevent it. BC ideology was eclipsed by Charterism, not only because the ANC offered the strategic advantages already described, but also because the international pressure that the liberation struggle needed to help make the government receptive to basic change could not readily be brought to bear on behalf of a movement that seemed to be espousing black chauvinism. An inestimable advantage that the ANC possessed in its competition with the PAC and Black Consciousness groups for international support was that its official ideology transcended race in the name of a common humanity.

The American civil rights movement had succeeded in overcoming legalized segregation by appealing to a similar, color-blind ideology of human rights that it shared with enough white Americans to constitute a working majority in 1964 and 1965. Its failure to move beyond formal rights to substantive equality provoked the Black Power reaction. In South Africa a comparable failure to move decisively beyond the repeal of apartheid toward the goal of equal opportunities for blacks and whites could also lead to the resurgence of racialism and ethnocentrism among blacks. But a government responsible to a black majority has a better chance of satisfying the aspirations of those who have been victimized by centuries of racism than one that continues to be dominated by descendants of their historic oppressors.

Notes

INTRODUCTION

1. This essay has a complicated history and has been in a constant state of revision for the past seven years. It originated as an address to a plenary session of the American Anthropological Association in November 1989. I was asked to speak generally about the historical meaning of racism, an invitation that forced me to think in broader terms than I had previously found necessary. Shortly thereafter I presented it as a paper at a Newberry Library seminar on race in American history. Publication was supposed to follow, but the projected book of contributions to the seminar never made it into print. In June 1991 I presented a revised version at an international conference on racism in Paris. The proceedings of this conference were published in French, and my paper appeared as "Une histoire comparée du racisme: réflexions générales" in *Racisme et modernité,* ed. Michel Wieviorka (Paris, 1993), 42–53. I gave it in a slightly different form as the keynote address to the first meeting of the American Studies Association of Southern Africa in June 1992 at Pietermaritzburg, South Africa. The USIA, which had helped to sponsor the conference, circulated the proceedings in mimeographed form. I made a lot of copies and gave them to anyone who was interested. Finally, the same text was published as "Reflections on the Comparative History and Sociology of Racism" in a remarkable little magazine devoted to antiracist opinion and scholarship—*Race Traitor,* no. 3 (Spring 1994), 83–98. When I came to revise it for this volume, I expanded it considerably in order to clarify and refine the argument and make it reflect my current thinking about race and racism as fully as possible.

2. George M. Fredrickson, "Thorstein Veblen: The Last Viking," *American Quarterly* 11 (1959), 403–415.

3. George M. Fredrickson, "Ibsen's Antichrist: A Study of *Hedda Gabler*," *Symposium* 12 (1958), 117–132.

4. George M. Fredrickson, *The Inner Civil War: Northern Intellectuals and the Crisis of the Union* (New York, 1965; second ed., Urbana, 1993).

5. I note in chapter 3 that a reading of Hartz's *The Founding of New Societies: Studies in the History of the United States, Latin America, South Africa, Canada, and Australia* (New York, 1964) first piqued my interest in comparisons of the United States and South Africa. The book included essays by specialists on each of the cases treated, and Leonard Thompson's piece on South Africa introduced me to aspects of that country's history that lent themselves to comparison with the United States. But, as indicated later in this introduction, it was Pierre van den Berghe's *Race and Racism* that brought South African white supremacy into my field of vision in a way that compelled me to think seriously about it. My current views on American exceptionalism can also be found in chapter 3.

6. George M. Fredrickson, *The Black Image in the White Mind: The Debate on Afro-American Character and Destiny, 1817–1914* (New York, 1971), 61; Pierre L. van den Berghe, *Race and Racism: A Comparative Perspective* (New York, 1967).

7. George M. Fredrickson, *White Supremacy: A Comparative Study in American and South African History* (New York, 1981), 3–53; James O. Gump, *The Dust Rose Like Smoke: The Subjugation of the Zulu and the Sioux* (Lincoln, Neb., 1994).

8. Two good examples of the effective use of comparative perspective to illuminate one case are Eric Foner, *Nothing but Freedom: Emancipation and Its Legacy* (Baton Rouge, 1983), which relates American slave emancipation to a range of transformations from forced to free labor in other parts of the world; and Alan Dawley, *Struggles for Justice: Social Responsibility and the Liberal State* (Cambridge, Mass., 1991), which highlights special features of the rise of the American liberal state in early to mid–twentieth-century America by comparing it to the growth of state responsibilities in Germany during the same period.

9. A classic example of comparative history of the second kind is Theda Skocpol, *State and Social Revolutions: A Comparative Analysis of France, Russia, and China* (Cambridge, U.K., 1979). For discussions of the methodology employed, see Theda Skocpol, ed., *Vision and Method in Historical Sociology* (Cambridge, U.K., 1984).

10. George M. Fredrickson, *Black Liberation: A Comparative History of Black Ideologies in the United States and South Africa* (New York, 1995).

11. See George M. Fredrickson, "Colonialism and Racism: The United States and South Africa in Comparative Perspective," in George M. Fredrickson, *The Arrogance of Race: Historical Perspectives on Slavery, Racism, and Social Inequality* (Middletown, Conn., 1988).

12. George M. Fredrickson, "White Responses to Emancipation: The American South, Jamaica, and the Cape of Good Hope," in *Arrogance of Race*, 236–253.

13. Fritz Redlich, "Toward a Comparative Historiography: Background and Problems," *Kyklos* 11, no. 3 (1958), 386.

14. A study of the intellectual roots of postmodernism that views aestheti-cism as its defining feature is Allan Megill, *Prophets of Extremity: Neitzche, Heidegger, Foucault, Derrida* (Berkeley, 1985).

15. Pauline Marie Rosenau, *Post-Modernism and the Social Sciences: Insights, Inroads, and Intrusions* (Princeton, 1992), 105.

16. My sense of the logical fallacies of extreme relativism and of radical postmodernism in general has been strongly influenced by Richard J. Bernstein, *The New Constellation: The Ethical-Political Horizon of Modernity/Post-Modernity* (Cambridge, Mass., 1993), as well as by various writings of Jürgen Habermas, especially *The Philosophical Discourse of Modernity*, trans. Frederick G. Lawrence (Cambridge, Mass., 1993).

17. David Harvey, *The Condition of Postmodernity* (Cambridge, Mass., 1990). I am somewhat uncomfortable, however, with the deterministic impli-cations of Harvey's essentially Marxian analysis.

CHAPTER 1

1. Some discussions of the nature of comparative history that present varying definitions and approaches are Fritz Redlich, "Toward a Comparative Historiography: Background and Problems," *Kyklos* 11 (1958), 362–389; William H. Sewell, "Marc Bloch and the Logic of Comparative History," *History and Theory* 6 (1967), 208–218; Robert F. Berkhofer, Jr., *A Behavioral Approach to Historical Analysis* (New York, 1969), 250–269; C. Vann Woodward, "The Comparability of American History," in *The Comparative Approach to American History*, ed. Woodward (New York, 1968), 3–17; Carl Degler, "Comparative History: An Essay Review," *Journal of Southern History* 34 (1968), 425–430; and Maurice Mandelbaum, "Some Forms and Uses of Comparative History," unpublished paper delivered at the Convention of the American Historical Association, San Francisco, 1978.

2. This approach is employed in many of the essays in Woodward, ed., *Comparative Approach*.

3. A large proportion of the articles in the excellent journal *Comparative Studies in Society and History* (1958–) are actually of this nature.

4. Much work in comparative sociology can thus be excluded. A search for uniformities that can be described only on a very abstract plane clearly in-hibits a detailed comparison involving the kinds of variables that historians normally stress.

5. Charles Tilly, Louise Tilly, and Richard Tilly, *The Rebellious Century, 1830–1930* (Cambridge, Mass., 1975), constitutes a major methodological contribution to comparative historical analysis. But the fact that its compar-isons are limited to closely related Western European societies places it outside the scope of this essay.

6. For a defense of the "historicist" approach to comparative history, see Redlich, "Toward a Comparative Historiography." A historian who de-fends the social-scientific mode is Lee Benson. See especially Benson's pro-posal for a comparative approach to the causes of the American Civil War based on "typologies, analytic models, theories of internal war" in *Toward*

the Scientific Study of History: Selected Essays (Philadelphia, 1972), 309–326.

7. *The Dynamics of Modernization: A Study in Comparative History* (New York, 1966).

8. *Social Origins of Dictatorship and Democracy: Lord and Peasant in the Making of the Modern World* (Boston, 1966).

9. Black, *Dynamics of Modernization*, 7.

10. See Cyril E. Black, ed., *Comparative Modernization: A Reader* (New York, 1976).This collection contains some essays on the comparative history of modernization. Particularly notable is "Education and Modernization in Japan and England," by Marius B. Jansen and Laurence Stone (214–237), originally published in *Comparative Studies in Society and History* 9 (1967), 208–232.

11. Cyril E. Black et al., *The Modernization of Japan and Russia: A Comparative Study* (New York, 1975).

12. New York, 1969. Wolf describes and compares agrarian uprisings in Mexico, Russia, China, Vietnam, Algeria, and Cuba.

13. *The Modern World-System: Capitalist Agriculture and the Origins of the European World-Economy in the Sixteenth Century* (New York, 1974). An essay that applies some of the insights of Moore and Wallerstein to the comparative study of revolutions is Theda Skocpol, "France, Russia, and China: A Structural Analysis of Social Revolutions," *Comparative Studies in Society and History*, 18 (1976), 175–210.

14. See especially Walker D. Wyman and Clifton B. Kroeber, eds., *The Frontier in Perspective* (Madison, Wis., 1957); Richard Hofstadter and Seymour Martin Lipset, eds., *Turner and the Sociology of the Frontier* (New York, 1968); and David Harry Miller and Jerome O. Steffen, eds., *The Frontier: Comparative Studies* (Norman, Okla., 1977). Actually most of the essays published or reprinted in these collections are not directly comparative but deal exclusively with individual frontiers. Important exceptions are A. L. Burt, "If Turner Had Looked at Canada, Australia, and New Zealand When He Wrote about the West"(Wyman and Kroeber, 59–77); Marvin W. Mikesell, "Comparative Studies in Frontier History" (Hofstadter and Lipset, 152–171); and David Henry Miller and William W. Savage, Jr., "Ethnic Stereotypes and the Frontier: A Comparative Study of Roman and American Experiences" (Miller and Steffen, 109–137).

15. Billington, "The Frontier," in *Comparative Approach,* ed., Woodward, 77.

16. Lipset, "The Turner Thesis in Comparative Perspective: An Introduction," in *Turner,* ed., Hofstadter and Lipset, 12.

17. Jack D. Forbes, "Frontiers in American History and the Role of the Frontier Historian," *Ethnohistory* 16 (1968), 207.

18. See chapter 2.

19. Hartz, *The Founding of New Societies: Studies in the History of the United States, Latin America, South Africa, Canada, and Australia* (New York, 1964), with contributions by Kenneth D. McRae, Richard M. Morse, Richard N. Rosecrance, and Leonard M. Thompson.

20. Hartz, *The Liberal Tradition in America: An Interpretation of American Political Thought Since the Revolution* (New York, 1955).

21. Hartz, *Founding of New Societies,* 3.

22. Lang, *Conquest and Commerce: Spain and England in the Americas* (New York, 1975).

23. See Frank Tannenbaum, *Slave and Citizen: The Negro in the Americas* (New York, 1946); and Stanley Elkins, *Slavery: A Problem in American Institutional and Intellectual Life* (Chicago, 1959).

24. Klein, *Slavery in the Americas: A Comparative Study of Cuba and Virginia* (Chicago, 1967).

25. Davis, *The Problem of Slavery in Western Culture* (Ithaca, N.Y., 1966), 223–288. A provocative earlier attack on the Tannenbaum-Elkins thesis appeared in Marvin Harris, *Patterns of Race in the Americas* (New York, 1964), 65–94. But its thin documentation and polemical tone limited its influence among historians.

26. Davis, "Slavery," in *Comparative Approach,* ed. Woodward, 130.

27. See Franklin W. Knight, *Slave Society in Cuba during the Nineteenth Century* (Madison, Wis., 1970) and *The African Dimension in Latin American Societies* (New York, 1974), 5–49; Carl N. Degler, *Neither Black nor White: Slavery and Race Relations in Brazil and the United States* (New York, 1971), 25–92; and H. Hoetink, *Slavery and Race Relations in the Americas: An Inquiry into Their Nature and Nexus* (New York, 1973), 3–86.

28. Davis, *Problem of Slavery in Western Culture,* 262.

29. Genovese, "The Treatment of Slaves in Different Countries: Problems in the Application of the Comparative Method," in *Slavery in the New World: A Reader in Comparative History,* ed. Laura Foner and Eugene D. Genovese (Englewood Cliffs, N.J., 1969), 203.

30. Donald L. Horowitz, "Color Differentiation in the American Systems of Slavery," *Journal of Interdisciplinary History* 3 (1973), 509–541.

31. See David W. Cohen and Jack P. Greene, eds., *Neither Slave nor Free: The Freedmen of African Descent in the Slave Societies of the New World* (Baltimore, 1972); Stanley L. Engerman and Eugene D. Genovese, eds., *Race and Slavery in the Western Hemisphere: Quantitative Studies* (Princeton, 1975); and Vera Rubin and Arthur Tuden, eds., *Comparative Perspectives on Slavery in New World Plantation Societies,* Annals of the New York Academy of Science, vol. 292 (New York, 1977).

32. Genovese, *The World the Slaveholders Made: Two Essays in Interpretation* (New York, 1969), 3–113.

33. Toplin, *The Abolition of Slavery in Brazil* (New York, 1971).

34. Toplin, "The Specter of Crisis: Slaveholder Reactions to Abolitionism in the United States and Brazil," *Civil War History* 18 (1972), 129–138.

35. Davis, *The Problem of Slavery in the Age of Revolution, 1770–1823* (Ithaca, N.Y., 1975).

36. George M. Fredrickson, "After Emancipation: A Comparative Study of White Responses to the New Order of Race Relations in the American South, Jamaica, and the Cape Colony of South Africa," and Woodward "The Price of Freedom," in *What Was Freedom's Price?,* ed. David G. Sansing (Jackson, Miss., 1978), 71–92 and 93–113.

37. Wilson, *Power, Racism, and Privilege: Race Relations in Theoretical and Sociohistorical Perspectives* (New York, 1973).

38. *Comparative Studies in History and Society* 16 (1974), 309–328.

39. A study of my own, *White Supremacy: A Comparative Study in American and South African History* (New York, 1981), attempts a detailed and systematic comparison of white-supremacist attitudes, ideologies, and policies.

40. Miers and Kopytoff, eds., *Slavery in Africa: Historical and Anthropological Perspectives* (Madison, Wis., 1977).

41. Cooper, *Plantation Slavery on the East Coast of Africa* (New Haven, 1977), 1–20.

42. By Peter Kolchin, who has presented papers on this topic at historical meetings.

43. London, 1973.

44. Paulson, *Women's Suffrage and Prohibition: A Comparative Study of Equality and Social Control* (Glenview, Ill., 1973).

45. Thompson, *Women in Stuart England and America: A Comparative Study* (Boston, 1974).

46. Rupp, *Mobilizing Women for War: German and American Propaganda, 1939–1945* (Princeton, 1978).

47. Kelley, *The Transatlantic Persuasion: The Liberal Democratic Mind in the Age of Gladstone* (New York, 1969).

48. Higham, "Immigration," in *Comparative Approach,* ed. Woodward, 96–98.

49. Shannon, "Socialism and Labor," in ibid., 238–252.

50. Wilbur R. Miller, *Cops and Bobbies: Police and Authority in New York and London, 1830–1870* (Chicago, 1977).

51. Tom Bowden, *The Breakdown of Public Security: The Case of Ireland, 1916–1921, and Palestine, 1936–1969* (Beverly Hills, Calif., 1977).

52. In addition to the works already cited, however, a small number of comparative essays or articles deserve to be mentioned. Daniel Walker Howe, "The Decline of Calvinism: An Approach to Its Study," *Comparative Studies in Society and History* 14 (1972), 302–327, is a good example of how to compare the fate of a common set of ideas in different societies. C.K. Yardley's "The 'Provincial' Party and the Megalopolises: London, Paris, and New York, 1850–1910," ibid., 15 (1973), 51–88, is an important attempt at comparative urban history, a field that remains surprisingly underdeveloped. John A. Garraty, "The New Deal, National Socialism, and the Great Depression," *American Historical Review* 78 (1973), 907–944, represents the first results of an inquiry into the effects of the Depression on major industrial nations. It demonstrates the usefulness of examining the impact of an international cataclysm, such as a depression or a world war, on two or more comparable societies.

53. Tufts University, however, is in the process of establishing one.

CHAPTER 2

1. The books discussed in this essay are Howard Lamar and Leonard Thompson, eds., *The Frontier in History: North America and Southern Africa Compared* (New Haven, 1981); Richard Elphick and Hermann Giliomee, eds.,

The Shaping of South African Society, 1652–1820 (Cape Town and London, 1979); and Shula Marks and Anthony Atmore, eds., *Economy and Society in Pre-Industrial South Africa* (London, 1980).

   2. Lamar and Thompson, *The Frontier in History,* 7.

   3. Ibid., 188–191.

   4. See for example, Michael Paul Rogin, *Fathers and Children: Andrew Jackson and the Subjugation of the American Indian* (New York, 1975); and Francis Jennings, *The Invasion of America: Indians, Colonialism, and the Cant of Conquest* (Chapel Hill, N.C., 1975).

CHAPTER 3

   1. George M. Fredrickson, "Comparative History," in *The Past before Us: Contemporary Historical Writing in the United States,* ed. Michael Kammen (Ithaca, 1980), 459. This essay is reprinted as chapter 1 of this volume. For a call for a broader definition of comparative history than appears there, see Peter Kolchin, "Comparing American History," *Reviews in American History* 10 (Dec. 1982), 74–75.

   2. Raymond Grew, "The Comparative Weakness of American History," *Journal of Interdisciplinary History* 16 (Summer 1985), 93; Ian Tyrrell, "American Exceptionalism in an Age of International History," *American Historical Review* 96 (Oct. 1991), 1033.

   3. Seymour Martin Lipset, *Continental Divide: The Values and Institutions of the United States and Canada* (New York, 1990).

   4. Aristide R. Zolberg, "How Many Exceptionalisms?," in *Working-Class Formation: Nineteenth Century Patterns in Western Europe and the United States,* ed. Ira Katznelson and Aristide R. Zolberg (Princeton, 1986), 430–431. See also Charles A. Ragin, *The Comparative Method: Moving beyond Qualitative and Quantitative Strategies* (Berkeley, 1987), 17. Norbert MacDonald, *Distant Neighbors: A Comparative History of Seattle and Vancouver* (Lincoln, 1987).

   5. See especially P. B. Evans, D. Rueschmeyer, and T. Skocpol, eds., *Bringing the State Back In* (Cambridge, U.K., 1985).

   6. Liah Greenfield, *Nationalism: Five Roads to Modernity* (Cambridge, Mass., 1993).

   7. Ian Tyrrell, *Woman's World / Woman's Empire: The Women's Christian Temperance Union in International Perspective, 1880–1930* (Chapel Hill, N. C., 1991).

   8. David Brion Davis, *The Problem of Slavery in Western Culture* (Ithaca, N.Y., 1967); David Brion Davis, *The Problem of Slavery in the Age of Revolution, 1770–1823* (Ithaca, N.Y., 1975); George M. Fredrickson, *Black Liberation: A Comparative History of Black Ideologies in the United States and South Africa* (New York, 1995).

   9. This conclusion could be drawn from much recent literature on comparative slavery and race relations, some of which is cited in following notes.

   10. Jean-Claude Lamberti, *Tocqueville and the Two Democracies,* trans. Arthur Goldhammer (Cambridge, Mass., 1989), 2.

11. Louis Hartz, *The Liberal Tradition in America* (New York, 1955).

12. Louis Hartz, *The Founding of New Societies: Studies in the History of the United States, Latin America, South Africa, Canada, and Australia,* with contributions by Kenneth D. McRae, Richard M. Morse, Richard N. Rosecrance, and Leonard M. Thompson (New York, 1964). My interest in the comparative history of the United States and South Africa was awakened by *The Founding of New Societies.*

13. See Frank Tannenbaum, *Slave and Citizen: The Negro in the Americas* (New York, 1946); and Stanley M. Elkins, *Slavery: A Problem in American Institutional and Intellectual Life* (Chicago, 1959).

14. Marvin Harris, *Patterns of Race in the Americas* (New York, 1964); Davis, *Problem of Slavery in Western Culture,* 233–288; Carl Degler, *Neither Black nor White: Slavery and Race Relations in Brazil and the United States* (New York, 1971).

15. Degler, *Neither Black nor White,* 226–232.

16. Alexis de Tocqueville, *Democracy in America,* ed. Phillips Bradley, trans. Henry Reeve (2 vols., New York, 1948), I, 373–374, quoted in Degler, *Neither Black nor White,* 258–259. (The first bracketed phrase is Degler's.) Other works of the 1970s that linked the growth of democracy and the rise of racism (without making explicit or extensive comparisons) include George M. Fredrickson, *The Black Image in the White Mind: The Debate on Afro-American Character and Destiny, 1817–1914* (New York, 1971); and Edmund S. Morgan, *American Slavery—American Freedom: The Ordeal of Colonial Virginia* (New York, 1975).

17. Ross Evans Paulson, *Women's Suffrage and Prohibition: A Comparative Study of Equality and Social Control* (Glenview, 1973); Richard J. Evans, *The Feminists: Women's Emancipation Movements in Europe, America, and Australasia, 1840–1920* (London, 1977).

18. Stanley Greenberg, *Race and State in Capitalist Development* (New Haven, Conn., 1980); George M. Fredrickson, *White Supremacy: A Comparative Study in American and South African History* (New York, 1981); John Cell, *The Highest Stage of White Supremacy: The Origins of Segregation in South Africa and the American South* (Cambridge, U.K., 1982).

19. I compare my work with that of Cell and Greenberg and discuss the special features of my interpretation in George M. Fredrickson, *The Arrogance of Race: Historical Perspectives on Slavery, Racism, and Social Inequality* (Middletown, 1988), 254–269.

20. I deal with some of these issues in Fredrickson, *Black Liberation.* The case for black agency in emancipation and Reconstruction is effectively made in Eric Foner, *Reconstruction: America's Unfinished Revolution, 1863–1877* (New York, 1988).

21. Peter Kolchin, *Unfree Labor: American Slavery and Russian Serfdom* (Cambridge, Mass., 1987); Shearer Davis Bowman, *Masters and Lords: Mid-19th-Century U.S. Planters and Prussian Junkers* (New York, 1993). See chapter 4 for a detailed discussion of these works.

22. Ann Shola Orloff and Theda Skocpol, "Why Not Equal Protection? Explaining the Politics of Public Spending in Britain, 1900–1911, and the United States, 1880s to 1920," *American Sociological Review* 49 (Dec. 1984),

726–750; Ann Shola Orloff, *The Politics of Pensions: A Comparative Analysis of Britain, Canada, and the United States, 1880–1940* (Madison, 1993); Theda Skocpol, *Protecting Soldiers and Mothers: The Political Origins of Social Policy in the United States* (Cambridge, Mass., 1992).

23. On the method, see Theda Skocpol and Margaret Somers, "The Uses of Comparative History in Macrosocial Inquiry," *Comparative Studies in Society and History* 22 (April 1980), 174–197.

24. The work of Ann Shola Orloff and Theda Skocpol draws on Stephen Skowronek, *Building a New American State: The Expansion of National Administrative Capacities, 1877–1920* (New York, 1982). On this explanation of American distinctiveness, see Orloff, *Politics of Pensions,* 215–217.

25. Daniel Levine, *Poverty and Society: The Growth of the American Welfare State in International Comparison* (New Brunswick, 1988).

26. Greenfield, *Nationalism,* 19.

27. Jack A. Goldstone, *Revolution and Rebellion in the Modern World* (Berkeley, 1991), 49. In *White Supremacy,* I found that material interests played a more important role in the making of South African segregation than in the rise of Jim Crow in the South. However, Cell, in *The Highest Stage of White Supremacy,* assumed similar patterns of causation—which he derived from the neo-Marxist historiography on South Africa.

28. This is what I have attempted to do in *Black Liberation.*

29. Alisa Klaus, *Every Child a Lion: The Origins of Maternal and Infant Health Policy in the United States and France, 1890–1920* (Ithaca, 1993). For a summary of some of her findings, see Alisa Klaus, "Depopulation and Race Suicide: Maternalism and Pronatalist Ideologies in France and the United States," in *Mothers of the New World: Maternalist Politics and the Origins of Welfare States,* ed. Seth Koven and Sonya Michel (New York, 1993), 188–212, esp. 188–189. The other essays in this collection deal with single cases, although the editors make some comparative observations in their introduction.

30. Olive Banks, *Faces of Feminism: A Study of Feminism as a Social Movement* (Oxford, 1981). A more recent comparison of British and American feminism makes a commendable effort to deal with differences as well as commonalities. Unfortunately, it came to my attention too late to be discussed in this essay. See Christine Bolt, *The Women's Movements in the United States and Britain from the 1790s to the 1920s* (Hemel Hempstead, U.K., 1993).

31. Donald Meyer, *Sex and Power: The Rise of Women in America, Russia, Sweden, and Italy* (Middletown, Conn., 1987).

32. John Dower, *War without Mercy: Race and Power in the Pacific War* (New York, 1986).

33. See, for example, Alan Dawley, *Class and Community: The Industrial Revolution in Lynn* (Cambridge, Mass., 1976); and Sean Wilentz, *Chants Democratic: New York City and the Rise of the American Working Class* (New York, 1984).

34. Katznelson and Zolberg, eds., *Working-Class Formation.*

35. Jeffrey Haydu, *Between Craft and Class: Skilled Workers and Factory Politics in the United States and Britain, 1890–1922* (Berkeley, 1988).

CHAPTER 4

1. Peter Kolchin, *Unfree Labor: American Slavery and Russian Serfdom* (Cambridge, Mass., 1987), and Shearer Davis Bowman, *Masters and Lords: Mid-19th-Century U.S. Planters and Russian Junkers* (New York, 1993).

CHAPTER 5

1. Michael Banton, *Race Relations* (New York, 1967), 8; Pierre van den Berghe, *Race and Racism: A Comparative Perspective* (New York 1967), 11. Recognizing the narrowness and limited applicability of his definition, Banton used the term "racialism" to cover the attitudinal and institutional aspects of racial domination, and van den Berghe's perceptive treatment of the sociohistorical role of race in the United States, Brazil, Mexico, and South Africa took account of the implicit or assumed character of racism in situations where its full ideological expression was absent or muted. But neither transcended the notion that a belief in genetic or biological determinism had to be present.

2. Richard J. Herrnstein and Charles Murray, *The Bell Curve: Intelligence and Class Structure in American Life* (New York, 1994); Dinesh D'Souza, *The End of Racism: Principles for a Multiracial Society* (New York, 1995). See also my review of D'Souza, *New York Review of Books,* 19 October 1995, 10–15.

3. George M. Fredrickson, *The Arrogance of Race: Historical Perspectives on Slavery, Racism, and Social Inequality* (Middletown, Conn., 1988), 189–205. This essay on "The Social Origins of American Racism" was originally published in 1971.

4. Barbara J. Fields, "Ideology and Race in American History," in *Region, Race, and Reconstruction: Essays in Honor of C. Vann Woodward,* ed. J. Morgan Kousser and James M. McPherson (New York, 1982), 150–151.

5. Max Weber, *Economy and Society: An Outline of Interpretive Sociology,* ed. Guenther Roth and Claus Wittich (Berkeley, 1978), 385–398, 926–939.

6. Donald L. Horowitz, *Ethnic Groups in Conflict* (Berkeley, 1985), 41–54.

7. See John Rex, "The Concept of Race in Sociological Theory," in *Race and Racialism,* ed. Sam Zubaida (London, 1970), 35–55.

8. On the Barakhumin as a minority caste analogous to African Americans in their social position and the problems they face, see John Ogbu, *Minority Education and Caste* (New York, 1978).

9. See F. James Davis, *Who Is Black? One Nation's Definition* (University Park, Pa., 1991).

10. Fredrickson, *The Arrogance of Race,* 210–211; Herbert Blumer, "Race Prejudice as a Sense of Group Position," *Pacific Sociological Review* 1 (1958), 3–7.

11. See David R. Roediger, *The Wages of Whiteness: Race in the Making of the American Working Class* (London, 1991); and *Toward the Abolition of Whiteness: Essays on Race, Politics, and Working Class History* (London, 1994).

12. See Carl Degler, *Neither Black nor White: Slavery and Race Relations in Brazil and the United States* (New York, 1971); Marvin Harris, *Patterns of Race in the Americas* (New York, 1964); and Eric Foner, *Reconstruction: America's Unfinished Revolution* (New York, 1988).

13. For an example of the effective use of the Weberian triad to analyze race politics, see Ira Katznelson, *Black Men, White Cities: Race, Politics, and Migration in the United States, 1900–1930, and Britain, 1948–1968* (London, 1973).

14. On the complicated and sometimes antagonistic relationship between nationalism and racism, see Benedict Anderson, *Imagined Communities: Reflections on the Origin and Spread of Nationalism* (London, 1983).

15. See I. K. Sundiatta, "Late Twentieth Century Patterns of Race Relations in Brazil and the United States," *Phylon* 48 (1987), 62–76.

16. On the ideological shifts and their significance, see Stanley Greenberg, *Legitimating the Illegitimate: State, Markets, and Resistance in South Africa* (Berkeley, 1987), and Julie Frederikse, *The Unbreakable Thread: Non-racialism in South Africa* (Bloomington, Ind., 1990).

17. W.E.B. Du Bois, *Dusk of Dawn: An Essay toward the Autobiography of a Race Concept* (New York, 1940), chap. 7; *Report of the National Advisory Commission on Civil Disorders* (New York, 1968), 1.

18. William Julius Wilson, *The Declining Significance of Race: Blacks and Changing American Institutions* (Chicago, 1978); and *The Truly Disadvantaged: The Inner City, the Underclass, and Public Policy* (Chicago, 1987).

CHAPTER 6

1. See Harvey Mansfield's foreword to Pierre Manent, *Tocqueville and the Nature of Democracy* (London, 1996).

2. The revival of the Tocquevillian view of the French Revolution was manifested in François Furet, *Penser la Révolution française* (Paris, 1978). On Tocqueville's "unwitting" contribution to the exceptionalist view of the American past that prevailed in the 1940s and 1950s see George M. Fredrickson, "From Exceptionalism to Variability: Recent Developments in Cross-National Comparative History," *Journal of American History* 82 (September 1995), 591–594. A prime example of the use of Tocqueville to support the liberal consensus view of American history is Louis Hartz, *The Liberal Tradition in America* (New York, 1955).

3. Jean-Claude Lamberti, *Tocqueville and the Two Democracies,* trans. Arthur Goldhammer (Cambridge, Mass., 1989), 134, 176, and passim.

4. Alexis de Tocqueville, *Democracy in America,* trans. George Lawrence, ed. J. P. Mayer (Garden City, 1969); Lamberti, *Tocqueville and the Two Democracies,* 2–4 and passim.

5. Tocqueville's generalizations about the dangers of privatism and statism in a democratic society in volume two of *Democracy in America* are, as Lamberti points out, based mainly on his perception of French tendencies.

6. Roger Boesche, *The Strange Liberalism of Alexis de Tocqueville* (Ithaca, N.Y., 1987); Adam S. Kahan, *Aristocratic Liberalism: The Social and Political Thought of Jacob Burkhardt, John Stuart Mill, and Alexis de Tocqueville* (New York, 1992).

7. See chapters 6 and 7 of Frederick Merk, *Manifest Destiny and Mission in American History* (New York, 1963). Similar qualms about the futility of

uplifting "inferior races" reemerged as a theme of American anti-imperialist discourse at the end of the century.

8. See Joseph-Arthur de Gobineau, *Essai sur l'inégalité des races humaines* (Paris, 1853–1855). An English translation was published in the United States in 1856.

9. Alexis de Tocqueville, *Selected Letters on Politics and Society*, ed. Roger Boesche (Berkeley, 1985), 297–301, 342–344.

10. James T. Schleifer, *The Making of Tocqueville's Democracy in America* (Chapel Hill, N. C., 1980), 45–46, 66–67.

11. Tocqueville, *Democracy in America*, 317–320.

12. Ibid, 321–339 (quote on 327).

13. Ibid, 340–363 (quotes on 341, 342, 356). On the concept of *Herrenvolk* democracy, see George M. Fredrickson, *The Black Image in the White Mind: The Debate on Afro-American Character and Destiny, 1817–1914* (Middletown, Conn., 1987, orig. pub. 1971), 61–64 and passim.

14. Tocqueville, *Democracy in America*, 257, 356. One striking example of liberal pessimism about black-white equality is the racial thought of Abraham Lincoln. See George M. Fredrickson, *The Arrogance of Race: Historical Perspectives on Slavery, Racism, and Social Inequality* (Middletown, Conn., 1988), 54–72. For a recent manifestation see Andrew Hacker, *Two Nations: Black and White, Separate, Hostile, and Unequal* (New York, 1992).

15. Tocqueville, *Democracy in America*, 316.

16. Quoted in Tzvetan Todorov, *On Human Diversity: Nationalism, Racism, and Exoticism in French Thought*, trans. Catherine Porter (Cambridge, Mass., 1993), 192.

17. For a good account of Tocqueville's views on slavery in the French colonies, see Matthew Mancini, *Alexis De Tocqueville* (New York, 1994). 103–119 (quote on 115).

18. My discussion of Tocqueville's views on Algeria is based on Melvin Richter, "Tocqueville on Algeria," *Review of Politics* 35 (1963), 362–398; André Jardin, *Tocqueville*, trans. Lydia Davis and Robert Hemenway (New York, 1988), 318–342; Alexis de Tocqueville, *De la colonie en Algérie*, ed. Tzvetan Todorov (Paris 1988); and Todorov, *On Human Diversity*, 191–207.

19. Richter, "Tocqueville on Algeria," 385; Todorov, *On Human Diversity*, 194–202; Tocqueville, *Algérie*, 60–61.

20. Richter, "Tocqueville on Algeria," 381–388; Todorov, *On Human Diversity*, 195–196.

21. Richter, "Tocqueville on Algeria," 364; Todorov, *On Human Diversity*, 199–202.

22. Tocqueville, *Algérie*, 53–54.

23. Tocqueville, *Algérie*, 141–142; Richter, "Tocqueville on Algeria," 375.

24. Quoted in Jardin, *Tocqueville*, 322.

25. Tocqueville, *Algérie*, 178–179; Richter, "Tocqueville on Algeria," 367. (I use Richter's translation of this remarkable passage.)

CHAPTER 7

1. Among the major studies comparing slavery in the United States and Latin America are Frank Tannenbaum, *Slave and Citizen: The Negro in the Americas* (New York, 1946); Marvin Harris, *Patterns of Race in the Americas* (New York, 1964); Herbert S. Klein, *Slavery in the Americas: A Comparative Study of Cuba and Virginia* (Chicago, 1967); David Brion Davis, *The Problem of Slavery in Western Culture* (Ithaca, N.Y., 1966), 223–288; Carl N. Degler, *Neither Black Nor White: Slavery and Race Relations in Brazil and the United States* (New York, 1971); and *Comparative Perspectives on Slavery in New World Plantation Societies,* ed. Vera Rubin and Arthur Tuden (New York, 1977). For comparisons with slavery in South Africa, see George M. Fredrickson, *White Supremacy: A Comparative Study in American and South African History* (New York, 1981), 54–135. Comparative perspectives on slavery elsewhere in Africa can be found in *Slavery in Africa: Historical and Anthropological Perspectives,* ed. Suzanne Miers and Igor Kopytoff (Madison, Wis., 1977); Frederick Cooper, *Plantation Slavery on the East Coast of Africa* (New Haven, Conn., 1977); and *The End of Slavery in Africa,* ed. Suzanne Miers and Richard Roberts (Madison, Wis., 1988). The latest extension of the scope of comparative slavery studies is Peter Kolchin, *Unfree Labor: American Slavery and Russian Serfdom* (Cambridge, Mass., 1987).

2. Although they disagree sharply on whether or not how slaves were treated had a determining effect on postemancipation race relations, or indeed on the question of what, if any differences there were in the harshness or leniency of servitude in the areas being compared, the books cited in note 1 by Tannenbaum, Harris, Klein, and Degler all attribute the creation of enduring racial patterns to the kinds of distinctions and modes of stratification that developed in the context of a slave society.

3. See *The Destruction of Slavery,* series 1, vol. 1 of *Freedom: A Documentary History of Emancipation,* ed. Ira Berlin et al. (Cambridge, U.K., 1985).

4. William Julius Wilson's work drew my attention to how an increase of black resources during World War II made effective protest more likely in the postwar period. See *Power, Racism, and Privilege: Race Relations in Theoretical and Socio-Historical Perspective* (New York, 1973), 122–127.

5. See Aldon D. Morris, *The Origins of the Civil Rights Movement: Black Communities Organizing for Change* (New York, 1984).

6. My view of current black-white relations has been influenced by two books by William Julius Wilson, *The Declining Significance of Race: Blacks and Changing American Institutions* (Chicago, 1978) and *The Truly Disadvantaged: The Inner City Underclass and Public Policy* (Chicago, 1987). I agree with Wilson that economic class has become relatively more important in recent years as a determinant of black disadvantage but would not go quite so far as he does in deemphasizing the current role of racial attitudes. Racial prejudice continues to exist and may never entirely disappear, but it can be made less harmful and even neutralized to a considerable extent by successful efforts to empower blacks economically and politically.

7. Florestan Fernandes, *The Negro in Brazilian Society* (New York, 1971), 210–220; and I.K. Sundiatta, "Late Twentieth Century Patterns of Race Relations in Brazil and the United States," *Phylon* 48 (1987), 71.

8. See Degler, *Neither Black nor White*.

9. Fernandes, *Negro in Brazilian Society*, 300–301, 416–417, 430.

10. Fredrickson, *White Supremacy*, 239–254.

11. This point is made by Shula Marks in *The Ambiguities of Dependence: Class, Nationalism, and the State in Twentieth-Century Natal* (Baltimore, Md., 1986), 5.

12. Fredrickson, *White Supremacy*, 255–281.

13. Ibid., passim.

14. Recent works on the connection of black America and black South Africa include the following: J. Mutero Chirenje, *Ethiopianism and Afro-Americans in Southern Africa, 1883–1916* (Baton Rouge, 1987); James Campbell, "Our Fathers, Our Children: A History of the African Methodist Episcopal Church in the United States and South Africa," unpublished Ph.D. dissertation, Stanford University, 1989; William Manning Marable, "African Nationalist: the Life of John Langalibele Dube," unpublished Ph.D. dissertation, the University of Maryland, 1976; Robert A. Hill and Gregory A. Pirio, "Africa for the Africans: the Garvey Movement in South Africa, 1930–1940," in *The Politics of Race, Class, and Nationalism in Twentieth-Century South Africa*, ed. Shula Marks and Stanley Trapido (New York, 1987); Tim Couzens, "Johannesburg, 1918–1936," in *Industrialization and Social Change in South Africa: African Class Formation, Culture, and Consciousness, 1870–1930*, ed. Shula Marks and Richard Rathbone (London, 1982); and David B. Coplan, *In Township Tonight! South Africa's Black City Music and Theatre* (New York, 1985).

15. These generalizations and those that follow are based on work in progress.

CHAPTER 8

1. See George M. Fredrickson, *White Supremacy: A Comparative Study in American and South African History* (New York, 1981); Idem, *The Arrogance of Race: Historical Perspectives on Slavery, Racism, and Social Inequality* (Middletown, Conn., 1988), 216–269; John W. Cell, *The Highest Stage of White Supremacy: The Origins of Segregation in South Africa and the American South* (Cambridge, U.K., 1982); and Stanley B. Greenberg, *Race and State in Capitalist Development* (New Haven, Conn., 1980).

2. Fredrickson, *White Supremacy*, xx.

3. *Black Liberation: A Comparative History of Black Ideologies in the United States and South Africa* (New York, 1995).

4. Thomas Karis and Gail M. Gerhart, *Challenge and Violence*, vol. 3 of *From Protest to Challenge: A Documentary History of African Politics in South Africa*, ed. Thomas Karis and Gwendolen M. Carter (Stanford, Calif., 1977), 205.

5. See Fredrickson, *Black Liberation*, chaps. 2, 4, 7 for surveys of the history of black separatism in the United States and references to the principal secondary sources on this ideological tradition.

6. See ibid., chaps. 2 and 4; J. Mutero Chirinje, *Ethiopianism and Afro-Americans in Southern Africa, 1883–1916* (Baton Rouge, 1987); Robert Edgar, "Garveyism in Africa: Dr. Wellington and the American Movement in the Transkei," *Ufahumu* 6 (1) (1976), 31–57.

7. Thomas Karis, *Hope and Challenge,* vol. 2 of *From Protest to Challenge,* ed. Karis and Carter (Stanford, 1973), 328.

8. See Fredrickson, *Black Liberation,* chap. 7; Gail M. Gerhart, *Black Power in South Africa: The Evolution of an Ideology* (Berkeley, 1978); Robert M. Fatton, *Black Consciousness in South Africa: The Dialectics of Ideological Resistance to White Supremacy* (Albany, 1986); and N. Barney Pityana et al., *The Bounds of Possibility: The Legacy of Steve Biko and the Black Consciousness Movement* (Cape Town, 1991).

9. See Fredrickson, *Black Liberation,* chap. 5, for a full discussion of these and subsequent efforts of Communists to put themselves in the forefront of black liberation struggles in the United States and South Africa. The notes for this chapter contain references to the major secondary sources on blacks and Communism in the two societies during the period between the mid twenties and the late forties.

10. See Robin D. G. Kelley, *Hammer and Hoe: Alabama Communists during the Great Depression* (Chapel Hill, N.C., 1990).

11. See Fredrickson, *Black Liberation,* chap. 6. The fullest account of black political thought and action during the postwar era is Tom Lodge, *Black Politics in South Africa since 1945* (London, 1983).

12. Adam Fairclough, *To Redeem the Soul of America: The Southern Christian Leadership Conference and Martin Luther King, Jr.,* (Athens, Ga., 1987), 7–8 and passim.

13. For a full discussion of the evolution of Black Power ideology, see Fredrickson, *Black Liberation,* chap. 7, and John T. McCartney, *Black Power Ideologies: An Essay in African-American Political Thought* (Philadelphia, 1992).

14. See Stokely Carmichael and Charles V. Hamilton, *Black Power: The Politics of Liberation in America* (New York, 1967), 44–56.

15. On King's embrace of social radicalism, see especially David Garrow, *Bearing the Cross: Martin Luther King, Jr., and the Southern Christian Leadership Conference* (New York, 1986), 527–624.

16. Steve Biko, *Black Consciousness in South Africa,* ed. Arnold Mallard (New York, 1978), 98.

17. See Gerhart, *Black Power,* 257–299.

18. A good account of South African developments in the 1980s is contained in Anthony Marx, *Lessons of Struggle: South African Internal Opposition to Apartheid, 1960–1990* (New York, 1992).

19. For a discussion of the expert opinion of the late 1980s, see George M. Fredrickson, "Can South Africa Change?," *New York Review of Books,* 26 October 1989, 48–56.

CHAPTER 9

1. This dissertation has been published in David J. Garrow, ed., *Martin Luther King and the Civil Rights Movement,* vol. 1 (Brooklyn, 1989), 58–126.

2. Peter Walshe, *The Rise of African Nationalism in South Africa: The African National Congress, 1912–1952* (Berkeley, 1971), 13.

3. See Robert A. Hill and Gregory Pirio, "'Africa for the Africans': The Garvey Movement in South Africa," in *The Politics of Race and Class in Twentieth-Century South Africa*, ed. Shula Marks and Stanley Trapido (London, 1987), 209–253.

4. These connections are revealed in the Xuma papers at the University of Witwatersrand in Johannesburg.

5. See Gail M. Gerhart, *Black Power in South Africa: The Evolution of an Ideology* (Berkeley, 1978), 273–281.

6. Julie Frederikse, *The Unbreakable Thread: Non-Racialism in South Africa* (Bloomington, Ind., 1990).

7. James H. Cone, *Martin & Malcolm & America: A Dream or a Nightmare* (Maryknoll, N.Y., 1991), 209, 258.

8. *The Autobiography of Malcolm X,* with the assistance of Alex Haley (New York, 1965), 27.

9. See Cone's *Black Theology and Black Power* (New York, 1969), and *A Black Theology of Liberation* (Philadelphia, 1970).

10. See Dwight N. Hopkins, *Black Theology, U.S.A. and South Africa* (Maryknoll, N.Y.), 1989.

11. Cone, *Martin & Malcom,* 108.

12. The radicalization of King's social thought is demonstrated in David J. Garrow, *Bearing the Cross: Martin Luther King, Jr., and the Southern Christian Leadership Conference* (New York, 1986).

13. Cone, *Martin & Malcolm,* 213–214, 226, 234–235.

14. Ibid., 294.

15. Ibid., 15.

16. Ibid., 211.

17. Frederikse, *Unbreakable Thread,* 100.

18. See Louise Kretzchmar, *The Voice of Black Theology in South Africa* (Johannesburg, 1986).

19. Frederikse, *Unbreakable Thread,* 161.

20. Benjamin Pogrund, *Sobukwe and Apartheid* (New Brunswick, N.J.), 1991. See also Donald Woods, *Biko* (New York, 1979).

21. For a detailed discussion of the debates of the 1950s, see chap. 11.

22. Pogrund, *Sobukwe,* 252.

23. See Tom Lodge, *Black Politics in South Africa since 1945* (London, 1983), 201–230.

24. Ibid., 210–223, is an example of the less flattering assessments of how helpful the liberals really were.

25. Pogrund, *Sobukwe,* 205.

26. In a pamphlet of 1966, the Liberal party called for "a combination of private enterprise and public ownership" and a program for redistributing land to African peasants. Two years later the party dissolved rather than comply with a new law prohibiting interracial political organizations.

27. Pogrund, *Sobukwe,* 231.

28. Ibid., 253.

29. Garrow, *Bearing the Cross*, 405.

30. Quoted in Hugh Davis Graham, *The Civil Rights Era* (New York, 1990), 174.

CHAPTER 10

1. The standard historical account of the South African movement of the 1950s can be found in Tom Lodge, *Black Politics in South Africa since 1945* (London, 1983), 33–230. A valuable sociological analysis written at the time is Leo Kuper, *Passive Resistance in South Africa* (London, 1956). Documents relating to the struggle can be found in Thomas Karis and Gwendolen M. Carter, eds., *From Protest to Challenge: A Documentary History of African Politics in South Africa, 1882–1964*, vols. 2 and 3 (Stanford, Calif., 1973, 1977).

2. A vast historical literature on the civil rights movement now exists. A good overview is Harvard Sitkoff, *The Struggle for Black Equality, 1952–1980* (New York, 1981). A selection of interpretive essays by some of the most prominent historians of the movement is Charles W. Eagles, ed., *The Civil Rights Movement in America* (Jackson, Miss., 1986).

3. African American influence on black political thought in South Africa before the apartheid era is detailed in Peter Walshe, *The Rise of African Nationalism in South Africa: The African National Congress, 1912–1952* (Berkeley, 1971). On the black American religious connection with South Africa, see J. Mutero Chirenje, *Ethiopianism and Afro-Americans in Southern Africa, 1883–1916* (Baton Rouge, 1987), and James T. Campbell, "Our Fathers, Our Children: The African Methodist Episcopal Church in the United States and South Africa," (unpublished Ph.D. dissertation, Stanford University, 1989). I explore some of these connections in *Black Liberation: A Comparative History of Black Ideologies in the United States and South Africa* (New York, 1995).

4. Harold R. Isaacs's study of black Negro opinion on Africa, *The New World of Negro Americans* (New York, 1964), suggests that awareness of Africa increased during the 1950s, but that most of it was focused on West Africa and especially on Kwame Nkrumah and the successful movement for independence in Ghana. My own impression from a variety of sources is that intense interest in South Africa did not develop until after Sharpeville. On the petition of the Council on African Affairs, see Gerald Horne, *Black and Red: W.E.B. Du Bois and the Afro–American Response to the Cold War* (Albany, 1986), 185. A review of *The Crisis* for 1952 and 1953 (vols. 59, 60) turned up a number of references to the injustices perpetrated by the government under the banner of apartheid, but the only way readers would have known about the Defiance Campaign was from publication in January 1953 of the text of the petition to the United Nations. See *The Crisis* 60, 38.

5. On the fate of the March on Washington Movement, see especially Paula F. Pfeffer, *A. Philip Randolph, Pioneer of the Civil Rights Movement* (Baton Rouge, 1990), passim. The effect of McCarthyism on CORE is described in August Meier and Elliott Rudwick, *CORE: A Study in the Civil Rights Movement, 1942–1968* (New York, 1973), 63–71.

6. Interactions between African American and black South African ideologies and movements are dealt with in some detail in my *Black Liberation*. On the South African bus boycotts of the mid 1950s, see Lodge, *Black Politics*, 153–187. For King's comments on the South African boycott, see *The Christian Century*, 10 April 1957, 447. The one tenuous link I have been able to find between South African nonviolence and Montgomery is the reference to the use of Gandhi's methods in South Africa in a November 1955 speech by Harris Wofford that was brought to King's attention at the beginning of the boycott. The speech is printed for the first time in David Garrow, ed., *We Shall Overcome: The Civil Rights Movement in the 1950's and 60's*, vol. 3 (Brooklyn, 1989), 1151–1162 (Reference to South Africa on 1160).

7. Works that emphasize Gandhi's influence on King include David Levering Lewis, *King: A Biography* (Urbana, 1970); John J. Ansbro, *Martin Luther King, Jr.: The Making of a Mind* (Maryknoll, N.Y., 1982); and James P. Hanigan, *Martin Luther King, Jr., and the Foundations of Nonviolence* (Lanham, Md., 1984). Taylor Branch argues in *Parting the Waters: America in the King Years, 1954–1963* (New York, 1988), that King modified Gandhi's ideas in the light of Reinhold Niebuhr's critique of them. The Gandhian statements of purpose for SCLC and SNCC can be found in Miller, Rudwick, and Broderick, eds., *Black Protest Thought in the Twentieth Century* (Indianapolis, 1971), 302–308. An examination of nonviolence in South Africa that stresses the use of a Gandhian model is Leo Kuper, *Passive Resistance*.

8. See David Garrow, *Bearing the Cross: Martin Luther King, Jr., and the Southern Christian Leadership Conference* (New York, 1986), 66–73, and Adam Fairclough, *To Redeem the Soul of America: The Southern Christian Leadership Conference and Martin Luther King, Jr.* (Athens, Ga., 1987), 23–26, for accounts of how Glenn Smiley of FOR and Bayard Rustin, one of the founders of CORE, persuaded King to adopt an explicitly Gandhian rationale for the Montgomery bus boycott during its early days. The image of Gandhi in the black American consciousness is ably described in Sudarshan Kapur, *Raising Up a Prophet: The African-American Encounter with Gandhi* (Boston, 1992).

9. On Gandhi in South Africa see Maureen Swan, *Gandhi: The South African Experience* (Johannesburg, 1985). Early ANC interest in nonviolence is shown in Karis and Carter, *From Protest to Challenge*, vol. 1, 62, 65–66, 108. There is no authoritative readily available history of the Indian Passive Resistance Campaign, but much can be learned about it from recent collections of the speeches and writings of its two principal leaders. See Dr. Joseph M. Dadoo, *His Speeches, Articles, and Correspondence with Mahatma Gandhi* (Durban, 1991), and *Monty Speaks: Speeches of Dr. G. M. (Monty) Naiker* (Durban, 1991).

10. See Dan T. Carter, *Scottsboro: A Tragedy of the American South* (London, 1973), 248–251 for an account of the Communist Party's "March on Washington" of 1931 to protest the Scottsboro verdict. For other examples of Communist-led nonviolent protest in the 1930s, see Mark Nason, *Communists in Harlem during the Depression* (Urbana, Ill., 1983), passim, and Sinclair

Drake and Horace R. Cayton, *Black Metropolis: A Study of Negro Life in a Northern City* (New York, 1962), vol. 1, 85–88.

11. See Pfeffer, *Randolph,* 45–88 and passim. For discussions of the realistic side of King's use of nonviolence, see Garrow, *Bearing the Cross,* 273–274; Branch, *Parting the Waters,* 85–87; and Fairclough, *To Redeem the Soul,* 51–53. Garrow argues that King began as a naive Gandhian, but Branch and Fairclough believe that King had always been committed to a practical or realistic conception of nonviolent action.

12. On the ANC Youth League and the Programme of Action, see Walshe, *Rise of African Nationalism,* 349–361, and Karis and Carter, *From Protest to Challenge,* vol. 2, 301–339.

13. *Speeches of Albert John Luthuli* (Durban, 1991), 41–44 and passim. See also Luthuli, *Let My People Go: An Autobiography* (London, 1962). Despite the spelling that appears in both of these titles, 'Lutuli' is now generally accepted as correct.

14. Carter and Karis, eds., *From Protest to Challenge,* vol. 2, 487.

15. Quoted in Lewis, *King,* 93.

16. See Leo Kuper, *An African Bourgeoisie: Race, Class, and Politics in South Africa* (New Haven, Conn., 1965), 101–103 and passim, and Alan Cobley, *Class and Consciousness: The Black Petty Bourgeoisie in South Africa, 1924 to 1950* (New York, 1990).

17. Steven M. Millner, "The Montgomery Bus Boycott: A Case Study in the Emergence and Career of a Social Movement," in *The Walking City: The Montgomery Bus Boycott,* ed. David Garrow (Brooklyn, 1989), 512–513.

18. The localized basis for the southern movement is set forth effectively in Aldon D. Morris, *The Origins of the Civil Rights Movement: Black Communities Organizing for Change* (New York, 1984). My view of the South African movement derives principally from Lodge, *Black Politics.* Lodge discusses the peculiarities of the Eastern Cape on 45–60 and passim.

19. See Lodge, *Black Politics,* 170–171 on the ANC's failure in Alexandria. My understanding of how SCLC operated is based primarily on Morris, *Origins* and Fairclough, *To Redeem the Soul.*

20. Morris in *Origins* emphasizes the local religious basis of the Civil Rights movement, but note also the critique of Morris's argument by Clayborne Carson in *Constitutional Commentary* 3 (Summer 1986), 616–621. Carson believes that Morris "should have discussed the conflicts within the church regarding racial militancy and noted the large number—perhaps a majority—of southern black clergymen who did not become active in the Civil Rights movement or allow their churches to be used for civil rights meetings." (620–621). Lodge in *Black Politics* describes the grass-roots religiosity of the Defiance Campaign on 43–44 and the PAC's overture to the Independent African Churches on 81. The subject of religious influences on the South African protest of the 1950s has not been adequately studied, and generalizations must be made with caution.

21. For an earlier formulation of these contrasts of political context, see George M. Fredrickson, 'The South and South Africa', in *The Arrogance of Race: Perspectives on Slavery, Racism, and Social Inequality* (Middletown, Conn., 1988), 254–269.

22. Sheridan Johns and R. Hunt Davis, eds., *Mandela, Tambo, and the African National Congress: The Struggle against Apartheid, 1948–1990* (New York, 1991), 193. (Excerpted from the *Washington Times*, 22 August 1985.)

23. See Lodge, *Black Politics*, 196–199.

24. *Christian Century*, 10 April 1957; Lewis, *King*, 259; King quoted in Branch, *Parting the Waters*, 599.

25. Martin Luther King, Jr., "Address on South African Independence," London, U.K., 7 December 1964. Library and Archives of the Martin Luther King, Jr., Center for Nonviolent Change, Atlanta, Ga.

26. Ibid., 2; Address of Dr. Martin Luther King on 10 December 1965 for the benefit of the American Committee on Africa, Hunter College, New York City. Martin Luther King, Jr., Center, Library and Archives.

27. Good accounts of recent developments in South Africa are Anthony W. Marx, *Lessons of Struggle: South African Internal Opposition, 1960–1990* (New York, 1992), and Richard Price, *The Apartheid State in Crisis, 1975–1990* (New York, 1991). An explicit repudiation of "passive resistance" on behalf of the ANC was made by Oliver Tambo in 1966. (Johns and Davis, *Mandela, Tambo*, 134). I learned of the extent to which the UDF represented a revival of Gandhism during the course of an interview in South Africa in July 1993 with Mewa Rambgobin, a leader of the Indian community and former treasurer of the UDF. For him, the domestic protest in South Africa during the 1980s, which featured a boycott of elections and leaders going to jail without paying fines or making bail, was a vindication of some of the nonviolent methods that Gandhi had employed in the liberation of India.

CHAPTER 11

1. For comparisons of white supremacy, see George M. Fredrickson, *White Supremacy : A Comparative Study in American and South African History* (New York, 1981); John W. Cell, *The Highest Stage of White Supremacy: The Origins of Segregation in South Africa and the American South* (Cambridge, U.K., 1982); Stanley B. Greenberg, *Race and State in Capitalist Development: Comparative Perspectives* (New Haven, Conn., 1980); and several of the essays in Howard Lamar and Leonard Thompson, eds., *The Frontier in History: North America and Southern Africa Compared* (New Haven, Conn., 1981). Studies of the connections between African American and black South African ideologies and movements include J. Mutero Chirenje, *Ethiopianism and Afro-Americans in Southern Africa, 1883–1916* (Baton Rouge, 1987); James Campbell, *Songs of Zion: The African Methodist Episcopal Church in the United States and South Africa* (New York, 1995); Robert A. Hill and Gregory A. Pirio, "'Africa for the Africans': The Garvey Movement in South Africa," in *The Politics of Race, Class, and Nationalism in Twentieth-Century South Africa*, ed. Shula Marks and Stanley Trapido (London, 1987), 209–253; Robert Edgar, "Garveyism in Africa: Dr. Wellington and the American Movement in the Transkei," *Ufahuma* 6, no. 1 (1976), 31–57; Tim Couzzens, "Moralizing Leisure Time: The Transatlantic Connection, 1918–1936," in *Industrialization and Social Change in South*

Africa, 1870–1930, ed. Shula Marks and Richard Rathbone (London, 1982), 314–337; David Coplan, In *Township Tonight! South Africa's Black City Music and Theatre* (Johannesburg, 1985); and David H. Anthony III, "Max Yergan in South Africa: From Evangelical Pan-Africanist to Revolutionary Socialist," *African Studies Review* 34 (1991), 27–55. I have made use of some of this work in my broader comparative study, *Black Liberation: A Comparative History of Black Ideologies in the United States and South Africa* (New York, 1995). This essay is adapted from chapter 7 of that work.

2. See Fredrickson, *Black Liberation,* 265–267.

3. Gail M. Gerhart, *Black Power in South Africa: The Evolution of an Ideology* (Berkeley, 1978), 273–281 and passim.

4. Julius Lester, *Look Out, Whitey! Black Power's Gon' Get Your Mama!* (New York, 1968), 91. On earlier manifestations of African American black nationalism, see Fredrickson, *Black Liberation,* chaps. 2 and 4.

5. The shifting attitudes in SNCC are well described and analyzed in Clayborne Carson, *In Struggle: SNCC and the Black Awakening of the 1960s* (Cambridge, Mass., 1981), 111–211, passim. On CORE's similar evolution toward separatism and away from nonviolence, see August Meier and Elliott Rudwick, *CORE: A Study in the Civil Rights Movement, 1942–1968* (New York, 1973), 374–408.

6. A good account of the Meredith march can be found in Carson, *In Struggle,* 206–211. Carmichael did not actually invent the term Black Power, even in the context of the mid 1960s. Adam Clayton Powell, for one, had used it earlier. Carmichael was not even the first to use it on the Meredith march; but his usage was the first to be widely publicized.

7. Lester, *Look Out, Whitey!,* 100.

8. Gayraud S. Wilmore and James H. Cone, eds., *Black Theology: A Documentary History* (Maryknoll, N.Y., 1979), 27; Nathan S. Wright, Jr., *Black Power and Urban Unrest: Creative Possibilities* (New York, 1967), 61.

9. Wright, *Black Power and Urban Unrest,* 7; Wright, "The Crisis Which Bred Black Power," in *The Black Power Revolt,* ed. Floyd Barbour (Boston, 1968), 116–117.

10. Stokely Carmichael and Charles V. Hamilton, *Black Power: The Politics of Liberation in America* (New York, 1967), 44–45.

11. Stokely Carmichael, *Stokely Speaks: From Black Power to Pan-Africanism* (New York, 1971), 35, 97.

12. For Carmichael's revolutionism of 1968, see ibid., 134–136.

13. This discussion is based mainly on Manning Marable, *Race, Reform, and Revolution: The Second Reconstruction in Black America* (Jackson, Miss., 1991), 86–148 (quote 110); John T. McCartney, *Black Power Ideologies: An Essay in African American Political Thought* (Philadelphia, 1992); and William L. Van Deburg, *New Day in Babylon: The Black Power Movement in American Culture, 1965–1975* (Chicago, 1992), 112–191. Conspicuous separatists (or in William Van Deburg's terminology "territorial nationalists"), in addition to those named above, included the poet Imamu Baraka (Leroi Jones) and Imari Obadele I (Richard Henry), founder of a sect called the Republic of New Africa. Prominent among those that political scientist John McCartney

labels "countercommunalists"—but whom I prefer to call, in accordance with the terminology of the late sixties and Van Deburg's classifications, "revolutionary nationalists"—were (in addition to Newton and other Black Panther leaders like Eldridge Cleaver) James Foreman, the former SNCC leader, and Robert L. Allen, author of the book that made the strongest case for a black-led revolution against American capitalism: *Black Awakening in Capitalist America* (New York, 1969).

14. Perhaps the most articulate and thoughtful of those who defined Black Power in this way was Shirley Chisolm, the first black woman to serve in Congress and, in 1972, the first African American to mount a serious campaign for the presidential nomination of one of the major parties. On Chisolm's significance among "the Black Power pluralists," see McCartney, *Black Power Ideologies*, 151–165. For a more general discussion of the pluralist tendency, see Van Deburg, *New Day in Babylon*, 113–129.

15. See Van Deburg, *New Day in Babylon*, 193–291, for an extensive treatment of the impact of Black Power on African American and American culture.

16. On the "hiatus of the 1960s," see Gerhart, *Black Power in South Africa*, 251–259.

17. On NUSAS in the 1960s, see Gerhart, *Black Power in South Africa*, 257–259; Tom Lodge, *Black Politics in South Africa since 1945* (London, 1983), 322–323; and Baruch Hirson, *Year of Fire, Year of Ash: The Soweto Revolt: Roots of a Revolution* (London, 1979), 65–68.

18. Gerhart, *Black Power in South Africa*, 259–270; Hirson, *Year of Fire*, 68–84; Robert Fatton, *Black Consciousness in South Africa: The Dialectics of Ideological Resistance to White Supremacy* (Albany, 1986), 63–80; N. Barney Pityana, Mamphela Ramphele, Malus Mpumlwana, and Lindy Wilson, eds., *The Bounds of Possibility: The Legacy of Steve Biko and Black Consciousness* (Cape Town, 1991), 154–178 and passim.

19. Gerhart, *Black Power in South Africa*, 288–290; Aelred Stubbs, ed., *Steve Biko—I Write What I Like* (San Francisco, 1978), 80–86 (quote on 86).

20. Stubbs, ed., *Biko—I Write What I Like*, 67. It is also worth noting, however, that BC, like the PAC, was willing to tolerate the permanent presence of whites in South Africa. According to the SASO policy manifesto of 1971, "South Africa is a country in which both black and white live and shall continue to live together." (B. A. Khoapa, ed., *Black Review*, 1972 [Johannesburg, 1972], 40.)

21. Stubbs, ed., *Biko—I Write What I Like*, 49–53; Khoapa, ed., *Black Review*, 1972, 42–43.

22. See Gerhart, *Black Power in South Africa*, 277, for an analysis of this similarity. Gerhart, however, creates confusion when she writes that "the term black by the late 1960s in the United States had become a loose synonym for 'nonwhite'—a new catchall term encompassing all victims of racial discrimination." Clearly one had to have some specifically African ancestry to qualify as "black." Other nonwhites, such as Asians and Native Americans, have never been so designated. Hence, curiously enough, the South African designation became broader than the American. It parallels in its usage the newer American designation "people of color," which was popularized by the multicultural

movement of the 1980s. On the earlier and more racialistic conceptions of black nationalism in the United States, see Fredrickson, *Black Liberation,* chaps. 2 and 4. There may, however, be some reason to be skeptical about the depth and clarity of BC's inclusive concept of blackness. BC literature actually devoted more attention to the value of specifically African cultural traditions as a basis for identity than was fully consistent with the view that the common victimization of Africans, "Coloured," and Indians had given blackness a purely political meaning.

23. Lodge in *Black Politics in South Africa* provides the basis for this comparison, although he does not actually make it explicitly. (See 83–86 and 323–324.)

24. Sipho Buthelezi, "The Emergence of Black Consciousness: An Historical Appraisal" in *The Bounds of Possibility,* ed. Pityana et al., 124–128.

25. On the religious character and association of BC, see especially Fatton, *Black Consciousness in South Africa,* 107–119, and Hirson, *Year of Fire,* 78–81. On the role of religion in Biko's life and thought, see Lindy Wilson, "Bantu Steve Biko: A Life," in *Bounds of Possibility,* ed. Pityana et al., 20, 43–44. N. Barney Pityana, the second most important of the original student leaders, became a clergyman and eventually the director of the World Council of Churches' Program to Combat Racism.

26. The best source on the development of black theology is Wilmore and Cone, *Black Theology: A Documentary History.* Among its major expressions were Albert B. Cleage, *The Black Messiah* (New York, 1968); James H. Cone's *Black Theology and Black Power* (New York, 1969), *A Black Theology of Liberation* (Philadelphia, 1970), and *God of the Oppressed* (New York, 1972); and Gayraud S. Wilmore, *Black Religion and Black Radicalism* (New York, 1972). A work that shows the connections between American and South African versions is Dwight N. Hopkins, *Black Theology: USA and South Africa* (Maryknoll, N.Y., 1989).

27. James H. Cone, *A Black Theology of Liberation,* 7. Buthelezi quoted in Louise Kretzschmar, *The Voice of Black Theology in South Africa* (Johannesburg, 1986), 62.

28. See Kretzschmar, *The Voice of Black Theology,* 43–70.

29. Cone, *Black Theology of Liberation,* 6; Buthelezi quoted in Hopkins, *Black Theology: USA and South Africa,* 99; Cone quoted in Basil Moore, ed., *The Challenge of Black Theology* (Atlanta, 1973), 48; Allan Boesak, *Farewell to Innocence: A Socio-Ethical Study of Black Theology and Black Power* (Johannesburg, 1976), 78. For a discussion of the differences, see Kretzschmar, *The Voice of Black Theology,* 65–68.

30. Khoapa, ed., *Black Review,* 1972, 42.

31. Gerhart, *Black Power in South Africa,* 276. Emphasis added.

32. Stubbs, ed., *Biko—I Write What I Like,* 69; Steve Biko, *Black Consciousness in South Africa* (New York, 1978), 99.

33. Stubbs, ed., *Biko—I Write What I Like,* 132–136.

34. See Anthony Marx, *Lessons of Struggle: South African Internal Opposition, 1960–1990* (New York, 1982), 39–60, 194–195; and Geoff Budlender, "Black Consciousness and the Liberal Tradition," in *Bounds of*

Possibility, ed. Pityana et al., 234–235. For a good example of white leftist criticism of BC, see Hirson, *Year of Fire*, passim.

35. See Marx, *Lessons of Struggle*, 64–72; and Lodge, *Black Politics in South Africa*, 328–339.

36. Keith Mokoape, Thenjiwe Mtintso, and Welile Nhlapo, "Towards the Armed Struggle," in *Bounds of Possibility*, ed. Pityana et al., 142–143; Marx, *Lessons of Struggle*, 91–105.

37. Budlender, "Black Consciousness and the Liberal Tradition," in *Bounds of Possibility*, ed. Pityana, et al., 235.

38. Good accounts of black politics in South Africa in the 1980s can be found in Marx, *Lessons of Struggle*, 106–234; Robert M. Price, *The Apartheid State in Crisis: Political Transformation in South Africa, 1975–1990* (New York, 1991), 152–219; and Steven Mufson, *The Fighting Years: Black Resistance and the Struggle for a New South Africa* (Boston, 1980).

39. Revealing statements of former Black Consciousness supporters who embraced nonracialism as a more advanced form of struggle can be found in Julie Fredrickse, *The Unbreakable Thread: Non-racialism in South Africa* (Bloomington, Ind., 1990), 114–115, 134–135, 161–162.

40. See Price, *The Apartheid State*, 166–167, 251, and passim.

41. On the debates within the Black Consciousness movement in the mid 1970s, see Marx, *Lessons of Struggle*, 75–85.

Index

African National Congress (ANC), 89,
129, 137, 138, 141, 143, 146–47,
149–51; 159–69; 195; and Black
Consciousness, 207–8; Communist in-
fluence in, 160, 166–167; and policy of
multiracialism, 197; Youth League of,
179. *See also* nonviolent resistance
Alabama Sharecroppers Union, 141
Alexandria bus boycott, 176, 182
Algeria, 111–15
American exceptionalism, 98; and post-
emancipation race relations, 124
American frontier, 36–45; and the Turner
thesis, 27–28
American Historical Association, 36
American Indians, 38–40, 42–44, 45,
103, 106, 114
American Quarterly, 2
American slavery, 30–33, 67–73, 185,
225; and capitalism, 71–73; and
Christian ethics, 110; as a paternalistic
institution, 71–72, 79; and Russian
serfdom, 68–70, 72; and southern
planters, 68, 70–73; and the
Tannenbaum-Elkins thesis, 30–31; in
Tocqueville's experience, 102; and
Weber's theory, 90. *See also* race
"American way of life." *See* Turner thesis
Anglo-Boer War, 37, 127
apartheid: and cultural determinism, 81;
destruction of, 146, 187–88; domestic
resistance to, 143, 207–8; and the
frontier experience, 45–46; key elements of, 46, 92; policies, 128; and the

rise of industrial capitalism, 46. *See
also* African National Congress; nonviolent resistance
Azanian Peoples Organization (AZAPO),
139, 146, 208

Banton, Michael, 79
Bell Curve, 81
Biko, Steve, 5, 145, 196–97, 204–6, 211
Billington, Ray Allen, 28
Birth of a Nation, 90
Black, C. E., 25–26
"Black Capitalism." *See* capitalism
Black Consciousness (BC), 128, 138,
145–46, 158, 189–212, 235–36;
African American influences on, 195,
198–99, 203, 229; ANC view of, 161;
compared to Black Power, 208–12;
failings of, 211; and nongenetic black-
ness, 198; and Pan-Africanism,
198–99, 207–8; political consequences
of, 206; and religious beliefs, 200–3;
roots of, 196–97; *See also* Biko, Steve;
Frederikse, Julie
Black Image in the White Mind, 4
"black is beautiful," 195, 199, 208
Black Liberation, 9, 10, 12
Black Muslims, 137–38. *See also*
Malcolm X
black nationalism. *See* nationalism
Black Panther party, 145, 194, 206, 210
Black People's Convention (BPC), 196,
200, 205
Black Power, 192–93

Compositor: Publication Services
Text: 10/13 Sabon
Display: Optima
Printer: Edwards Bros.
Binder: Edwards Bros.